D0385227

# The Modern Netherlands

# The Modern Netherlands

FRANK E. HUGGETT

115009

DJ 109 .H84

 ⌐ **LIBRARY**
SOUTHERN SEMINARY

PRAEGER PUBLISHERS
New York · Washington · London

15873

Published in the United States of America in 1971

Praeger Publishers, Inc.
111 Fourth Avenue, New York, N.Y. 10003, U.S.A.
5 Cromwell Place, London, S.W.7. England

© 1971 by Pall Mall Press Ltd, London, England
Library of Congress Catalog Card Number: 75-143491
All rights reserved

No part of this publication may be reproduced, stored in a
retrieval system or transmitted in any form or by any means,
electronic, mechanical, photocopying, recording or otherwise,
without the prior permission of the Copyright owner

Printed in Great Britain

# Contents

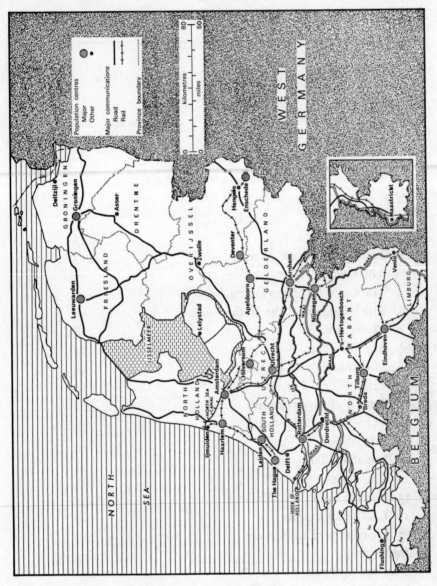

The Netherlands: Political and Communications Map

# Preface

The terminology relating to the Low Countries has been, and still is, somewhat confused, so that many foreigners use the word 'Holland' to describe the country which should more accurately be known as the Netherlands. The latter term is used throughout this book to describe the present-day country, while the word 'Holland' is reserved for the province of that name (which is now divided into two—North and South Holland). The term the 'Low Countries' is used to describe the whole of the area of the present-day Netherlands and present-day Belgium, whose fortunes have been so closely intertwined in history. In the sixteenth century, they both formed part of the Seventeen Provinces, until the Dutch in the United Provinces of the north revolted successfully against the rule of the Spanish Habsburgs.

※

In the writing of this book I have received much help from many Dutch men and women in all walks of life in all regions of the country. Without exception, they have all given very generously of their knowledge and of their time, and even though none of them is named here individually, I would like them to accept this general tribute to their kindness and generosity. I have also been greatly assisted in my research by numerous official and unofficial institutions. To them, also, I would like to record my thanks and particularly to the Leergang

*Preface*

Buitenlandse Betrekkingen, the Genootschap Nederland-Engeland and the Ministry of Cultural Affairs, Recreation and Social Welfare, who have given me special help. None of the individuals or institutions is in any way responsible for the facts or opinions expressed in this book. I should also like to thank Mrs Dorothea Gray for typing the manuscript.

೫

£ sterling = 8·68 guilders
$1 = 3·6 guilders

# I

# Before the Revolt

THE NETHERLANDS is today one of the most densely populated countries in the world, but originally it presented so few natural attractions that it was only thinly populated. In the south-west, the great rivers, the Rhine, the Meuse (Maas) and the Scheldt created a huge swampy delta—a fragmented region of small and large islands, lakes and shifting dunes of sand, which were stirred ceaselessly into new patterns by the wind and waves—a region inimical to settled life. In the far north, there was a long line of sand dunes, penetrated in places by rivers, and so frequently breached by incursions of the sea, that they were broken up into a series of small, bleak, sandy islands, called the Frisian Islands. On the mainland there was a low-lying peaty swamp, which was frequently flooded. The sea, indeed, often penetrated as far inland as the slightly higher ground of Drenthe. But even the higher regions consisted to a large extent of sandy heath, which offered few attractions for settlers.

Nevertheless, people did live there. Archaeologists have unearthed evidence of stone-age settlements in some of the higher regions; but the northern part remained mainly uninhabited until about 400 BC when some tribes migrated westwards from Germany, in search of space and better grazing lands. It was these tribes, the Frisians, who began to create the means for civilised settlement that nature had so gratuitously failed to provide. Working initially with their bare hands, they scooped up the peaty mud from the marshlands and transported these heavy loads in baskets, and later on a kind of sled, to the chosen site for their settlements, building there, over the course of many years, huge mounds, called *terpen*, which sometimes rose as high as 30 feet above the normal sea-level and ranged from 5 to 40 acres in extent. On these artificially constructed mounds they later built their farmhouses, which were long wooden structures with steeply sloping roofs, characteristic of the farmhouses in Friesland today. In addition, they constructed smaller mounds called *wieren*, which, so archaeologists have discovered, were uninhabited, but used as refuge mounds for cattle stranded in the floods. At least 600 *terpen* were built in what is now the province of Friesland, and another 400 in the province of Groningen, where the mounds were known as *wierden*. Some mounds are still extant, such as those which form the centre of Leeuwarden, capital of the province of Friesland.[1] But many more have been swept away by the sea. It has been estimated that the total amount of clay and mud moved to build these mounds in the northern region was 100 million cubic yards, against the 3·5 million cubic yards content of the Great Pyramid of Giza.[2]

In this forbidding swampy region, the Frisians lived an isolated and independent life, their only contact with the rest of Europe being by sea, rivers or the primitive tracks which ran east from Stavoren and south from Groningen.[3] Further south, in the higher regions between the Rhine and the Meuse, there lived another tribe—the Batavi. Both tribes became subject to

Roman rule. The Batavi became more romanised than the Frisians, some of them forming the bodyguard of the Julian dynasty. But Roman rule was never total in the northern regions, as the Romans made their main defence line on the Rhine and penetrated beyond only to make occasional sorties against the Germanic tribes along the Weser and the Elbe.

It was on one of these excursions in AD 47 that Pliny saw the tribes living on their *terpen* in the desolate region around the mouth of the Ems, where the vast tide of the ocean swept in a flood over the measureless expanse of marshland twice in every twenty-four hours. He described how the miserable race resembled 'sailors in ships when the water covers the surrounding land, but shipwrecked people when the tide was retired'. The inhabitants made nets from the sedge and rushes growing in the marshes to catch the fish escaping on the ebb-tide.[4]

This region held terrors even for the Romans. Describing the shores of one lake Pliny said:

> they were occupied by oaks, which grow with extreme eagerness and these when undermined by the waves or overthrown by blasts of wind carry away with them vast islands of soil in the embrace of their roots, and thus balanced, float along standing upright, so that our fleets have often been terrified by the wide rigging of their huge branches, when they seemed to be purposely driven by the waves against the bows of the ships at anchor for the night, which thus were unavoidably compelled to engage in a naval battle with the trees.[5]

These natural terrors, and the isolation, gave the inhabitants a certain measure of protection against incursions from the south at least.

Nevertheless, the whole of the Low Countries was invaded by the Franks after the Roman grip started to weaken in the third and fourth centuries. The Romans retreated before the Frankish invaders to the safer river line of the Rhine and, by the end of the fourth century, they retained their hold only in the south-eastern corner of the Netherlands. Eventually, the whole of the Low Countries was overrun by the Franks. One of their warlords, Clovis, pressed on into Gaul, where he married a Christian princess and adopted her faith. Returning to the Netherlands, he attempted to subdue the Frisians, who were opposed to both Frankish rule and the Christian religion. It was a lengthy struggle. As Bernard H. M. Vlekke says: 'Christendom did not conquer German paganism until the Frankish kings had established their political supremacy on the battlefields. The murder of St Boniface, the German apostle, in AD 754 near Dokkum in Friesland, marked the last violent outbreak of pagan resentment against the newly organised Christian Church. Eventually, under Charlemagne's rule, a certain degree of political and religious unity came to the Netherlands.'[6] Even so, the unity was extremely fragile.

More important for the future course of the country's development were the activities of the Frisians themselves, which opened the way to physical security and commercial prosperity. Although they went on living on their *terpen* until about AD 1000, for at least two centuries before that they had started to dike the coast and to reclaim the land. Initially, a group of mounds were joined together and protected from the sea by a high embankment, or dike. Later they set themselves the more ambitious task of building a sea wall round the north-eastern region. An ancient document declared 'that we Frisians shall establish and control a sea fortress, a golden band which shall encircle all Friesland, in which each portion of dike shall be the same as the next, and against which the salt sea shall thrust both by day and by night'.[7] This formidable feat was carried out mainly with shovels and sleds. But the golden band, or hoop, was repeatedly breached; even in 1894, 1916 and 1953, there were serious breaks in the present sea defences.[8]

It was the sea that shaped the history of the Netherlands. As one of the earliest writers on the country said: 'The sea may well be termed, not only a neighbor but also a member of the low countreys, as well for ye great benefite that it bringeth to them: as also for the harme that it doth them when it rageth.'[9] Although the Netherlands was unendowed with any natural harbours—apart from a number of creeks, most of which were extremely shallow—it was situated in a very favourable position for voyages round the coasts of Denmark and through the Kattegat into the Baltic, to the ports of Scandinavia, Poland and Russia. It was the Frisians who first showed that, although the sea could never be ignored, it could be controlled by dikes and also used for very profitable voyages. They began the Baltic trade which was to become the whole basis of the future prosperity of the country, the 'mother', the 'vital nerve' and 'soul' as it has been variously called.[10] But as has been the case in the country's history so frequently, trade and war were to be intimately linked. It was these same sea routes that the Norsemen, or Vikings, used in reverse from about 840 onwards, when they returned year after year to pillage, to kill and to burn, penetrating far up the rivers and the creeks to strike at Frisian strongholds. Towards the end of the ninth century, the greater part of Friesland and what are now the provinces of Holland were under Viking domination. The invasions, combined with the effects of a particularly disastrous series of floods, weakened the Frisians' power, which they never regained to such an extent again.

The fragile unity under Charlemagne's rule was soon dissipated after his death. By the Treaty of Verdun in 843, his empire was divided into three parts with the whole of the Low Countries coming under the rule of Lothair. But this middle kingdom, an improbable compilation of conflicting groups squeezed between the French and German kingdoms, soon broke up into a tangle of petty states and principalities. The Netherlands came under German suzerainty. At this time, the most important town in the Netherlands was the religious and trading centre of Utrecht and the German emperor deputed the bishop to be his representative in the Netherlands. After the Viking raids had lessened towards the end of the tenth century, the bishopric of Utrecht tried to extend its influence. By 1075, the powers of the counts of Friesland had been broken, but the bishopric was less successful in crushing the counts of Holland, who had established themselves in what is now North Holland early in the tenth century. Gradually, the counts of Holland extended their power southwards and, in 1018, succeeded in seizing Dordrecht, where they erected a toll house to collect dues from passing vessels. East of Utrecht, too, the counts of Gelderland built up a strong principality. But the really important developments in the Low Countries as a whole were taking place further south, in what is now northern Belgium. There, during the tenth and the eleventh centuries, the counts of Flanders established a wealthy and powerful principality which eventually extended its frontiers to Normandy and to the islands of Zeeland.[11] Flanders was favourably situated on the trade routes of northern Europe and had somewhat less tendency to disastrous flooding. The town of Bruges soon became the major trading and commercial centre of northern Europe; in the Netherlands, the development of towns occurred much later.

The main reason for the late development of towns in the Netherlands was the fact that much of the country was still in a state of physical instability. The appearance of the coastal region was very different from today's neat pattern of polders intersected by dikes, dams and canals. The Frisian Islands extended much further south, breaking up into a series of smaller sand dunes and islets which reached as far south as Schagen. The present province of North Holland was covered with lakes, some of which formed inlets of the Zuider Zee. Further south, in what is now South Holland and Zeeland, the wide estuary of the Scheldt, Meuse and Rhine, formed a kaleidoscope of innumerable small fragments of sandy land and larger islands ceaselessly shaken by wind, wave and tide into new patterns.

For towns to develop in the Netherlands there had to be not only, as elsewhere, a particular reason, such as the meeting of trade routes, but also a physical opportunity. Sometimes, the latter was provided naturally, where the confluence of two rivers produced, as it often does, a natural eminence. But more often, the opportunity had to be created by draining, consolidating or raising the site above the flood level before any building could commence. Even then, large buildings in the coastal area had to be supported on deeply driven piles; the town hall, now the royal palace, of Amsterdam—directly in the centre of the city—rests on 13,659 piles.[12]

Most of the Netherlands was poor in natural resources; the main activities being dairy farming, fishing and salt refining. It was this lack of natural resources that forced the inhabitants into their traditional role of carriers. By the twelfth century, ships were sailing from the ports of Kampen, Zwolle and Deventer on the river Ijssel, through the Zuider Zee and into the Baltic. For many centuries, cargoes of herrings and salt from the coast and butter and cheese from Friesland, were taken to the Baltic ports while timber and grain were brought back.

By the end of the following century, the increased traffic along the Rhine, in salmon, eels and wine in particular, and the general expansion of overseas trade, had stimulated the growth of ports further south in Holland and Zeeland. Dordrecht was one of the first ports to benefit from the Rhine traffic. When the river Zwyn, which gave Bruges its outlet to the sea, began to silt up at the end of the fourteenth century, Middelburg in Zeeland, became one of the main centres for the trans-shipment of goods for both Bruges and Antwerp, which had no sizeable mercantile marine of its own.

Because of the shallow waterways, most Dutch ships were small; the largest at the time was that known as the 'hulk' with a capacity of 250 tons. Many Dutch ships were built abroad, like the 'hulk', which was constructed mainly in Prussian yards; but when the Hanse banned members from making ships for non-members in 1413, shipbuilding became more common in Holland and Zeeland, particularly at Dordrecht which had had a shipbuilding industry since the thirteenth century at least. Around 1450, the Hollanders introduced the caravel—the ship used by Columbus on his voyages—into northern Europe.[13] In the fifteenth century, a new form of joint ownership, which was to be so characteristic a feature of the economic structure of the future Dutch republic, gave the maritime provinces a commercial edge over their foreign rivals. More and more ships came to be owned not by one man alone, but by a group of shareholders. Not only was the risk more widely spread, but as the master of the vessel was often also one of the shareholders, he had a direct interest in the care of the ship and the sale of the cargo.[14] By the end of the fifteenth century, the ships of Holland and of Zeeland were familiar in most of the ports of northern Europe. To England they brought wine and salt from France, corn from Normandy, herrings from Norway, timber and corn from the Baltic, and fish, vegetables, madder, teazles, linen, tiles and many other products from the Low Countries.[15]

By that time, too, there had been some development in home industries and manufacture. Grain was imported and beer exported. An extensive export trade in salted herrings—the staple diet of the poor until the nineteenth century—was built up after William Beukels of Zeeland discovered, in the fourteenth century, that herrings could be preserved by salting them in barrels. The development of the ports and towns was already shaping the future power centre of the Netherlands, the *randstad* or rim town, composed of the major towns of Amsterdam, Haarlem, Leiden, The Hague, Delft, Schiedam, Rotterdam and Dordrecht, around the central moor of Holland, which contains today nearly a half of the total population of the country. Dordrecht was one of the most ancient ports and Amsterdam, the present-day capital, was fast developing; The Hague, the present seat of government, was the site chosen in 1247 by Count William II of Holland for a castle; while Haarlem and Leiden were already important centres for the manufacture of coarse cloth which found a ready market overseas. In these small towns, men who were often merchants, shippers and manufacturers at the same time, were laying the foundations for the rich oligarchy which was to flourish so fruitfully in the Dutch republic of the seventeenth century.

The process of diking and damming continued but not without grave setbacks, such as the disastrous night of November 18, 1421—St Elizabeth's Day—when the Meuse dikes were breached. Seventy-two villages were submerged; an estimated 10,000 people drowned; and thousands of acres of land were flooded, some of which have not been reclaimed to this day. Flooding was caused not only by nature, but also by man himself. The central moor of Holland was then a region of hundreds of small and large lakes, some of them created by peasants who dug up peat to burn as fuel and who used the salt-laden ashes for preserving herrings and meat. In stormy weather, these man-made lakes flooded the surrounding lands. This practice of digging up peat was not prohibited until the sixteenth century.

From the very earliest times, a strong foundation had been laid for the future economic development of the Netherlands—in land reclamation, the carrying trade and general commerce. But the line of political development was less clear. The Low Countries still remained a patchwork of separate principalities, with one lord extending his domains as his power increased, only to be replaced by another as his power waned. The dukes of Burgundy came nearest to creating some unity in their attempts to restore and re-create the middle kingdom. On June 19, 1369, Philip the Bold, duke of Burgundy, married Marguerite, daughter and heiress of the count of Flanders, Louis de Maele. On the death of the count in 1384, Philip became the ruler of Flanders, Artois, Nevers, Franche-Comté and the towns of Antwerp and Malines. By marriage alliance, diplomatic skill and the acquisition of new territories, he laid the foundations for a revived middle kingdom.[16] This ambition was pursued even more eagerly by his successors, particularly Philip the Good, 1419–67, who by war, marriage and purchase, greatly extended his dominions. By 1433, they included Holland and Zeeland. It was not until the reign of Charles v, 1519–55, after the Burgundians had been linked by marriage with the Habsburgs, that the provinces of Friesland, Utrecht, Overijssel, Groningen and Gelderland came under his control.[17] The ambition of re-forming a middle kingdom had been achieved; but this Burgundian-Habsburg circle of the Seventeen Provinces was to have only a brief existence.

Differences between the maritime provinces in the west and the land provinces in the east remained extreme; the inhabitants of Gelderland, Drenthe and Overijssel had different racial origins, different economic interests and a different social structure from the inhabitants of the west. Even within the maritime provinces themselves, there were numerous rivalries and differences. For example, throughout the early Middle Ages, Holland

9

and Zeeland had conflicting commercial interests: 'the Zeeland towns wanted to keep and to improve their trade with England, while the towns of North Holland, which felt the competition of the English in the Baltic and in the Bay of Bourgneuf, sometimes upset this trade.'[18] People's allegiance was to towns, or to provinces at the most: an examination of entries made by over 10,000 students and artists from the Low Countries in the registers of Italian universities and academies has shown that, up to 1560, they described themselves as Friso, Geldrus, Zelandus, Hollandus, etc.[19]

The power structure in the various provinces showed considerable variation. In the maritime provinces of Holland and Zeeland, the lack of physically stable land had prevented the growth of a powerful rural class of landowners. The main power rested in the hands of the top 'regent' class of wealthy urban merchants, whose investments had created the towns out of marshy swampland, giving them a personal, passionate attachment to the towns, which was stronger than that current among other town dwellers of those times. The regent class had originated among the officers of the guilds, which had spread from Flanders and Brabant to Holland and Zeeland in the thirteenth and fourteenth centuries. By the fifteenth century, these guild officers looked upon their tenure of office as a matter of established right. Under the Burgundians, the powers of the regent class were regularised through the grant of charters and privileges to the towns, which made the closed community of twenty to eighty rich and influential regents, in each of the large towns, a ruling, self-perpetuating oligarchy. The charters made them regents for life, or until they went to live elsewhere, and gave them the power to co-opt successors. It was the regents who chose the burgomaster and aldermen, who were responsible for local taxation and the administration of justice. They also dominated the states (provincial councils) of Holland and Zeeland. Each state was composed of delegations from the towns and from the nobility. Protocol was observed in the meetings of the states, as the nobility was given precedence.[20] But real power rested with the regents, as each of the towns had one vote each, while the nobility as a whole had only one. In Holland, the clergy was not represented at all. The power structure in the other provinces showed considerable variation. In Utrecht, for example, the seat of ecclesiastical government, the clergy possessed considerable power in the states. In Gelderland, where towns had not developed to such an extent as in the maritime provinces, the nobility and landowners had more power. While in Friesland, the most isolated and the most historic of the provinces, the peasants remained a force with which to be reckoned.

Very sensibly, the early Burgundian rulers tried to lead these separate provinces towards unity—not to impose it. In celebration of his marriage to Isabel of Portugal, Philip the Good instituted in 1430, the Order of the Golden Fleece. This was designed to attract allegiance to himself, rather than to provincial lords, by granting members a number of exceptional privileges, including exemption from trial in all courts but those of their own chapter, and the right to be considered for the highest government posts. In 1465, Philip summoned a States-General (*Staten-Generaal*) composed of representatives from the provincial states. Its main purpose was to raise money, but it had no power to do so until it had attained the consent of each separate principality. Even then, representatives of the eastern and north-eastern provinces, which were acquired only during the reign of Charles v, guarded their independence even more jealously and only attended meetings of the States-General for formal purposes: demands for money had to be made individually to them. In addition, the Burgundians appointed a stadtholder (or lieutenant-governor) in the various provinces, though he sometimes officiated in more than one province at a time. The stadtholder, who sometimes also commanded the forces in the area, had the right of nomination to some municipal offices and other powers, but control over finance remained firmly in the hands of the states, which in Holland and Zeeland—the wealthiest provinces in the Netherlands—meant the towns (i.e. the regent class). Much power was already held by this self-perpetuating urban oligarchy of about ten thousand people, which was to become the main force in the Dutch republic.[21]

But the later Burgundian rulers proved to be far less tolerant of provincial rights—particularly in religion. Lutherism spread first into the Low Countries from Germany; later in the 1530s and the 1540s, the Mennonites (so-called from the name of one of their leaders Menno Simons, an ex-priest from Friesland), gained a hold in Friesland and Holland, particularly Amsterdam; while later on, in the 1550s and the 1560s, Calvinism started to spread northwards from the southern, Walloon provinces of what is now Belgium. Of all these, it was the creed of Calvinism, with its mass appeal, which was to gain most support in the Netherlands. But to the Burgundians, all three creeds were but differing aspects of the same heresy. Charles v attempted to stamp out Protestantism by introducing the Inquisition, but some of the towns and provinces resisted it successfully by claiming that it was a breach of their charters and privileges.

In 1555, Charles v announced his intention of abdicating and retiring to a monastery. Although he was also the king of Spain and the German emperor and thus ruled over vast possessions in Europe and the Americas, Charles had been born in Ghent and therefore looked upon the Low Countries as his home. Philip II, his son who succeeded him, had spent nearly all his life in Spain, and had no such personal attachment. For four years he lived unhappily in Brussels and then retired to Spain, leaving his half-sister, Margaret, duchess of Parma, as regent. Even before Philip departed for Spain in 1559, there had been clashes between him and his subjects. Philip had requested a nine-years' subsidy from the States-General, which it countered by asking for the withdrawal of 3,000 Spanish troops stationed in the Low Countries. Both parties accepted the requests grudgingly.

Relations became more strained after his departure. In 1559, Philip obtained the pope's sanction to increase the number of bishops in the Low Countries (who were now to be appointed by the crown), to reorganize the bishoprics and to make the new archbishop of Malines primate of the Low Countries. This idea of reorganizing the bishoprics was not new; Charles v had planned to do it, though he never put it into effect. The reorganisation of the bishoprics was a sensible measure and was long overdue. But it was seen by the Protestants as a stiffening of the measures against heretics; by the nobility as a curtailment of their privileges of appointing their sons to high ecclesiastical rank; by the existing bishops as a diminution of their own status; and by the abbots, whose endowments were being used to finance the new sees, as plain robbery.

It was this neglect of the interests of the establishment which helped to swell the opposition to Philip's rule. At first, and indeed for many years afterwards, they were not opposed to the monarchy as such, or even to the Inquisition. It was far more a question of who knew best how to rule. Philip was challenged by some of the highest nobility, including the count of Egmont, the count of Hoorn and William of Orange (known as William the Silent), Philip's own stadtholder in the provinces of Holland, Zeeland, Utrecht and Franche-Comté. By 1564, they had persuaded Philip to order the much hated Cardinal Granvelle, first archbishop of Malines, to leave the country. But their victory was more apparent than real. Though Granvelle was blamed at the time for the severities to heretics, later research has shown that it was not he, but Philip, who was primarily responsible.[22] Granvelle went; but the seeking out of heretics went on with even greater vigour.

Rebellion was still far distant, though rumblings of it could now be heard. In the words of one seventeenth-century historian: '. . . what with the discontent of great ones, who thought themselves neglected, and the jealousies of the people, who were afraid of being oppress'd by the Inquisition, all men were ready and dispos'd for tumults.'[23] The lead was now taken by the lesser nobility. In the spring of 1566, about five hundred of them, led by the count of Brederode, petitioned Margaret for some moderation of the edicts against heresy. They, too, were reasonable in their demands. They stressed that they were not against the monarchy or even against the edicts, which had 'some ground and just title'. But their greatest fear was that if there was no mollification there might 'follow a mutinie and generall sedition, tending to the miserable ruin of the whole country'. They suggested that new laws should be made 'by the advice and consent of all the generall-states assembled, to provide accordingly, by other fit and convenient meanes, without such apparent dangers'.[24] They were just as much concerned with preserving old privileges as the new religion.

Although the nobles were contemptuously dismissed by one of Margaret's advisers as mere beggars ('ces gueux'), she told them that she would diminish the Inquisition's activities while she awaited the king's reply to their petition. To the Calvinists, this seemed to be an incredible victory. Preachers emerged from their hiding places to hold services in the open, which thousands attended. This new liberty induced some of the Calvinists to incite mobs of unemployed weavers in the Walloon provinces of the south to take their revenge upon the established church by breaking images and burning pictures, and this wave of iconoclastic fury spread rapidly throughout the Low Countries.

To Philip, this revolt seemed part of a vast international Protestant conspiracy. Everywhere, the forces of Protestantism—Huguenots, Breton sailors, English privateers—seemed to be on the attack. After some hesitation, Philip decided to send in the duke of Alva with a force of 10,000 Spanish troops to crush the most serious manifestation of this conspiracy.[25] Alva entered the Low Countries in August 1567 and established himself in Brussels. By the autumn, he had set up the Council of Troubles, which soon became popularly known as the Council of Blood, to persecute all the main heretics and rebels. Egmont and Hoorn were arrested and William the Silent would have been, had he not already fled to his brother's estates at Dillenburg in Germany. In April 1568, exiled nobles and burghers, supported by Huguenot soldiers and arms, and subsidised by money from Protestants who remained in the Low Countries, made a three-pronged attack upon Alva's forces. It was easily crushed. In reprisal, more executions took place in Brussels, among the victims being Egmont and Hoorn, Catholic though they were. The duke of Alva had succeeded in his task of imposing Spanish rule over the Low Countries; but the revolt had begun.

# 2

---

# The Eighty Years' War

THE STRUGGLE against Spain was part of a much larger 'indescribably complicated series of conflicts' which involved 'the issue of the powers of the assemblies of estates against the centralising policies of kings; the new religions and the old; and the international rivalry of Valois and Habsburg'.[1] There is no need to follow the course of the complex interaction of events in the Low Countries in any detail; only to isolate those strands which were significant for the future development of the Netherlands.[2] But it is essential to realise from the start that the revolt took place not only in the northern provinces which were eventually to band together as the Dutch republic, but also in the southern provinces which were very much later to become modern Belgium. Motley's view that this was only a struggle between the democratic, freedom-loving Protestants in the northern provinces against the tyrannical rule of Catholic

Spanish emperors, has been completely discredited by Pieter Geyl. Initially, the whole of the Low Countries was involved, and a major part was taken by the burghers of the cities in Flanders and Brabant. But in correcting one error of historical interpretation, Geyl himself to a certain extent substituted another, by imposing on the subject matter his own ambitions for a greater Netherlands, in which the present-day Netherlands and the Dutch-speaking regions in the northern part of what is now Belgium, would be accepted as an historical entity. But these two areas were neither as similar as Geyl would have us believe, nor as different as Motley imagined. There was great rivalry between the merchants of the port of Antwerp and those of the northern ports, such as Amsterdam. The lines of religious conflict did not coincide with provincial or state boundaries. It is true that the two regions shared a common language which had developed from the Flemish spoken in Flanders and not, as is sometimes erroneously stated, from a variety of Low German, or Platt Deutsch.[3] But the Dutch spoken in the Netherlands still had undertones of Frisian, the language initially spoken throughout many parts of the country. Moreover, language as such did not achieve any real political or nationalistic significance until very much later. There can be no simple explanation of the complex interaction of events involved in the revolt against Spain.

Although so much excellent work has been done on this subject, there still remain gaps in our understanding of both the Dutch and Spanish motivations and actions.[4] Partly the confusion comes from purely semantic reasons. The Dutch description of the struggle known as the Eighty Years' War parcels the chaos of events into a unity, implying a single set of causes, a continuity of aim and a single enemy, none of which existed. Relations with England, for example, altered greatly. From 1585 to 1587, Robert Dudley, earl of Leicester, was actually governor-general of the Netherlands; yet, by the end of the struggle, England and the Netherlands were on the verge of war. The struggle, which persisted over a period which was then equivalent to nearly three whole generations, had a multiplicity of causes; economic, political, social and religious, and, perhaps more important for true understanding, it was as much a battle for internal power as a revolt against a common enemy. Throughout the struggle, the conflicting forces sought to stamp their particular pattern upon the Netherlands: ambitious nobles, most of them of foreign extraction, angled for the crown; the Calvinists wanted to establish a theocracy, a little kingdom of God's grace upon earth; while the merchants wanted to expand their trade and to protect their profits. The nobles played the commanding part in the struggle; the Calvinists took the most extreme role; victory in the end, however, went to neither, but to the rich merchants of Amsterdam, a city which had kept out of the fight altogether for the first ten years. The final outcome was not the start of something fresh, but the triumph of something very old, of the medieval city-state of Amsterdam, the last time, as Violet Barbour so perceptively says, 'in which a veritable empire of trade and credit could be held by a city in her own right, unsustained by the forces of a modern unified state'.[5]

The Dutch republic was shaped to a large extent by the course of the actual struggle itself. During this period, its strength as a maritime power developed greatly. This was responsible to a large extent for its victory against Spain, and also led to a vast expansion of its trade, the consolidation of the powers and riches of the merchant class in Amsterdam, and the voyages of overseas discovery and the creation of an empire. The religious conflict, too, was also settled in this period, not in a way that either the Catholics or the Calvinists would have chosen, but more on the basis of an earlier tradition of toleration, epitomised by Erasmus. And the peculiar state structure of the Dutch republic, in which the regents retained power, but had a stadtholder, who if he was strong enough could act almost like a king, was also consolidated during this time. All of these factors—trade, religious toleration and the dualistic form of government—had enormous consequences for the future of the country, so that it is no exaggeration to say that even now, when the Netherlands has become a highly industrialised country, these factors remain of paramount significance. It was during this eighty-year period that the framework for the country was formed.

Though many of these main issues were not to be finally decided until after his death, one person has become intimately and inevitably linked with the struggle for independence from Spanish rule: William of Orange. Few other leaders have been so praised, both within his own lifetime (though not exclusively so) and for 400 years after his death. For Clark, there is no doubt that he was great; he had 'no equal in constancy and purpose'.[6] For Wedgwood, he was 'one of that small band of statesmen whose service to humanity is greater than their service to their time or their people'.[7] And even Geyl, who in his preface to the first edition of *The Revolt of the Netherlands* appears to be critical of Motley for his hero worship of William, has few words of criticism for the leader in the book itself. It is easy to understand why this should be so. William's story in all of its aspects—from his many marriages to his death by an assassin's bullet at Delft on July 10, 1584—is full of romantic appeal. Yet there were a number of hesitations, evasions, military and even political misjudgements in his career. In the early days, William hopelessly underestimated the part that the Calvinists were to play in the successful outcome of the struggle. Indeed he wished at one time to minimise their powers as much as possible. In 1568, he launched a premature attack against the duke of Alva which was a complete fiasco, whereas if he had waited for a couple of years, until he had collected more money, and until the people were suffering under Alva's new 10 per cent purchase tax, he might have gained more popular support. He failed again, in his self-appointed task, extremely difficult though it was, of keeping the Seventeen Provinces united, though there was still some chance of this during the confused years of 1576–8, with the signing of the Pacification of Ghent. Under this, the states of Holland and Zeeland and the States-General representing the other provinces, agreed that Spanish troops should be compelled to leave the Low Countries and that the Seventeen Provinces themselves should decide on the question of religious toleration. But neither William, nor other contenders, could obtain sufficiently wide support to act on this resolve. In May 1579, the southern provinces and towns of Hainaut, Artois, Lille, Douai and Orchies concluded the Treaty of Arras in which they pledged their loyalty to Philip on condition that he upheld their rights and privileges. A few days later, Holland, Zeeland, Utrecht and Gelderland signed the Union of Utrecht, by which they agreed to resist foreign intervention in their affairs as if they were one province—the United Provinces—and to establish freedom of worship. The division between north and south had not been irrevocably fixed (the fate of Flanders and Brabant had still to be decided), but the two treaties provided rallying points for rival forces.

But William persisted in believing that unity could be maintained, though only with the help of outside powers and foreign princes. He had no faith in the ability of the Low Countries to achieve independence for themselves or, indeed, any desire for it. In this he was essentially conservative. He was fighting not for new freedoms but for old privileges. He wanted not so much a republican leadership as a new emperor or monarchical overlord who would respect the ancient rights of the provinces. To him, the new monarch's nationality and religion was a matter of some indifference.

Relatively poor though his family was, it was nevertheless a minor branch of one of those medieval sets of international princely families with the whole known world as their parish: William, who was born in Germany without high hopes of power, had unexpectedly inherited large estates in the Low Countries and in France through the premature death of a cousin. In his personal life, William remained untouched by the religious fanaticisms of the age; not necessarily through conviction, but far more probably through political convenience, he was, in his lifetime, Lutheran, Catholic and Calvinist in turn. There was, therefore, to him nothing contradictory in forcing a Catholic and a foreign prince—the duke of Anjou —as 'Defender of the Liberties of the Netherlands' upon the reluctant States-General in 1580–1. William viewed his support of Anjou pragmatically; he had money, troops, was a brother of the French king and suitor of Queen Elizabeth—'her little frog'. But the admission of Anjou led only to what might have been expected; his attempt to take over Antwerp by force, to crush the towns and to obtain from the States-General the final sovereignty that it was reluctant to concede in full to anyone.

But the monarchical principle was never finally abandoned. Initially, neither on the part of William nor of the separate provinces, had there been resistance to the king as such, but more to his incompetent ministers and counsellors. The numerous pamphlets of those times show that initially, at least, the rebels' main grievance was the overriding of their privileges, granted in such charters as the Joyeuse Entrée of Brabant, which allowed the people to rebel against a tyrannical ruler.[8] But there was no general agreement on the form the new government should take. There was considerable support for some form of democratic rule, with some of the more extreme Calvinists advocating a Geneva-style confederation based on Ghent, with 'an insane disregard of strategic possibilities'.[9] But monarchical support remained strong. The southern nobility and the Catholics eventually made their peace with Philip; even the north accepted the duke of Anjou, until by his attack on Antwerp he showed that he had no respect for the rights of towns. William, with his desire to keep the Low Countries united, possibly as a patrimony that he could eventually take over himself, always refused to commit himself too closely. Under Anjou, he remained the trusted lieutenant. William, perhaps, was too sly to claim the ultimate prize which could only be his when all other possible contenders had been tried and their inadequacies revealed. (By a misrendering of the old Dutch *schluwe* into the Latin *taciturnus*, William has come down in history as William the Silent instead of William the Sly.[10]) But before it could be revealed if this was his ultimate intention, he had been assassinated.

Whatever William's ultimate motives may have been, he personified the spirit of resistance in his resourcefulness, his indomitable courage and his personal popularity, fortified by his ability to be all things to all men (a nobleman in the south and a plain Calvinist in the north). He was anything but the simple spirit of romantic myth; but a hard-headed statesman, a tireless worker and a ceaseless propagandist. It was not until after his assassination that the need for similar protection and leadership was greatly felt. There began a frenzied search to find some successor. Sovereignty was offered first to Henry III of France and then to Queen Elizabeth. Both of them rejected it. In despair, the States-General made Robert Dudley, earl of Leicester, governor-general. He accepted the title much to Elizabeth's extreme vexation. He soon proved himself to be tactless politically, incompetent militarily and within two years he was forced to resign.

The constitutional problem was never solved. The Dutch republic always remained a state in search of a monarch, alternating between periods when a stadtholder—a constitutional monarch in all but name—was in office, and others when the States-General ruled alone. The will for the seven provinces of the north to coexist as a nation did not precede the revolt, but was fashioned by the circumstances and the course of the revolt itself.

An equal indecisiveness prevailed in the religious sphere. This was a troubled period of religious turmoil throughout northern Europe and particularly so in the Low Countries with its geographical situation at the crossroads of northern Europe, the meeting place for both trade and ideas. In different forms—Lutheran, Calvinist and Anabaptist—the new religions penetrated all parts of the Low Countries; none was entirely Catholic, none completely Protestant. Indeed, there were remarkable variations even between neighbouring towns. It was for men of deep religious conscience, a very personal and interior question; for many more, it was often a mere matter of convenience and outward show. But in the Low Countries, the religious question became inextricably intertwined with the political. As the Spanish armies swept across the flat plains of Flanders and Brabant, up to the great rivers, or drove up the eastern flank of higher ground towards Friesland and Groningen, the Protestants in those areas were forced to remain in silent subjection to an alien faith, or to flee abroad or to the safer regions of Holland and Zeeland protected by their natural marshy creeks or man-made dikes. As the Protestants consolidated their strength in these two latter provinces, the Catholics were faced with a similar choice; to flee south, where they could practise their religion openly, or adopt an outward show of a false piety and maintain their true religion only in their hearts and homes. At the same time, the growing Calvinist strength in these two provinces persuaded many Protestants to return there from their exile abroad. This cross-migratory process was slow but inevitable; the religious composition of the north and the south varied with the fortunes of war. Nevertheless, its final effect was to give the north—the provinces that were to form the Dutch republic—a Protestant complexion, with Catholic tinges, while the south remained, outwardly at least, loyal to the older faith.

The Calvinists played the most extreme—and initially, at least—the most successful part in the revolt. Their main instrument was the *Gueux de mer* (sea beggars) who had taken the insult hurled at them in the days of their petition to Margaret of Parma and transformed it into a title of their faith, if not of their honour. Their fierce fleets of unemployed sailors and mercenaries of many nations—Germans, Danes, Scots, French, English as well as native-born Netherlanders—led by Calvinist nobles, were a wild, merciless, undisciplined, piratical force. The Beggars had been formed in August 1569, when Lancelot de Brederode and five of his friends signed a declaration of perpetual enmity towards the duke of Alva.[11] William had granted them letters of marque: from their mastheads fluttered the Orange flag with the lion of Nassau. With Elizabeth's permission, they used English ports, and later the port of La Rochelle held by the Huguenots, as bases for their marauding attacks upon Spanish vessels and for commando-style raids against churches and monasteries on the coasts of Friesland and Groningen. But there were serious disagreements between William and the Beggars. He believed that it was only with the aid of foreign powers that the freedom of the Low Countries could be secured; they believed that native faith and foreign mercenaries would suffice. He thought that the excesses of their actions would offend the faithful Catholics in the Low Countries; they saw the struggle from the start as a crusade. It was this divergence of views that caused William to try to curb their activities by ordering that there should be a minister on each ship, regular services, a ban on foreign mercenaries and stricter discipline and order. At the same time, he ordered that the booty should be divided into three equal parts; one for the officers, one for the men and one for himself.[12]

The Beggars, however, continued to act in their former ruthless ways, desecrating churches, tyrannising priests and taking prisoners. To prisoners from whom they could hope for no ransom, they were merciless; they were shot, or their feet and hands were tied together before they were thrown into the sea. The fanatical William de la Marck, lord of Lumey—who became the self-styled leader of the Beggars after the death of the lord of Dolhain in 1572—instituted a form of counter-inquisition against the monks and prelates in the towns that his forces tyrannised. It was common practice for him to call the 'Abbot and his Fryers into a Chamber, where hee forced them to denie their Masse and to preach against it, in case they would not be hanged'.[13]

It was the Beggars, however, who achieved the first real success in the struggle, by giving the rebels—and William himself —their first firmly established bases in the Low Countries, initially in the estuaries of the great rivers and then throughout Holland and Zeeland. Although there were to be many more courageous victories than these, the establishment of these bridgeheads was absolutely vital to the rebels' future success.

On April 1, 1572, the Beggars captured the town of Brill (opposite present-day Rotterdam). Although there are varying accounts of this feat, it appears that the capture of the town came about by chance and the decision to hold it as an afterthought.[14] A fleet of about twenty-five Beggars' ships had been attacking vessels off the coasts of Holland when a storm forced them to drop anchor off Brill. When a sailor from the shore told them that the Spanish garrison had been called away to restore order in Utrecht, the Beggars disembarked and, in the silence of the evening, stole up to the town and gained admittance by setting fire to one of the gates. After pillaging houses and churches, they installed themselves in an abandoned house to celebrate their success before returning to their ships. One of their leaders, William de Blois, lord of Treslong, suggested that, as Elizabeth had just banned them from using English ports, they should fortify the town and hold it in the name of William. The next day, the flag of Orange was fluttering for the first time from the walls of a town in the Low Countries.

Initially, William failed to grasp the significance of this success, but his brother Louis, with his better military sense, seized on its importance immediately and urged the Beggars to take Flushing which commanded the sea approaches to the port of Antwerp. Within a few days the Beggars had taken this important stronghold and within a few months they had raised the flag of Orange in most of the towns of Holland and Zeeland, with the exception of Amsterdam. It was an astonishing victory; even though Alva was distracted at that time by a threat from France, it was in complete contradiction to William's thesis that the revolt could succeed only with the aid of outside powers. In fact, it was the curtailment of such aid, which provided the impetus for the Beggars to establish their first bridgehead.

The Spanish troops, under the count of Bossu, had no success in expelling the Beggars from the maritime towns and little more in raising popular feelings against them. The Beggars had several factors in their favour. They were urged on by their faith, their hopes of plunder and their recklessness. Their leaders—lesser nobles exiled from their own lands—were desperate men, with nothing to lose and everything to gain. For years, they and the country gentlemen, who were also prominent among the Beggars, had suffered economically, as growing inflation reduced the profits from their estates. Now, as town after town fell to them, fellow exiles sailed across the North Sea from England to join them, taking the places of those town regents who had fled, or who had been expelled from office for being too favourable to the Catholic cause. The Beggars were fighting for the resumption of their privileges and position under the banners of a new reformed faith.

Although the regent class included some Protestants and perhaps many more who were willing to pose as such in public, they were as a class, Catholic and conservative; they had a vested interest in preserving the *status quo*. It was not so with the ordinary citizens and the working classes. Both had been hard-pressed by Alva's proclamation of a 10 per cent purchase tax on all goods in March 1572—the notorious 'Tenth Penny'—while unemployment had become particularly high among one of the major working class groups in these maritime provinces—the fishermen. Calvinism, with its powerful and pertinent appeal of predestination—the salvation of the elect—gained many adherents among the fishermen. Some of them went to join the rebel forces; those who remained in the towns acted as a fifth column for the Beggars. The speedy victories of the Beggars were made possible by these conflicts in the towns between the regents and the Catholic clergy on one hand, and the citizens and unemployed on the other.[15]

Like many revolutionary parties, the Calvinists soon divided into rival factions of moderates and extremists. As is again quite common in such situations, the dispute centred on the correct interpretation of the master works. The conflict started between Jacobus Arminius and Franciscus Gomarus, professors of theology at Leiden University. The complex ramifications of their conflict need not concern us here.[16] Ostensibly the argument was over predestination. The Arminians—later known as Remonstrants—believed that the elect did not automatically achieve salvation, but merely the chance of attaining it; the Gomarists, known later as counter-Remonstrants, believed implicitly and finally in the inevitable salvation of the elect. Much of the conflict centred on the 'correct' interpretation of two basic documents, the Heidelberg catechism and the confession of faith, composed in 1561 by Guy de Bray, a Calvinist from the southern provinces of the Low Countries. Although the argument became formalised into austere intellectual and theological forms, in essence it involved a far more important issue, which has been central to the whole ideological development of western Europe since the Reformation: the conflict between a

doctrinaire view, represented by the Gomarists, and a latitudinarian view, represented by the Arminians. While the former
believed entirely in the rigidity of doctrine, the latter allowed
the action of individuals some free play. (This dichotomy of
views still persists in Dutch Protestantism.)

What started as an academic dispute in a university soon
spread to engulf the whole nation, with various provinces supporting different sides. The dispute would have had fewer consequences if the two most powerful men in the Netherlands
—the stadtholder and the advocate of Holland—had not
become involved on different sides.

The office of stadtholder had not ceased with William but
had continued as a curious political anomaly from the days of
Spanish rule. In 1585, William's second son, Maurice of Nassau,
had been appointed stadtholder of Holland and Zeeland to
counter the growing power of the earl of Leicester. Five years
later, he was appointed stadtholder in three other provinces—
Utrecht, Overijssel and Gelderland. His cousin, William Louis,
was stadtholder in Friesland and Groningen. As stadtholder,
Maurice had considerable political powers, including the right
of appointing a considerable number of municipal magistrates
who, in their turn, chose the representatives in the states of
Holland; but his main aptitudes and interests were military.
Not only was he commander-in-chief of the land and naval
forces of the province of Holland, but in 1588, the States-
General had appointed him captain-general and admiral-
general of the whole republic. A position of equally great
authority was held by the advocate of Holland, who presided
over the meetings of the states of the province, acted as foreign
secretary and led the Holland delegation in the States-General.
This position, which was then held for life, was occupied from
1586 by Johan van Oldenbarnevelt, one of William's lieutenants
in the early stages of the struggle.* Oldenbarnevelt was the
major political force in Holland.

*After Oldenbarnevelt's execution, the title of the office was changed to
council-pensionary (*raad-pensionarius*). The office could be held for five years
only, with the right of re-election.

Initially, these two men worked successfully in close collaboration under the strain of Parma's brilliant compaigns in 1578–89, which reduced the republic again to a basic holding of Holland, Zeeland and Friesland. Then, like Alva before him, Parma was forced to turn his attentions southwards to France. This fortuitous opportunity was seized by Maurice, who, in a series of brilliant campaigns from 1590 onwards, succeeded in regaining much of Groningen, Drenthe and Overijssel and in establishing a bridgehead around Breda, south of the great river estuaries, which was probably the main turning-point in the struggle against Spain. But by the end of the century, stalemate had developed with both sides struggling futilely each summer over the possession of a few towns. The continuance of the indecisive struggle proved financially exhausting to both Spain and to the Dutch republic. In 1609, Oldenbarnevelt was responsible for concluding a twelve-year truce, in which Spain recognised the republic as 'free states'.

Oldenbarnevelt's great political victory failed to please all men and all classes at home. The Calvinists looked upon the truce as a capitulation; the merchants of Amsterdam wanted to form a West India Company to compete against the Spanish and the Portuguese in their American possessions; while Maurice, himself, thought that his powers as stadtholder would be less in a republic at peace than they would be in a state of war. The three together formed a very powerful party interested in reopening the war. It was again the more extreme Calvinists who took the lead in opposition to Oldenbarnevelt by reviving their demands for a national synod in which they hoped to have the Arminians denounced. Oldenbarnevelt, who favoured moderation, managed to resist their demands for a number of years, but in May 1617, the States-General by a majority of one, declared in favour of calling a national synod. In August of the same year, Oldenbarnevelt persuaded the states of Holland to agree to set up militias in the towns, to guard against any disturbances or coercion by the forces of the republic. This was a direct challenge to Maurice's authority that he could not ignore. Throwing in his lot completely with the counter-Remonstrants, he travelled from town to town dismissing Remonstrant regents and disbanding militias.

In August 1618, he had Oldenbarnevelt and others arrested on the authority of the States-General. Tried before a specially-summoned court, composed largely of counter-Remonstrants and members of the 'war' party, Oldenbarnevelt was condemned to death at his sham trial for a whole catalogue of 'crimes', including supporting unorthodox religious teachings and accepting presents from foreign powers. He was executed in May 1619.

The counter-Remonstrants achieved only a partial victory at the synod of Dordrecht held contemporaneously with Oldenbarnevelt's trial. They succeeded in having Arminianism proscribed, some of its ministers banished and Leiden University purged. But they failed to secure the total theocracy they had sought; the civil authority retained its control over Catholic estates sequestered during the war and also kept its right to be consulted on the appointment of ministers. The Calvinist church became the recognised, though not the established, church of the Netherlands.[17]

This was the nearest the Netherlands ever came to ideological excess. With the death of Maurice in 1625, and his replacement as stadtholder by the more moderate Frederick Henry, there was a return to reason and the teachings of Erasmus, in which religion was viewed far more as a philosophy of life than one of supernatural salvation. This 'humanistic religion' had some notable adherents in the Low Countries, including Georgius Cassander, Dirck Volckertsz Coornhert and Justus Lipsius.[18]

Although Catholics also suffered, being excluded from public office and forbidden to worship in public, Catholicism never disappeared. Wealthy Catholics built chapels upon their estates and, in the towns, Catholic merchants created chapels in the upper storeys of their houses.* In the captured 'generality'

*One of these, now preserved as a museum though it was in public use until 1887, may be seen in the house built by the merchant Jan Hartman in Amsterdam in 1661. The lower storeys are furnished with a plain simplicity, but a narrow winding staircase leads to an ornate chapel of Our Lord in the Attic, which runs the whole length of two adjoining houses. In 1681, there were twenty-six known chapels of this kind in Amsterdam.

lands of the south, which were administered by the States-General, there were always (as there still are) many Catholics. Towards the end of the eighteenth century, one writer estimated that one-third of the Dutch were Catholics. Throughout the seventeenth century, the persistence of the older faith was revealed in numerous proclamations made by the civil power, similar to the one of February 1651, forbidding people to attend Catholic services held in foreign embassies in the Netherlands, and another of December 1655, prohibited the inhabitants of four towns from interfering with Protestant services. The religious problem was settled pragmatically. The Catholics were discriminated against in public, but allowed to worship in private; while the Calvinists never gained the degree of public recognition that they desired.

# 3

# The Golden Age

THE REAL VICTORY in the Eighty Years' War went to the rich merchants and regent classes in the towns of the maritime provinces, particularly those in Amsterdam. It was in these towns that in the midst of war the golden age of the Dutch republic flourished. These self-perpetuating oligarchies kept their own self-interest resolutely before them. Their voices could not be ignored any more than their financial subsidies; it was they who profited most from the war and they who paid for much of it. Not that they remained totally unaffected by the politico-religious struggle; in its long course scarcely any man could be. Nevertheless, for ten years the Amsterdam regents succeeded in keeping the city out of the fight against Spain, even though it lay in rebel territory and was blockaded and besieged by Beggar forces. Their motives for doing so were based partly on an internal power struggle within the city itself. During the first half of the sixteenth century, a new class of wealthy merchants had arisen who had been kept out of power by the established regents. In 1567, a number of the new rich, who had repeatedly complained about corruption in the city's administration, had been forced to flee and had later joined William's forces.[1] It was only by keeping out of the war that the established regents could keep these new men from seizing power. Although the rebel blockade 'nearly annihilated' the city as a commercial centre, the regents continued in their allegiance to Spain.[2] Eventually, however, it was the threat to their trade raised by the blockade that persuaded them to join the rebel cause. They had succeeded in beating off a rebel attack in November 1577; but 'the towne of Amsterdam, beeing thereby brought into, great feare of surprize, and having bin long beseeged both by water and land, resolved to fal to an agreement with the Estates of Holland, which was made upon the 8. of February, 1578'.[3] The returned Calvinist merchants soon replaced the Catholic regents; monks and priests were expelled from the town. Amsterdam became as fiercely pro-rebel as it had once been anti-rebel, supporting the counter-Remonstrants for a time, but becoming more moderate again once their commercial objects had been achieved with the founding of the Dutch West India Company after the truce had expired.

The rise of Amsterdam as a trading centre was spectacular. There were two main phases of expansion. The first occurred approximately between 1550 and 1590, and the second approximately between 1600 and 1620, after the Spanish had captured Antwerp in 1585, thus crippling the trade not only of the port itself, but also to a certain extent that of the Zeeland ports which were dependent on it. By the beginning of the seventeenth century, Amsterdam had three-quarters of all the Dutch trade through the Sound between Denmark and Sweden into the Baltic. Twenty-seven per cent of the republic's total finances came from Amsterdam.[4]

As Antwerp declined, people and prosperity shifted north to Amsterdam. The city became crowded with foreign refugees and merchants, and its boundaries thrust out into the surrounding countryside in a rash of land reclamation and speculation as new homes were built to accommodate the growing population. The population of the city rose from approximately 30,000 in 1567 to an estimated 105,000 in 1622 and to approximately 200,000 by 1675.[5] Some of the refugees were merchants who had fled from the Spanish-held southern provinces of what is now Belgium; tax returns from 1631 show that about one-third of the richest inhabitants in the city were of southern origin.[6] There was also a sizeable Jewish community, which totalled 20,000 by the end of the seventeenth century. Although there were some relatively prosperous Jews among the first group of refugees from Spain and Portugal, the native burghers had such a firm hold over the city's trade that there were only six Jews among the 1,500 biggest taxpayers in 1631. In addition, there were thousands of Protestant skilled workers who had fled from the industrial regions of what is now southern Belgium.

Partly as a consequence of this influx of capital and workers, a certain amount of industry developed in the Netherlands, but the basis of the regents' wealth was mainly, as it always had been, shipping and trade. Amsterdam was extremely favourably sited as a market for corn and spices. When ships returned to the main spice market of Lisbon at the end of August, it was too late for them to reach Danzig in the same year. Similarly, the Baltic corn fleets had to spend the winter in south European ports and return to their home ports in the spring. But both spices and corn could reach Amsterdam before the winter, and it was this favourable position that was the basis of the city's wealth.[7]

The size of the Dutch fleets remained a source of amazement to foreign observers during the seventeenth century. At the beginning of the seventeenth century, it was reported that a fleet of 800 to 900 ships had left Amsterdam for the Baltic in a period of three days. Colbert, the French statesman, said that the Netherlands had 15,000 to 16,000 ships out a world total of 20,000. And similar large estimates were made by Sir William Petty and Sir Walter Raleigh. But probably all of them were exaggerated. A more reliable estimate made by the states of

Holland in 1636, put the number of Dutch ships trading to the Baltic, Norway and France at just over a thousand.[8] Whatever the actual size of the Dutch merchant marine, there is little doubt that it was extremely large. The Sound tolls register shows that even by the last quarter of the sixteenth century, more than half the ships passing through the Sound were Dutch. And in ship design and construction the Dutch led the world with their development of the *fluit*, or flyboat, a cheap freighter, which first appeared in the 1590s.

The Amsterdam merchants placed profits before patriotism. They supplied the Spanish forces with grain; invested in Dunkirk privateers preying on other Dutch shipping; bought munitions from Liège and sold them to the highest bidder. For these activities they should not be too harshly condemned: such impartial speculation was not uncommon at that time; a sense of Dutch national identity had not been completely established; and the proceeds from this trade were essential to the successful prosecution of the war against the enemy, Spain. Nevertheless, the Amsterdam merchants were probably more grasping than most others.

In search of even greater profits, Dutch merchants extended the scope of their voyages. In 1590, for the first time, Dutch ships passed through the Straits of Gibraltar into the Mediterranean, trading first with Italy and then with the Levant. Shortly after that, Dutch vessels returned from the Gold Coast with a valuable cargo of ivory, gold and pepper. These maritime ventures were stimulated even more by the Spanish embargo on Dutch ships in peninsular ports towards the end of the sixteenth century. This exclusion from the spice markets encouraged merchants to send their ships to the source of the spices themselves. In 1595, Cornelius de Houtman sailed from Amsterdam and just over two years later returned from Java with a valuable cargo of spices. In the first half of the seventeenth century, they extended their voyages to all parts of the globe with Lemaire's and Schouten's voyage round Cape Horn in 1616, and Tasman's voyage to Tasmania and New Zealand in 1642, among many others.[9]

The Dutch United East India Company was established in 1602, with Amsterdam holding half the shares. Not only did the company make enormous trading profits, but it also laid the main foundations of the Dutch overseas empire, with its conquest of Java in the Dutch East Indies, the establishment of the Cape settlement in South Africa in 1652, and the conquest of Ceylon in 1656. The Dutch West India Company, formed in 1621 at the expiration of the twelve years' truce, was less successful, both in profitability (apart from Piet Heyn's capture of the Spanish silver fleet in 1628) and in the permanent acquisition of overseas territory, though this was not the original intention of either company. It captured Portuguese territory in Brazil, but never firmly established itself there. In 1626, Peter Minuit bought the island of Manhattan from the Indians for 60 guilders and established a settlement there, which he called New Amsterdam. (Less than forty years later, it was captured by the English and renamed New York.) But it was more successful in the West Indies. In 1634, it took possession of three islands in the Leeward Islands off the Venezuelan coast and at about the same time captured some of the Windward Islands. 'The Dutch flag became the only one in the world at that time to fly in five different continents.'[10] The achievements of the two million inhabitants of the Dutch republic in its golden age which lasted from approximately 1610 to 1680 (almost contemporaneous with the life of Rembrandt) were truly remarkable. It was the last great flourishing of the medieval city-state in a post-Reformation context.

Central to that development were the activities of the regent class of the province of Holland which constituted a close clan of relatives, friends and business acquaintances who monopolised the lucrative carrying trade. Christensen gives a fascinating account of the rise to wealth and power of one member of this class, gained from some of the earliest surviving papers of a regent's complicated financial and commercial transactions.[11] Claes Adriaensz van Adrichem was the son of a prominent corn merchant in the brewing city of Delft who in 1560, at the age of twenty-two, set up as a merchant on his own account.

Initially, he bought corn from the surrounding farms, but within ten years, he was also importing it from abroad. By then, he had taken a stake in another lucrative trade—the herring industry. His import-export business expanded so that he was soon dealing in salt, timber, flax and hemp and other naval stores. He appointed permanent factors, usually relatives, in many commercial centres overseas. Van Adrichem's papers show that he invested his profits in a variety of ways, including property in both town and country, short-term loans and mortgages; he also handled the investments of many members of his family. By 1585, he had become burgomaster of Delft and in 1597, he was admitted to the provincial government; from that time on, firmly established financially, he devoted himself more and more to public affairs.

Throughout the cities of Holland, and above all in Amsterdam, the regents lived a prosperous, secure life in their tall town houses. Even the most biased and envious foreign observers (and there were many of those) could not fail to be impressed by the wealth of the Amsterdam regents. One anonymous visitor remarked: 'Every Private House here looks like an Ale-house and is painted with Green, Red and White, and they are so sensible of their Country Villanies, that every Window has its Iron Gates, like our Jayle, in order to keep the Felon its owner out of harms way.'[12] The 'Iron Gates' were necessary because these houses were used more as business premises than homes; the top storeys were used as warehouses and the lower floors as store-rooms, for the merchants' treasures.[13] Apart from the extremely rich, very few merchants used any of the lower-storey rooms for living in. The kitchen was used only once a week; in winter, the family heated their food in a recess beside the kitchen and in summer, lived outside on the pavement.[14] Within the house itself, the maids and housewives constantly scurried to and fro, cleaning, polishing, scrubbing and sanding. Aglionby noted that some of the housewives were 'so curious, as not to let you come into their rubb'd rooms, without putting on a pair of Slippers, or making your own Shooes very clean. . . . Every day they rub and wash the lower Floors, and straw them with fine Sand, and make them so neat, that Strangers often make a scruple of spitting in them.'[15]

In paintings of Dutch interiors, the long-handled broom, the wooden bucket and the cleaning cloth are never far away. This ceaseless care was not motivated by a passion for cleanliness alone, but more by the merchants' concern to protect their investments. Owing to the absence of a royal court and the prevailing Calvinist discouragement of public display, there was a lack of opportunity for ostentation; physical shortage of land restricted investment in real estate. Instead, the prosperous merchants filled the rooms leading off from the neatly scrubbed, sanded and tiled corridors of their homes with tapestried furniture, gilded heads, delicate Delft ceramics, ornate spinets, precious tapestries, works of art in gold and silver (often made by Jewish refugees) and above all pictures. The home became both the symbol and the safeguard of success.

It is for its paintings that the golden age is still best known abroad. In that short period of about seventy-five years, a group of extraordinary artists were at work—Cuyp, Pieter de Hoogh, Frans Hals, Hobbema, Rembrandt van Rijn, the Ruysdaels, Jan Steen, Vermeer—to mention only some of the better known. Although some harbingers of their development may be found in the early Netherlandish school of paintings (which preceded the final division of the Low Countries), the Dutch painted a completely new world from other European schools, in which most mythologies were banished, each person and each object having its own validity and value. They produced a plain record of every-day events; women seated at, or by, their virginals, maids cleaning, interiors of town houses, country scenes of ruined aqueducts and castles, cloudy seascapes and frozen canals, with ships stuck in the ice, skaters, sleds and tall tents used as drinking booths. There is scarcely a smile or any other emotion, except for a rather sombre Calvinist earnestness of expression, a certain fixity engendered partly by the posed sense of occasion, but also by a deeper and more controlled feeling of a disciplined life. Everyone seems to be so purposeful, to know exactly what they are about, even if it is no more than posing by a virginal; it is an active, workaday world. Only in a few paintings, such as Nicolaas Maes' *A Sleeping Maid and her Mistress* do we find some comment: a maid is asleep before a pile of kitchen utensils, earthenware casseroles, plates and ladles, while her mistress stands by her side, her outstretched hand and her reproving look revealing her sense of slight distaste at such idleness—'Is this what we pay our servants for?' Yet even here, there is an overriding sense of reasonableness and gentleness; the mistress's clothes are not so very different from those of the maid and she looks as if she could do the work herself. The maid will not be kicked or cuffed as she would have been in many other countries; in fact, such actions were forbidden by law. This is a society which, within its contemporary limitations, was kind to maids, to the poor and to animals. The well-fed pet dog poses in so many of the pictures, brought in specially perhaps for the occasion, but even in the peasant's home the dog licks out the blue casserole on the floor, sharing what seems to be a skimpy meal for four, while in the austere churches the dogs run free or 'beg' to their masters by standing on their hindlegs. The bourgeois virtues of hard work, public courtesies and general probity reign supreme, so that even the odd scenes of mild debauchery have a furtive and artificial air.* Nudity is almost totally banished; the face, not the body, becomes the reflection of the soul. This is so even in Rembrandt's paintings which transcend all others; he, almost alone, was able to create a mythology out of contemporary portraits and to induce modern attitudes into mythology. In all, the Dutch school presents a remarkable record of a civilisation, which though it has vanished, still exercises great influence upon the Dutch.

But the contributions of the golden age in other spheres were almost as great, though less well known abroad: in international law, Hugo de Groot (Grotius); in astronomy and physical science, Christiaan Huygens; in literature, Joost van den Vondel; and in philosophy, Spinoza, the Amsterdam Jew.[16]

*In society itself debauchery did exist but it was rigidly controlled; the many brothels in Amsterdam were licensed by the town authorities.

The aggregate impact upon the rest of Europe was enormous; the Dutch style of life became extremely fashionable. Foreign visitors took home with them not only physical products, such as tiles, ceramics and tulip bulbs, but also ideas on architecture, agriculture and land reclamation. In architecture, for example, the Dutch extensive use of brickwork and of curled gables became also an English vogue. There was a great demand abroad for the services of Dutch hydraulic engineers.

The process of land reclamation, which had been going on for many centuries in the Netherlands, reached a climax in the first quarter of the seventeenth century, when 80,000 acres of land were permanently reclaimed, a total never since exceeded.[17] All over Holland, the dikemasters in their high pointed hats, baggy trousers and greased leather boots were at work reclaiming new land and strengthening and repairing existing sea defences. The boom in land reclamation was encouraged by the fact that during the early stages of the revolt against Spain, many hundreds of acres of land had been flooded, some of it deliberately, as on the most famous occasion in 1574, when two major dikes were breached to relieve the besieged town of Leiden. Speculators bought up the flooded land cheaply, hoping to make a quick profit. Though some of them doubtless did so, the work was expensive and not unattended by failure. Although the Beemster was eventually drained in 1610, many people lost money in an earlier attempt to reclaim it. Expense also prevented the most ambitious scheme of all, proposed by the notable engineer, Jan Leeghwater. An expert in the use of windmills for pumping out water, Leeghwater had proposed a carefully worked-out scheme for draining the 40,000-acre Haarlem lake by using 160 windmills. The project would have cost 3,600,000 guilders.[18] (The work was not completed until 1853, using steam-driven pumps, instead of windmills.) Nevertheless, the Dutch mastery of land reclamation, the art of building windmills and the planting of suitable crops on reclaimed land, created a demand for their engineers throughout Europe; they worked in England, Germany, France, Italy, Denmark, Sweden, Poland and Russia. At the same time, emigrant entrepeneurs and skilled workmen secured a hold on the economic activities of many European countries, particularly in the north. They played a prominent part in Iceland, England, Russia and Scandinavia, where the Swedish port of Gothenburg was built by Dutch engineers in the Dutch style.

Not all that the Dutch touched turned to gold. The vast influx of wealth and the relatively limited opportunities for investment encouraged financial speculation; one of the worst financial crashes occurred in 1637, when hundreds of investors lost money in 'bubble' companies set up to grow tulips.* And for the ordinary people and the sailors, on whom so much of the prosperity of the republic depended, this was anything but a golden age. There was much poverty and unemployment and the sailors were probably lower paid and worse fed than those of other nations. But the working classes during this period were probably only marginally worse off than those elsewhere, and in the maritime provinces at least there was probably better provision for their relief than in other European countries.

The full independence of the republic was finally recognised by Spain in the Treaty of Münster, 1648, even though it had already been established in principle at the beginning of the twelve years' truce in 1609. By the treaty, the republic was recognised as free and independent; it was allowed to retain the captured 'generality' lands in the south, and it obtained freedom of navigation in the East and West Indies. The small divided republic had succeeded in its fight against the world power of Spain to a degree that no other country had anticipated. But within a few years it was to face an even more formidable challenge, not from a Catholic king, but from a Protestant republic like itself.

---

*Tulip bulbs were so precious that they were grown in specially made silver tulip cups, which were highly ornate and decorated.

# 4

# The Collapse of the
# Dutch Republic

THE DUTCH republic suffered no sudden death, but survived
until the end of the eighteenth century when it was invaded by
the armies of revolutionary France. During the eighteenth century, there was still some scientific and philosophical achievements and the regents remained extremely rich, but the glories
of the previous golden age disappeared. Painting declined;
administration became increasingly corrupt; and both the
army and the navy became small and powerless.* One of the
prime reasons for this decline was the smallness of the population which, according to the most recent estimates, virtually
stagnated in the eighteenth century, increasing from just under
2 million in 1700, to only just over 2 million in 1795, the year
of the first truly national census.[1] The country was too small to

---

*Some recent Dutch research, however, has tried to show that the decline
was not so catastrophic as was once believed.

play a large part on the world's stage for long. It had over-strained itself, and was overshadowed and eventually eclipsed by bigger European powers. From the middle of the seventeenth century it had to face an increasing challenge, first from England at sea, and then from France on the land.

Throughout the seventeenth century, English envy of the Dutch pre-eminence in shipping and world trade had been growing. In 1651, England passed the Navigation Act, under which goods could be imported into England only in English ships or those of the producing country. This attempt to cripple the Dutch carrying trade had little immediate success, however, as Amsterdam was still too firmly established as a centre of world trade. In the following year, a naval war broke out between the two countries. The English objects were frankly commercial; Blake, the English admiral, was instructed, among other things, to 'interrupt and disturb' the Dutch trade to the Baltic.[2] The Dutch fleets, under their brilliant commanders Martin Tromp and Michael de Ruyter, came off somewhat worse in the various naval encounters and the Dutch sued for peace, which was restored in 1654. The war reduced Dutch trade 'noticeably, if not disastrously'.[3]

The peace did not last for long. In 1665, a second war broke out between the two countries. This went less well for the English, who captured only about half the amount of prizes they had done in the first.[4] Even more humiliating for the English was de Ruyter's brilliant attack on Chatham in June 1667, when part of his fleet forced its way through the boom at Gillingham on the river Medway and destroyed six large English warships.* The Dutch sailed off with a flagship, the *Royal Charles*, in tow.[5] Peace was restored by the Treaty of Breda, 1667, under which the English retained New Amsterdam which they had captured from the Dutch and the Dutch kept Surinam, on the north-eastern coast of Latin America, which they had taken from the English.

*In June, 1967, a Dutch warship sailed through a symbolic barrier of water thrown up by a fire-float in the river Medway as part of the celebrations of the tercentenary of de Ruyter's daring feat.

Within five years, however, the Dutch were forced to fight again. This time they had to face the powerful combination of England and France. Louis xiv intended to annex the strategically important Low Countries, by wresting the southern provinces from Spain and by invading the Dutch republic in the north. From these intentions the Dutch were saved by a combination of the well-tested naval skill of de Ruyter and the diplomatic and military expertise of the young prince of Orange, William iii. For twenty years previously, there had been no stadtholder in the major provinces and the country had been a republic in which Johan de Witt, the council-pensionary of Holland, was the most powerful figure. In 1672, he was murdered at the instigation of Orangist supporters, while William iii was swept into power as stadtholder on a wave of popular acclaim. William's whole policy was directed towards the isolation of France by coming to some accommodation with England. In 1674, two years after the war had started, he succeeded in making a separate peace with England. Three years later, he rounded off this achievement by marrying Mary, daughter of the duke of York, the future James ii. After James became king in 1685, William cultivated the growing opposition in England to the king's Catholicism and increasingly authoritarian rule. When a son was born to James, hopes of a Protestant succession under his daughter Mary were destroyed,* and leading Whigs and Tories in England combined to invite William to invade England. He did so in 1688, and in the following year, William and Mary were crowned joint sovereigns of England, while William remained also stadtholder of the republic until his death in 1702. After more than fifty years of bitter commercial rivalry between the two countries, they were at last in a position to present a united front against the real enemy—France. The wars against France lasted, with one brief uneasy interval, for the next twenty-five years, with the War of the League of Augsburg, 1689–97, and the War of Spanish Succession, 1701–13.

*James had become a Catholic in 1668 or 1669, but his brother Charles ii had insisted that James's daughter Mary be raised a Protestant.

The Dutch retained their independence, but at a great price. By the successive barrier treaties of 1709–15, they gained the right to garrison forts in what is now Belgium to protect themselves against any resurgence of French expansionism. But the long campaigns proved to be both militarily and financially exhausting for the Dutch; their national debt increased nearly fivefold between 1688 and 1713. Meanwhile, England by the Treaty of Utrecht, 1713, had laid the foundations of a vast overseas empire, which was soon to surpass that of its small ally and former rival. From that time on, the Dutch were to be increasingly dependent upon British naval power for retention of their empire overseas.

It was not surprising that the Dutch republic should have been so soon eclipsed as an international power. For almost a century and a half, from the outbreak of the revolt against Spain to the Treaty of Utrecht, it had been engaged almost continuously in war or preparation for war. No small country could withstand such a strain for so long. Nevertheless, it was also weakened by internal disputes between the stadtholders and the regents of Holland, whose interests were fundamentally opposed. The conflict between them flared up almost immediately after the Treaty of Münster, which ended the war against Spain. Although the size of the army was reduced, the province of Holland wanted to make it even smaller by disbanding some foreign mercenaries, reducing the number of officers and abolishing 'solicitors' who were paid a commission for recruiting soldiers. The stadtholder, William II, had six members of the states of Holland arrested and planned to seize Amsterdam, the heart of the incipient revolt. 'Certainly if he had taken Amsterdam', one contemporary writer avowed, 'he would have made himself Soveraign of these Countries, to have made slaves of these people of Holland. His intentions were to have seized upon the Banck there, and the stock of the town, which is many millions.'[6] To avoid a long siege and the possibility of civil war, the Amsterdam regents made peace with the stadtholder, but their interests were never finally reconciled. The Amsterdam regents wanted republican rule, a policy of neutrality and a strong navy, while the stadtholders continued to favour centralised control, an alliance with England and a strong army. These fundamental disagreements created a great internal weakness.

One of the reasons for the failure to solve this problem was the fact that the Dutch, through the pressures of these almost ceaseless wars, had been forced to act as a nation long before they ever created a formally constituted state.* They could preserve a large degree of unity in war, but much less in peace.†

An even bigger reason, perhaps, was the fact that the regents, in common with some republicans in Commonwealth England, were far in advance of their times in wanting a constitutional monarch, while the kings and princes and even rulers like Cromwell were unwilling to act in that capacity for long. Throughout the seventeenth and eighteenth centuries, with some rarer periods of co-operation, such as that between William III and Anthony Heinsius just before the outbreak of the War of the Spanish Succession, the regent classes and the stadtholders alternated in power. The first period of Orangist rule, under Prince Maurice, Prince Frederick Henry and William II, lasted from 1619 to 1650. This was followed by a period of republican rule under Johan de Witt, who was murdered in 1672. From 1672 to 1702 William III was stadtholder. Following his death, the country again came under republican rule until 1747 when William IV became stadtholder, and this period of Orangist rule under him and his son William V lasted, though with increasing ineffectiveness and some intervals, until 1795 when the country was subjugated by the revolutionary armies of France. The monarchical principle was never conceded in full nor finally abandoned; each province retained the right to choose its own

---

*This is in marked contrast to their southern neighbour, Belgium, which became a formally constituted state in 1831, even though it is still somewhat doubtful if it has become a nation.

†Even in the first Anglo–Dutch war, there was a great clash of interests between the needs of trade and the defence of the realm. Tromp and de Ruyter wanted to concentrate all available naval forces to destroy the enemy at sea, while the merchants wanted to use more warships to protect their convoys of merchantmen.

stadtholder until the middle of the eighteenth century when William IV was made stadtholder.*

In the same way, there was a great conflict of interests between the maritime provinces, particularly Holland, which wanted a strong navy, and the land provinces of Gelderland and Overijssel—usually the first to be invaded in war—who wanted a strong army. This became intertwined in the dispute between the stadtholders and the regents of Holland. The stadtholders also wanted a strong army, because it provided a base for their own internal power and because such a policy pleased the rural nobility on whom the stadtholders partly depended for support. Eventually a compromise was reached under which all provinces contributed towards both the army and the navy, but the net result was that both branches of the forces were under-subsidised. The republic attempted to solve the problem by trying to remain outside the conflicts of the eighteenth century. It succeeded in remaining neutral for part of the War of the Austrian Succession (1740–8) and for the whole of the Seven Years' War (1756–63). But neutrality only led to the further neglect of its forces and, by the end of the century, this had become so chronic that the republic lay open to humiliation by either sea or by land. Its naval weakness was strikingly revealed when England declared war on the republic for the fourth and final time in 1780, because of Dutch support for the Americans during their war of independence. The country which a century before had been able to send 100 warships to sea could muster only seventeen.[7] The army proved no more effective against the French invasion in 1794–5.

But whatever defence efforts had been made, the republic was too small to maintain its former position. The same factor was responsible for its being overtaken in the economic sphere. Its internal market was too small, its natural resources too scarce, its dependence on the carrying trade and finishing industries too great for it to be able to compete with the growing trading

---

*In the first stadtholderless period, there was a stadtholder in Friesland and Groningen, but the powerful provinces did not have one.

and industrial strengths of other European countries, particularly England. During the eighteenth century, and particularly after 1730, the republic was surpassed by larger nations in many industrial spheres. Dutch exports of linens, woollens, pottery and gin declined one after another during the century.[8] Even in the herring industry, the traditional 'golden Mines of this Countrey',[9] there was increasing competition from abroad. But in this, as in other well-established trades, such as diamond cutting, the republic maintained a strong position to the end; in 1780, the Dutch still supplied about one-half of the total demand for cured herring in Europe.[10] Industries declined because the industrialist classes were not powerful enough to get adequate protection by means of tariffs and subsidies as was happening in England and France at that time. (The main exception was in the herring industry.) The ruling classes, merchants still, were more concerned with reducing duties than in increasing them.

But in the changed economic circumstances of the eighteenth century, the merchants suffered as well. As other nations began to develop their own merchant fleets, there was less need to use Amsterdam—and the other Dutch ports—as an entrepôt. As the main trade routes shifted away from the ports of Holland, there was a catastrophic decline in the shipbuilding industry, which also had its repercussions on defence. The Dutch, who had led the world in ship design with their development of the fast, cheap flyboat, now lagged behind other countries, still building their old deep-waisted ships instead of the more sturdy flush-decked ships. Natural factors, too, created further difficulties for the Dutch maritime trade. The silting up of harbours struck the final blow at many ports such as Enkhuizen and Hoorn on the Zuider Zee which from the middle of the eighteenth century began to decline into the *dode steden* (dead towns) of the present day.* Today, all that remains of the former glory and bustling activity of Hoorn are the merchants' houses, the

---

*In 1932, they were finally cut off from their outlet to the sea by the completion of the Afsluitdijk (enclosing dam) linking North Holland and Friesland which transformed the Zuider Zee into an inland lake, the Ijsselmeer.

weighing hall, the town gates and the warehouses and, on the far side of the world, Cape Horn, named after his home town by William Schouten on his voyage around the coast of South America. At about the same time as these ports started to go into an irreversible decline, the seaworm* started to attack the timber defences against coastal flooding and the wooden piles had to be replaced by expensive imported stone. This led to further increases in the heavy taxation in the maritime provinces, where even in the early eighteenth century, land was 'taxed at forty pence per acre for the first cost of erecting the Dykes; thirty pence for throwing or milling off the Floods, that are caused by excessive Rains; and twenty pence per Acre for keeping the Dykes and Highways in repair'.[11] Most eighteenth-century observers agreed that the general level of taxation was much higher than in other countries—to pay for defence, dikes and the public debt. These taxes, which extended over a wide range of essentials, bore most heavily upon the working classes, but also affected the merchants too, though their opportunities for evasion were probably greater.

There was, however, no sudden decline in the merchants' wealth. What was once believed to be an abrupt ending of the republic's prosperity in about 1650, was in fact no more than a temporary recession, and there was a further period of economic development between 1680 and 1730, and another boom during the Seven Years' War.[12] The economic strength of the merchants, with their accumulated wealth, commercial expertise and world-wide contacts, proved to be more durable than either military power or international status. The merchants adapted to the changed economic conditions by lending their money abroad, where interest rates were higher than the profit they could now expect to make by trading ventures. This outflow of capital caused more unemployment at home and lessened the amount of capital available for home industries.

To be a merchant remained fashionable to the end of the republic; it was the goal of many ambitious sons. Long before

*The seaworm or teredo is not a worm, but a bivalve mollusc which bores into timber leaving large holes which eventually destroy it.

such developments had occurred elsewhere, merchants were living comfortable, secure and respectable lives in their dormitory suburbs where they retired 'when the hours of business are over . . . from the tumult and confusion of the city, to enjoy the tranquillity of a secluded village'.[13] In such villages as Broek, only six miles from Amsterdam, there were by the end of the republic about a hundred merchants' houses, many with wooden carvings dating from the seventeenth century over the doors, illustrating the origins of the family fortune—the young man setting off for the tropics, his work on the plantation run by slaves and his triumphant return as a wealthy man to his homeland. The village streets were scrupulously clean and each home had its little front 'garden' made of shells, broken glass and bits of china, screened by the fantastically ornate products of the topiarist's art.

By the end of the eighteenth century, many of the rich were living in homes furnished in a foreign style, with French furnishings and curtains, carpeted floors and chandeliers imported from England. Even the shapes of the rooms had changed from the severe, but very beautiful, cube-like proportions of the seventeenth century into something long and narrow similar to an English drawing-room or a French salon. The home was no longer a place for self-denying industry as it had been in the seventeenth century. 'The rich Dutch merchants love fine houses, and also to enjoy them. For they don't (like some of our English gentelmen) build fine houses, and live in some little office or corner thereof, shutting up every good room in them, unless for company; but if the Dutch have good apartments they live in them. . . .'[14] Travel, too, was cheap and easy in the cabins of 'handsome commodious barges', which provided a regular service along the canals leaving 'at the ringing of a bell, punctual to a moment, at their appointed hours'.[15] As a class, the merchants were content and prosperous. concerned above all with the interests of their own calling and of their own province and town.

In Amsterdam there were thirty-six council members for a city with a population of over 200,000. Their policies were pragmatically conservative. They could still adapt to the pre-vailing winds, as they had done so often in the past, but usually managed, in spite of all vicissitudes, to preserve eventually the *status quo ante*. During the eighteenth century, it probably be-came more difficult to get into the regent class or its attendant circles, which for many decades had been consolidating its com-mercial and political power by the intermarriage of sons and daughters. But the regent class, like the English aristocracy, was never completely closed to new entrants; it was the openness which made it so durable and also helped to save the country from revolution. During the eighteenth century, too, corrup-tion among the regents almost certainly increased. Nepotism and the sale of public offices, which had been banned in Hol-land in 1579, reappeared in the eighteenth century.[16] But in spite of the increased corruption, it never became entirely unreceptive to new ideas.

Towards the end of the century, some of the Amsterdam regents—men such as Abbema, Bicker, van Leyden and de Jonge—had adopted the new 'enlightened' ideas of French and English philosophers.* But most regents remained conservative. The new ideas gained adherents among some army and naval officers, merchants who had made their money but found their ambitions for power frustrated by the established regent class, some of the nobility in the 'land' provinces, but primarily, per-haps, among middle-class intellectuals, such as doctors and lawyers, and the manufacturers. By the middle of the eighteenth century, the economic structure of some of the land provinces, in particular, was beginning to change. In Overijssel, for exam-ple, the number of rich men with fortunes of over 10,000 guilders decreased between 1675 and 1758, while the number of men with middle-class incomes rose. The new middle classes, such as

---

*There was indeed a strong, native civilised tradition in the Netherlands, manifested in the spirit of religious tolerance, the unrealised desire for a constitutional monarchy and the relatively humane way of life. In some of the provinces there had been no public executions for a century and in Amsterdam, during the eighteenth century, the average number was only one a year. But this tradition lacked a political form and philosophical codification.

the linen manufacturers of Twente, were already providing mortgages on the castles of the impoverished nobility or taking over the castles themselves.[17]

These new forces coalesced into a pro-French Patriot movement which grew steadily in strength as the century drew to a close. Some of the regents in Holland, Friesland, Groningen and other provinces proved themselves to be capable, as they had been so often in the past, of accommodating the new forces by making temporary alliances with the Patriots. In other places, such as Utrecht and Amsterdam, new regents more sympathetic to the Patriot cause were only introduced by force. These changes provoked riots among the working classes, who were fairly solidly pro-Orange and anti-French. In this period of intellectual turmoil, new political alignments might have been permanently forged, but there were no men sufficiently capable of taking advantage of the opportunities. As the Patriots, with the help of the French, started to take over the towns, civil war seemed imminent; but the only decisive action the stadtholder, William v, could take was to retire to his estates in the eastern part of the country.

His German-born wife, Wilhelmina, was far more determined, arrogant and resourceful, than her weak, unimaginative husband, and she herself took control of the situation. In 1787, after two years of increasing disorder in the country, she was determined to return to The Hague. On her journey she was stopped and held by Patriot forces. The Prussian king, Frederick William ii, incensed by this insult to his sister and fearing a French annexation of the country, ordered his troops into the Netherlands. They met with scarcely any resistance. The Patriot forces in Utrecht, whose fortifications had been erected under the direction of French engineers, fled in disarray and most of the towns of Holland, such as Leiden and Haarlem, opened their gates to the Prussians without a fight. Throughout the province of Holland, the working classes, firm supporters of the House of Orange, celebrated William's return by erecting triumphal arches, dancing in the streets and wearing Orange favours.[18] The most ardent Patriots fled to Amsterdam, hoping still for some support from the French; but when none came, the gates of that city were opened too. The revolution had been easily crushed. Under Wilhelmina's direction, the councils of Amsterdam and those of other cities were purged of Patriots, many of whom were banned from holding office for life. A considerable number fled to France, from where many of them, such as General Daendals and Admiral de Winter, returned within less than a decade, riding into power again on the backs of the French revolutionary forces.

A stronger stadtholder might have taken advantage of these opportunities to consolidate his powers, but William was far too weak. In 1794, when the troops of revolutionary France were poised for their attack upon the Netherlands, William appealed to the regents for help. In October of that year, he went to Amsterdam to ask the regents to allow the dikes to be breached as they had so often been before in the defence of the country against Spain. His pleas were supported by a deputation of citizens. At first, the regents refused to see the deputation, but then agreed while 'an immense and irresistible multitude . . . filled the avenues of the stadhouse, the square and the adjacent streets, and maintained, during the conference of their deputies with the regents, a profound and terrible silence. . . .'[19] The regents told the deputation that the question of inundating the countryside had not yet been discussed. In fact, no resistance was ever shown and in January 1795, 5,000 French troops marched unopposed into the city. At the same time the stadtholder fled to England, where he died in 1806.

The old republic was dead. A new Batavian republic (named after the tribes who had rebelled against the Romans) arose to take its place. Within a few days, a provisional assembly at The Hague had swept away many of the features of the old regime— the stadtholderate and the old councils—and had established freedom of the press, of religion and universal suffrage. But when it came to formulating a constitution, the old divisions between advocates of provincial autonomy and centralised power reappeared in a new form of federalist and unitary groupings. But these disputes were more academic than real.

What was really to decide the fate of the country was what happened in Paris, not in The Hague; political and constitutional changes were to echo those of France. In 1798, the Unitarists, supported by the French, staged a *coup* and established a Directory of Five such as that which had just been set up in France. A year after Napoleon became emperor, the Netherlands was placed under the control of a 'grand pensionary' with dictatorial powers and in the following year, 1806, Napoleon's brother, Louis Bonaparte, was made king of the Netherlands. But he proved to be more interested in his own power than his brother's imperial schemes. He tried to reduce Dutch military and financial aid to France, and was accused by his brother of tolerating Dutch smuggling which breached the continental system designed to exclude English goods. In 1810, Louis abdicated and the country was then annexed by France. The continuance of the continental system, the increasingly heavy financial demands made by France, the introduction of conscription and the tightening of censorship, all helped to alienate large sections of the population against Napoleon. By November 1813, the French, threatened by an invasion of their own country, started to evacuate the Netherlands. Some of the regents proclaimed a provisional government in The Hague and invited the last stadtholder's son to return to the Netherlands. He arrived in The Hague on November 30, 1813, and assumed the title of William I, Sovereign Prince of the Netherlands, a few days later. By the end of May 1814, the whole of the country had been freed from French troops. Within less than a year, William had become king of the Netherlands, ruling over an enlarged territory, which included what is now present-day Belgium.

# 5

# The Kingdom of
the Netherlands

THE BRITISH idea of creating a strong buffer state against
France by bringing the former Austrian provinces of Belgium
under the Dutch crown was the last attempt ever made to
create a strong, united middle kingdom. If it had succeeded, it
would have had immeasurable consequences for the future
political stability of continental Europe; but it failed as rapidly
as all previous attempts had done. By the summer of 1814, plans
for the amalgamation under William had already been accepted
by the allied powers. At the same time, William himself was
secretly negotiating with the Prussians for the cession of his
hereditary Nassau estates in exchange for the Duchy of Luxemburg. While the proposals for the united kingdom were still
being discussed at the Congress of Vienna, Napoleon escaped
from his exile in Elba and landed in France. In March, 1815,
without waiting for the allies' formal approval, William

proclaimed himself king of the Netherlands. Later that year, the union was approved by the Congress of Vienna and William was appointed Grand Duke of Luxemburg, which, however, also remained a member of the German confederation.

William was faced with a most difficult task. There were so many differences between the Netherlands and Belgium that almost any action that pleased one of them would be almost bound to offend at least some section of the population in the other. The official religion of the Netherlands—even though it contained a large minority of Catholics—was Protestant; while Belgium was predominantly Catholic. There were differences of language, too. Flemish, the language from which Dutch itself had originated, was still spoken by the ordinary people in the northern Belgium, but to many Dutchmen then it seemed a provincial patois. Furthermore, the language of some of the wealthy people in northern Belgium, and of the whole of the south, was French. The Netherlands, with its long trading and carrying tradition favoured low duties, while southern Belgium, where some of the most advanced coal mines and metallurgical industries in the whole of continental Europe were situated, wanted protective tariffs. There were many other differences. Some of these problems could, doubtless, have been evaded or left untouched, but William, unlike his father, the last stadtholder, was not the man to shirk any task, however formidable. He was obstinate, decisive and determined—an enlightened despot from the eighteenth century with nineteenth-century commercial overtones.

He set about his task with great vigour. In 1816, he introduced a high protectionist policy to help industry, though it had to be modified only five years later because of growing discontentment among the Dutch merchants. In 1817, the king went into partnership with John Cockerill, who established a manufacturing works at Seraing, Liège, which was shortly to become the largest on the continent. Five years later, he founded the 'Société Générale des Pays-Bas pour favoriser l'industrie nationale'. Everyone, even foreigners, who offered to introduce useful industry, received protection and money, wrote the Austrian ambassador to Metternich some years later.[1] At the same time, Dutch interests were not neglected; the king invested in a new company, the Nederlandsche Handelsmaatschappij, founded in 1824 to revive the Netherlands' trade to the East Indies which had been virtually obliterated during the Napoleonic wars. Internal communications were improved by the construction of new canals and roads; while education, particularly at the university level, was encouraged in both countries. To help finance these projects, customs duties were increased and taxes were put on bread and meat. William ruled his kingdom with an iron hand. Ministers were appointed and dismissed at his will; he controlled the state's finance; and he personally ruled the overseas possessions, which had been restored to the Netherlands by Britain after Napoleon's defeat, except for the strategically important Cape Colony and Ceylon. There was a parliament, but members of the upper house were appointed by the monarch for life, while members of the lower house were elected indirectly by members of the provincial councils. Parliament had very limited powers and even these could be by-passed by making orders in council. There were also restrictions on press freedom and free association.

At first, however, there was no widespread opposition to William's rule. In the Netherlands, the House of Orange, with its evocations of past glory, still commanded widespread popular appeal. And the industrialists, manufacturers and professional classes were still not large or strong enough to oppose William's autocratic rule. It was different in Belgium. There, the manufacturers were becoming increasingly wealthy, partly as a result of William's protectionist policy. Yet they were still excluded from real power. There was growing resentment over the high incidence of taxation, the sharing of the public debt that they had not incurred, the large number of Dutch ministers and the restrictions on press freedom. Belgian Catholics, too, were incensed by William's closure of seminaries, while all the ruling classes were incensed by his decree that French should be replaced by Dutch as the official language in northern Belgium. The king's autocratic rule encouraged an incipient Belgian nationalism and in 1828, brought the Belgian Liberals and Catholics together in an official union of opposition. Two years later, in August 1830, the Belgian revolution broke out.[2]

After an attempt to crush the revolution by force of arms had failed, William appealed in October for the great powers to intervene. The following month they met in London. By this time, the British had lost some of their enthusiasm for the united kingdom; its growing strength posed a threat to British industry, and the need for a strong buffer state against France no longer seemed so acute. Mainly under British pressure, the great powers decided to accept the separation of the two countries. William opposed this decision. A few days after Leopold of Saxe-Coburg took the oath in Brussels as first king of the Belgians—on July 21, 1831—the Dutch army attacked and made a swift advance into Belgian territory. Leopold asked the French for help. The London conference met again and drew up a second treaty which was more favourable to the Netherlands. Under this Treaty of Twenty-four Articles, the Netherlands received about half of the province of Limburg from the Belgians and greater Belgian help in settlement of the joint national debt. The Belgians, who had claimed the whole of Luxemburg, were awarded only the western part of it. William still refused to accept the new treaty and kept the country on a war footing until growing domestic pressure and a realisation that he was going to be given no better terms by the great powers, made him accept the settlement in 1838. It was ratified in the following year. In October 1840, he abdicated in favour of his son, William II.

The dream of a greater Netherlands had vanished, though it was to be revived by the Flemish later in the century. Almost fifty years of autocratic rule—first under the French and then under William—had produced some striking changes in the Netherlands. There was a strong, central authority, with common taxes and the Napoleonic civil and criminal codes of law. But in many other ways it remained extremely backward. Members of the provincial councils, who chose the members of the lower house of parliament, were elected by the three estates of nobility, town and country. Parliament was dominated by conservatives, many of them descendants of the old regent classes, ennobled now under William's decree that anyone who could prove their family had been regents for three generations could claim a title. There was little industrialisation, agriculture was primitive and was to remain so for another forty years. William's policy of protecting industry had been of more benefit to the southern provinces of Belgium and to his own pocket, than it had been to the Dutch themselves. By 1840, the country had been brought to the verge of bankruptcy with a national debt of 2,200 million guilders, an arrears of interest of 35 million guilders and a large deficit on the budget. It was kept solvent only by a voluntary loan of 126 million guilders and the profits from the forced labour system which had been introduced into Java in the East Indies at the beginning of the 1830s.*³

But the forced labour system in Java and the associated revival of the carrying trade to the Indies, had created a new prosperous middle class, particularly in Amsterdam, who allied with the professional classes to demand a greater share of political power. These liberals, led by Jan Rudolf Thorbecke, were too small a minority in parliament to achieve reform by themselves. In 1844, their proposals for constitutional reform were overwhelmingly defeated by the conservatives. The only other possible ally were the Catholics, who in the 1840s constituted over one-third of the population. In theory, the constitution of 1815 had granted Catholics equal political and civil rights; but in practice they were hampered in establishing their own schools and new monastic orders and had an unrepresentative share of public offices.⁴

In return for parliamentary support on constitutional reform, the liberals promised the Catholics emancipation. But reforms might have been much delayed if the new king had been stronger. William II—who was in all essentials as weak as his grandfather, the last stadtholder—was alarmed by riots which followed the failure of the potato crops in 1845 and 1847, and the overthrow of Louis-Philippe of France in February, 1848.

*See Chapter 16 below for developments in the East Indies.

In the following month, he set up a commission to draft a reform of the constitution.

The commission, which consisted of four liberals and one Catholic, proposed numerous reforms, including the introduction of ministerial responsibility, an annual budget, parliamentary control over colonial affairs, freedom of the press, the right of assembly and freedom of religion and education. These proposals were too extreme to please the majority of conservatives in parliament so that 'Europe witnessed the unusual spectacle in the revolutionary year 1848 of a government committed to a rather far-reaching programme of constitutional reform attempting to persuade a reluctant parliament to comply with the spirit of the times'.[5] The conservatives were still so powerful that several concessions had to be made to them, including the election of the members of the upper house by the provincial councils instead of by direct election. But the main reforms were passed intact in October 1848.

Relative to what had happened and what was happening in some other European countries at this time, these reforms were scarcely revolutionary. The Catholic episcopal hierarchy was re-established in 1853, though it caused such a storm of protest among extreme Protestants and conservatives that it brought about the downfall of the Thorbecke administration. The lower house of parliament was now elected directly, but on an extremely limited franchise based upon the amount of taxes paid. The king's powers had been greatly decreased, but power was transferred to the government not to parliament. A parliamentary democracy did not evolve until twenty years later when parliament established the principle that the government was dependent on its support, by repeatedly voting down the budget.

Economically and industrially the country remained backward. There were developments in traditional spheres, with Leeghwater's seventeenth-century scheme for draining the Haarlemmermeer being completed in 1853 by means of steam-driven pumps. In the 1870s, the two major ports of Rotterdam and Amsterdam were both given improved approaches by canalising the river mouth from Rotterdam to the Hook of Holland and by building the North Sea Canal across the narrow strip of land from Amsterdam to Ijmuiden on the coast. This allowed ships to reach Amsterdam direct from the North Sea, instead of having to travel north up the coast and approach the port through the Zuider Zee. But development of newer means of transport met with great opposition from conservatives in parliament. By the middle of the 1840s, neighbouring Belgium had already created a comprehensive railway network, which covered the country in the shape of a cross; but by 1850, the Netherlands still had only 159 kilometres of track.[6] In the early 1860s, conservatives threw out a bill to build state-financed railways as Belgium had done, though a year later parliament reluctantly agreed to spend 10 million guilders annually for this purpose. Foreign capital and technicians played a large part in the development of railways in the Netherlands in the late 1860s and the 1870s.

Under liberal pressure a free trade policy was instituted in the early 1860s; and in 1870, the forced labour system was abolished in Java for all but the production of coffee crops.* The Netherlands continued to depend greatly on its overseas empire and the associated carrying trade for its income. Agriculture was backward, particularly in the south and east.† There were some improvements from the 1880s onwards, mainly owing to the development of farming co-operatives. From the middle of the century, there was some modernisation of the cotton industry in Twente in the east, of the woollen and linen industries in North Brabant in the south and some improvements in shipbuilding. But there was very little progress as a whole in heavy industry, partly due to the lack of raw materials. (Coal was not discovered in the southern province of Limburg until the present century.) In 1903, a group of Dutch industrialists reported that although iron and steel production was

*See Chapter 16 for details.

†The gnarled poverty of peasants in Nuenen, north-east of Eindhoven, may be studied in one of Van Gogh's better known early paintings, *The Potato Eaters*. He also produced many other paintings and drawings of peasants in this area between 1883 and 1885.

technically feasible, the market was too small.[7] It was not until German supplies were reduced during the First World War that Hoogovens (The Royal Netherlands Blast Furnaces and Steel Works) were opened at Ijmuiden on the North Sea Canal. The new foundations for the country's future prosperity were laid towards the close of the nineteenth century with the modest beginnings of Philips' factory at Eindhoven, set up with a staff of ten to make electric lamps; the Royal Dutch Petroleum Company established with a capital of 5 million guilders to exploit the oil resources of the East Indies; and the family firms of van den Bergh and Jurgens which made margarine. By the inter-war years, these had already developed into the international companies of Philips, Royal Dutch Shell and Unilever, before most multi-national companies of this size had appeared elsewhere. They still remain the main bulwarks of industry in the Netherlands.

Because of the late development of industry, the bourgeoisie had established itself in power long before an industrial proletariat had appeared, except in a few cities such as Amsterdam. This had enormous consequences for the future stability of the country. The late development of an industrial proletariat, combined with the traditional respect for the bourgeois way of life which has its roots deep in Dutch history, ensured that the Netherlands escaped prolonged clashes between the middle class and the working class which were so characteristic a feature of nineteenth-century history elsewhere in Europe. By the time the working classes had organised themselves, the middle classes were so firmly established in power that they could afford to make some concessions or to adopt a firm stand, almost as they wished.

Modern political parties did not appear until the last quarter of the nineteenth century. The first, founded in 1878, was the Anti-Revolutionary party (Anti-Revolutionnaire partij—ARP), which was started to combat the secularising effects of the French revolution. Its origins can be traced back to the Réveil movement which started in the Netherlands in the 1820s—some thirty years later than its English equivalent, the Clapham sect of William Wilberforce. Its adherents believed in a personal living piety, the divine authority of the Bible and in evangelical and philanthropic works.[8] Groen van Prinsterer, the historian-politician, laid the foundation for this party of orthodox Protestants, but he died just before it was formed. Its leader was Abraham Kuyper, who led a breakaway movement of more orthodox Protestants from the church in 1886.

In the previous year (1885), the liberals succeeded in forming their local associations into a union, but they could not agree on a unified programme and broke up into right- and left-wing factions. In 1894, the Social Democratic Labour party (Sociaal-Democratische Arbeiders partij —SDAP) was founded, and ten years after that the Roman Catholic State party (Rooms Katholieke Staats partij). The Catholics, however, with their virtual monopoly of votes in the two southern provinces and their network of parish priests, were probably the best organised of all, even before their party was officially constituted. The conservatives never tried to form a party, and their last representative lost his seat in 1891.

By the beginning of the present century, the parliamentary nucleus of one of the most characteristic features of Dutch contemporary society had already appeared. The parliamentary leaders represented blocs, some of them confessional, like the Catholics and the Protestants, and some of them secular, like the Socialists and the Liberals. The people were dependent on the deputies for the emancipation of their own bloc, while the deputies were dependent on the blocs for support at the polls. But nothing could be achieved in parliament—because none of the blocs was large enough to form a majority—unless the leaders were willing to co-operate with each other. There was toleration and accommodation at the top; and separation at the bottom. Even if there had been much desire for co-operation at the local level, such a development would have weakened the powers of the leaders, so, in the process of emancipation, more and more organisations were formed which sealed off one member of society from another according to their own particular ideology. Eventually, it was not only parliamentary parties, trade unions, schools and universities which were organised in this way; but also newspapers, radio and television stations, health and welfare services, football leagues and even public libraries. There was even a Catholic goat breeders association! This vertical division of society, which was much more rigid in the Netherlands than in most other countries, is known to the Dutch as *verzuiling*, or pillarisation.* Because it cut across social classes, it succeeded in maintaining a stable, if somewhat backward and divided, society for nearly fifty years. Each of the three main blocs—Catholic, Protestant and 'neutral'—contained about the same proportion of each socio-economic class as the population as a whole.

The main political issues until the First World War reflected these rivalries between the blocs. They were concerned with social reform, the extension of the franchise and the development of state or private, denominational schools. The Liberals and Catholics split over the schools issue and as the century progressed, the Catholics looked increasingly towards the ARP for support, who also wanted Protestant schools of their own. In 1889, after a Catholic-ARP coalition had come to power, some subsidies were given to existing private schools.

Pressure for extension of the franchise came mainly from left-wing Liberals inside parliament and from Socialists outside it. From 1848 to 1887, the franchise was still so severely restricted that only about 3 per cent of the population had the right to vote.[9] In 1887 and 1896, there were extensions of the franchise, which, however, was still based on property, income tax or educational qualifications. Nevertheless, this resulted in a progressive increase in the size of the electorate from 12·3 per cent of men in 1880 to 63·2 per cent in 1910.[10]

The real battle between the workers and the employers and the state occurred in the years before the First World War.

*Among sociologists there is still some dispute about the number of pillars. Some find four pillars, representing the more latitudinarian and orthodox Protestants, the Catholic and the neutral bloc; while others find Protestant, Catholic, Liberal and Socialist pillars. Others combine the last two into one 'neutral' bloc.

Because of late industrialisation, the development of unions and socialism took place later than in most other western European countries. The first craft workers unions, among them printers and diamond workers, were organised in the 1860s. In 1869, Dutch sections of the First International were set up in Amsterdam, Utrecht and The Hague, but they failed to gain much hold. In 1882, an extreme left-wing party, the Social Democratic Union, was founded and succeeded in returning one of its leaders, Domela Nieuwenhuis to parliament. But Nieuwenhuis, an ex-Protestant pastor, a lonely left-wing voice in a totally bourgeois parliament, rejected parliamentary means of reform and turned towards anarchism. Both anarchists and syndicalists were among the members of the National Labour Secretariat which was formed in 1893. In the following year, the more moderate SDAP was founded.

As the nineteenth century drew to a close, there were numerous clashes between the extreme left-wing and the employers. The last big trial of strength came in 1903 when strikes were called in the Amsterdam docks and on the railways. Parliament passed a law prohibiting strikes on the railways, which is still in force. Anarchists, syndicalists and Marxists combined to call a general strike, but it collapsed after only a few days owing to the lack of solidarity among the unions, poor organisation and the firm action of the government in occupying railway stations with troops. The failure of the strike caused the unions to form a socialist co-ordinating organisation, the Netherlands League of Trade Unions (Nederlands Verbond van Vakverenigingen—NVV), two years later. A few years after that, federations of Catholic and Protestant unions were also formed.

Before the First World War, there was some progress in social reform both by the state and by paternalistic employers. In 1874, a law was passed prohibiting the employment of children under twelve years of age, and in 1889, another law regulated the hours of work for women and children and youths from twelve to eighteen years of age. The first social insurance and industrial accidents acts were passed in 1901. Nevertheless industrial unrest continued and there was growing Socialist pressure for electoral reform and growing confessional demands for some settlement of the schools question. The government and party leaders became convinced of the need for some comprehensive reforms. On the eve of the First World War, two separate commissions, which included representatives of all the seven parties then in parliament, were set up to consider the franchise and schools questions. They reported during the war, and their recommendations were approved by the government and by parliament, virtually unchanged, in 1917.

This vast package deal which gave something to almost everyone was a supreme example of the Dutch flair for consensus politics. The schools issue was settled—forty years before the Belgians settled theirs—by giving subsidies to both state and private schools. Universal suffrage was introduced for men and women over the age of twenty-five. Under the Labour Act of 1919, the Socialists gained a 45-hour week (though this was subsequently raised to 48 hours) and old age pensions.[11] Party control was strengthened by introducing a system of proportional representation based on the list system. And *verzuiling* was preserved and, indeed, strengthened. This grand compromise was to shape the nature of Dutch society up until about 1965, when some even more fundamental changes started to occur.

Between the two world wars, conflicts in society diminished. The settlement of the schools issue created better relations between the confessional and the secular parties. The Socialists gradually abandoned their previous anti-monarchical policy, while the unions started to co-operate with the employers, particularly after the High Court of Labour was established for joint consultations in 1928. The slump of the 1930s had increased Communist strength in parliament to four seats by 1933, and there was also some growth in support for the Dutch National Socialist Party. Other small parties continued to spring up, so that in 1933, there were no less than fifty-four parties contesting the hundred seats in parliament! But government itself remained relatively stable.*

The Dutch continued to play only a minor role in foreign

*For the reasons see pp. 126–7 below.

affairs. After the final loss of Belgium in 1839, most people willingly accepted the country's diminution to a small-power status (though still with vast possessions overseas) and an isolationist policy was developed 'to a point, little short of perfection'.[12] This policy was not without its positive aspects. In 1891, T. M. C. Asser, a Dutch lawyer, succeeded in calling a conference in The Hague to codify international private law. Eight years later, the First Peace Conference was held at The Hague (though it was not convened by the Dutch), and just before the First World War, a Peace Palace was opened there, built with funds provided by Andrew Carnegie. As one writer on Dutch foreign policy says: 'The Hague, with its many international conferences, its Court of Arbitration and Permanent Court of International Justice, was heralded as the Peace Laboratory of the World.'[13]

But the main policy remained one of neutrality which sucessfully survived the Luxemburg affair, the Boer War and even the First World War. The Luxemburg affair was small and quite short-lived. After the Austrian-Prussian war of 1866, Napoleon III, alarmed by Prussia's growing strength, tried to buy the strategically situated territory of Luxemburg from William III of the Netherlands, who was also Grand Duke of Luxemburg. William believed that he had obtained Bismarck's consent to sell, but when the plan became known publicly in Germany there was such an outburst of rage, that William had to retract his offer. To avoid further dispute a conference of great powers was called, which, as in the case of Belgium previously, decided to guarantee the perpetual neutrality of Luxemburg.[14]

The outbreak of the Boer War caused even more internal stress for the Netherlands, as it involved a conflict between the country on whose protective sea power they had relied increasingly ever since the Treaty of Utrecht, and a people to whom they were bound by language, sentiment and religion. Pragmatically, the Dutch placed self-interest before involvement with the Boers, contented themselves with some bitter criticism of Britain in their press, received President Kruger of the Transvaal at The Hague, and offered to act as a mediator between the two sides. Not that they could have done much more anyway.

Their policy survived the First World War successfully. This was mainly because the Germans wanted to keep the Netherlands open as a pipeline for much-needed supplies of copper, rubber, ores and food, though this became increasingly difficult because of Allied control over imports into the Netherlands. Indeed, as the war progressed, the Netherlands found itself in an increasingly difficult position with the Germans increasingly reluctant and unable to supply coal and steel, and England unwilling to supply grain and fertilisers without some guarantee that there would be no exports to Germany. This balance of conflicting interests was only preserved by careful Dutch placation of both sides. During the war, the Netherlands provided asylum for thousands of Belgian refugees and, after it, for the German Kaiser.

There was doubtless a certain amount of self-satisfaction among the Dutch in their successful preservation of neutrality for just over a century. But that was abruptly shattered with the German invasion of May 1940.[15] A large part of Rotterdam and some of The Hague was destroyed; much of the land was flooded; approximately 400,000 Dutchmen were sent to work in Germany; hundreds of resistance workers were shot; and many Dutchmen were brought to the verge of starvation. The experience was just as devastating in a different way as Belgium's had been in the First World War. But something else, which at the time seemed to be just as catastrophic, occurred in 1949, with the loss of the major part of the Dutch overseas empire—the East Indies.* The combination of these two events made both changes in attitudes and widespread industrialisation necessary. In the last five years, this has brought about what many Dutchmen call the silent revolution, in which almost no segment of life has not been subject to intense questioning or rapid change.

Yet, there is still a continuing tradition which goes back many centuries; no country, least of all the Netherlands with its

* See Chapter 16 below.

impressive record in the past, can escape its own history. Even today, beneath the skin of society in the seventies, the skeleton of the Dutch republic can still be discerned in the great regional variety and intense attachment to towns and villages; the dominance of the provinces of Holland and their conurbation of large towns with their separate functions and interests; the emphasis on land reclamation (the newly-created polders in what was once the Zuider Zee); the international trading tradition (Royal Dutch Shell); the respect for an ordered bourgeois way of life and the pragmatic toleration at the top; the conflict between doctrinaire and latitudinarian views; the emphasis on religion; and a general humaneness (the Netherlands was one of the first countries to abolish capital punishment in 1870). No real comprehension of the modern Netherlands is possible without some understanding of its antecedents in the republic.

# 6

## Changes in Society

UNTIL A FEW years ago, Dutch society remained in many ways divided, closed and backward. Society was most rigidly structured, both vertically and horizontally. *Verzuiling* kept members of each bloc at a safe distance from each other. Horizontally, society was constructed in the form of a pyramid, presided over by God and the queen, which before the war had rested firmly on the broad, extensive base of the East Indies—a vast archipelago of some 3,000 islands with an area about seventy times larger than the small European power that ruled it. In between these two extremes, there were in descending order, the nobility; the old protestant families, some with centuries of public service, who provided many of the top administrators; the *burgerij*; and the mass of hard-working, devout, loyal farmers and fishermen, who accepted their lot with little complaint, and the industrial workers who seldom caused much trouble, except in Amsterdam, which has always been the most independent and radical city in the country.

The status of women and of youth was just as rigidly defined as social class. Although a woman reigned and women had been able to vote as early as they had in Britain, most women were still subservient socially, legally and domestically. They were unable to open a bank account without their husband's permission; in the public service, and in some private firms, as well, they could be dismissed if they married or became pregnant; their education was often neglected; and if they were divorced or widowed they had to endure what was called 'a year of grief' before they could remarry, so that any child born would gain their former husband's name.

Legal adulthood, also, was postponed longer than in most other western European countries. It was impossible to marry without parental consent before the age of thirty. Furthermore, there was a special age category for the upper and middle classes, between the end of student life, which might occur at the age of twenty-five or even thirty, and full adulthood. These young adults—*jongeren*—had finished their formal education, but had to remain in subordinate positions until they had proved their worth.[1]

From being one of the most backward countries in western Europe, the Netherlands has in the last decade or so caught up in many spheres and in some—such as immigration policy, some aspects of social welfare, culture and the arts—has surpassed other European countries. The status of women has changed considerably, though there are still fewer working wives than elsewhere in Europe and much more reverence for family life. The young, particularly in the large cities, are just as emancipated, free and committed as in other countries, but so far there has still been less change in the last bastion of the old closed structure—social class. (For the past five years an English-language, brightly written, well-produced magazine, *Holland Herald*, has been published which chronicles both the popular and serious transformations.[2])

Although women were given the vote shortly after the First

World War, other forms of emancipation were long delayed. It was not until January 1, 1957, that a woman was allowed, by law, to have a bank account of her own. In the same year, the law providing for the automatic dismissal of national civil servants upon marriage was rescinded. But municipalities were unaffected by this change and in 1969, there were still fifty-five of them which retained the right to dismiss married women.[3] Because of general staff shortages, this was rarely done; but at the time of writing the government had promised to make this illegal. In 1969–70, new laws were passed abolishing the 'year of grief' for divorcees, thus allowing them to remarry immediately, but not for widows.* And the age of marriage without parental consent was reduced from thirty to twenty-one.

Contraceptive devices and, since 1963, the 'pill', have been available almost everywhere on prescription. According to research carried out by one of the big drug companies, no less than 40 per cent of all Catholics practised some form of birth control, while one in eight Catholic women were taking the 'pill', against one in six women in the population as a whole.[4] The rate of illegitimate births was about 1·6 per cent in 1965—less than one-quarter of what it was in England at the same time.[5] This is not because there is a particularly high abortion rate. In fact, abortions are still illegal, but if a gynaecologist has consulted other doctors he is rarely prosecuted. It is estimated that there are approximately 2,000 abortions in Amsterdam clinics every year, while estimates for abortion in the country as a whole—both officially tolerated and illegal—range from 20,000 to 60,000.[6]

In her attitude to work, however, the Dutch woman still differs greatly from her contemporaries in other western European countries. At the top, there is a considerable degree of emancipation with twelve women deputies in parliament (out of a total of 150), a minister in the government, a president of a political party, several judges (including one in the supreme

---

*In parliament, it was argued that if a divorcee had a child during that year, it was more likely to be that of her new husband, while a widow's would more probably be that of her former husband!

court), an ambassador and about twenty women ministers in the main Protestant church. But at the middle level, the working wife is less common. The world of literature is still very much the preserve of men, and there are comparatively few women in journalism and in publishing. In society as a whole, the number of married women workers remains small. In 1960, it was only 6·8 per cent—against 27 per cent in Britain at that time—and of these about one-third were wives of small shopkeepers or of farmers. Since then the number of working wives has risen considerably. Even three years later, according to income tax statistics, the percentage had increased to 18·4, but out of this total of 497,658 women, only 29,971 had children.[7]

The traditional tendency for a woman to settle down as a housewife once she has had children still persists. It is caused partly by the lack of part-time work, low tax relief for working women and lack of nursery accommodation, but more perhaps even among young people, by the traditional Dutch respect for family life, with the mother as the central figure. Attitudes towards this, however, are also changing. One recent survey has shown that just over one-third of married women would like a job of some kind, though the majority of men were still opposed to it.[8]

Nevertheless, family life still remains more close than it does, for instance, in Britain. It is usually a two-tier family with grandparents living in their own house, on an old people's estate or in an old people's home. It is more unusual for young people to live away from home than it is in Britain; this is caused partly by the proximity of the main towns and the excellent communications and also by a more old-fashioned belief that young girls, in particular, should live at home. One twenty-year-old student told me that her parents were very opposed to her living alone in Utrecht.

Indeed, the unity of the family has been officially encouraged by making the wife and husband financially interdependent. When the law relating to women opening bank accounts was changed, it was stipulated at the same time that the couple's financial assets and liabilities should be a common responsibility. Thus, neither the husband nor the wife can sell their house or let part of it, without the other's permission; neither can make 'excessive' gifts to other people without the risk of being taken to court; and all hire purchase and mortgage agreements which are not signed by both partners are invalid.*[9]

This reverence for the family is revealed in many homes by the calendar on the wall with the birthday dates, not only of close relatives, but also of distant relatives and friends, carefully noted. In many offices, it is customary to make collections for birthday gifts to colleagues. The greatest time for present-giving is on December 5, the Feast of St Nicolas, and weddings. Not so long ago, weddings were even more magnificent than they are now, with the reception being held a week before the wedding. At present, it is usual among those who can afford it for the bride and bridegroom, accompanied by a small page in his 'topper' and a small bridesmaid in a long dress, to drive to the town hall in a coach and pair for the civil ceremony. After an optional church ceremony, a reception is held at the bride's home, with a formal wedding feast, and with long speeches from almost every male relative, to which the bridegroom is expected to reply. In a number of families it is customary for both the children and parents to exchange presents for major wedding anniversaries—copper (twelve and a half years), silver and gold. To celebrate a silver wedding, the parents and children in one rich family I know gave each other silver medallions of themselves.

The evening meal is still observed as a family occasion, not only for eating, but also for the exchange of opinions and gossip, though in towns the pressure of other activities has tended to reduce the amount of time that can be spent over it. In eating habits there has been less change than in many other aspects of life. The Dutch have retained their liking for *boterham* (bread

---

*Separate control of property can be, and is usually, retained by richer people who draw up a contract of settlement before marriage; it is possible to do so after marriage with a court's permission. Even so, certain of the restrictions noted above still apply.

and butter), which may be covered with anything from Dutch cheese to ground chocolate or 'hundreds and thousands'. (That is one reason for there being so many excellent sandwich bars in the towns.) Breakfast consists of bread, thin slices of cheese or preserved meats, jam and more often now, coffee rather than tea. Lunch is scarcely any different, though in some country areas a hot lunch is served. Most children and many workers and office workers take sandwiches for lunch. The main meal is dinner at about 6 p.m.—often the only hot meal of the day. The Dutch have some gastronomic specialities, such as raw herring dipped in onion which, so gourmets say, should be swallowed like oysters, not chewed. But their meals at home tend to be rather uniform: soup, which is frequently home-made, some kind of meat with large helpings of potatoes and other vegetables and a sweet. An aperitif—Geneva or Dutch gin or sherry—is often taken, and if any alcohol is consumed with the meal, it is usually beer. Cigars are excellent and cheap—about one-fifth of their price in Britain. As the Dutch prefer strong tobacco, many people smoke French cigarettes or roll their own.[10]

Like the British, the Dutch have gained a great gastronomic legacy from their former colonies. Almost every town has its Indonesian or Indo-Chinese restaurants, serving extremely copious and superlatively good dishes, such as *nasi* or *bami goreng*, and that gourmet meal for gluttons, *rijsttafel* (literally, rice table).*

On the surface, there are fewer differences in the way in which people of different social classes live, particularly in the big towns, than there are, for instance, in Britain. There is none of the ostentatious wealth and extremes of poverty, which shock

*The quality and the composition varies. One of the best I have ever had was at the Bali in Amsterdam, which was founded in 1952. Their *rijsttafel* consists of curried meat, meat in Java sauce, steamed meat, bean sprouts, tomatoes in special sauce, fried mushrooms, grilled pork on skewers, fried bananas, stuffed omelette, shrimp bread, vegetables in peanut sauce, cucumber in sour sauce, mixed sour fruit in sweet and sour sauce, fried coconut, peanuts, spices and soup which is used to moisten the central mound of rice on the plate. There is some controversy among former residents in the Indies as to how it should be eaten. Some say that the rice and side dishes should be mixed; while others, as at the Bali, say they should not.

Dutch visitors to Britain. In Amsterdam, there are only a few Rolls Royces and large American cars, and not many more expensive Mercedes. It is not considered demeaning to ride a bicycle: even the queen does. Around Utrecht, and to the east and north-east of it, there are some large houses and big estates, but they do not compare in number or in size with those that can still be found in most parts of Britain. Most houses and flats, many of which are rented even by the upper middle classes, do not differ radically from each other. As in Germany, there is more social democratisation of shopping, so that jewellers, chemists, leather shops, for example, are not selectively divided from each other by their class of customer, but sell a wide range of goods at all prices. There is a nobility, but even in the seventeenth-century republic, it was an unimportant element and did not constitute a political class at all.[11] Since the reign of William III, no new titles have been created, though foreign nobility who are resident in the country have the right to claim a Dutch title. At the other end of the social scale, there are few signs of obvious poverty. It is true that there are some slums in the large towns, such as the Schilderswijk area of The Hague—a series of bleak, desolate streets running parallel to each other, lined with mean terraced houses, where the undrawn curtains at night may reveal in one house a prostitute waiting for a customer and in the next a family in their barely furnished room containing a table, some chairs, a television set in one corner and a cot in another, and eating their main evening meal of mounds of potatoes and a little meat. But these slums are luxurious compared with the atrocious, dilapidated houses which may be found in similar areas of London or New York, and there are no coloured ghettos because immigrants are distributed throughout the country.

Yet social class is still important and quite rigidly fixed. It is not generally a popular subject for investigation. It is still largely true, as J. H. Huizinga has said, that the Dutch dismiss the subject as of little interest and 'not relevant to serious discussion of Dutch society'.[12] The nearest most Dutch people will come to acknowledging its existence is in some such vague phrase as: 'The Dutch are not nice to each other.' Yet all Dutchmen know—and a few of them are now prepared to admit—that it is still the most rigid aspect of society. Almost all expatriate and non-native writers on the country concur in believing that social distinctions are much greater there than in any other western European country. There is a great consciousness of ancestry and of accents. The first thing a Hague banker, whom I had met for the first time, showed me was a copy of his genealogical 'tree'. There is a whole range of class accents 'extending all the way from the Dutch equivalent of cockney through "common" and "genteel" (in various shades) to ,'upper class" and even "la-di-da" or, in Dutch, *haags*, the mannered, drawling speech of the *soi-disant* social elite in the Hague'.[13] According to some observers, adjustment to the received accent is 'almost indispensable for social ascent above a local level'.[14]

Opportunities for social advancement have increased now that the doors of universities have been opened wider to the working class. For a number of years, the big Dutch international companies have provided opportunities for some men to escape from their own social origins. But for most men it still remains extremely difficult to cross the bourgeois barrier in a generation—to become middle class in speech, way of life, taste and culture and to be accepted as such. For women it is even more difficult to ascend socially from a lower to a higher class. At upper-class parties and social gatherings, young women can still be asked outright for their mother's maiden name and their father's occupation. As a former Spanish ambassador to the Netherlands has said, it is considered 'right and proper to associate according to one's profession, one's position in it, one's age and one's class'.[15] What you are, and who you are, is still far less important than what your father was: in fact, the former are conditioned by the latter. People tend to live protectively in small, self-contained circles of their class contemporaries; there is very little easy mixing of the generations. Though these tendencies are now less marked among the young in general and the twenty-five- to thirty-year-old middle class, they still persist generally. As one writer has said of the Dutch: 'The separation of classes is still very much a fact in their informal social intercourse.'[16]

As a foreigner one becomes, as in any country, to a certain extent de-classed, so that it is possible to remain outside this structure. It needs a long acquaintanceship with the country to realise that it does exist. There are very few outward signs. The Dutch appear to be extremely polite to each other; though almost all of them deny that they are. On one occasion, I saw a man in a café spill a glass of beer over five men at a neighbouring table and he received in return nothing but good-humoured smiles. There is very little overt snobbery in the English sense at least; very few public resentments; few bad-tempered drivers, in spite of the narrow streets; and apart from street demonstrations, hardly any public violence. The Dutch appear to be a kind, peace-loving and tolerant people, and in fact they are—more so than they think.

The Dutch have a most complex attitude to themselves, accepting the most rigid stereotypes, yet questioning, or even denying the existence of other, more complimentary, attitudes. The reason for this strange phenomenon may be that, like the Scots, with whom they have so often been compared, they have had to live with foreign execrations for so long that they have come to believe some of them themselves. Many of the English terms relating to the Dutch—Dutch courage, double Dutch, Dutch auction, Dutch cap, I'm a Dutchman if . . ., talking to someone like a Dutch uncle—are far from complimentary. In a poll conducted by *Delta*, a number of Dutch intellectuals found no faults with the Dutch, but others thought them immature, cantankerous, earnest and lacking a sense of humour. The poet J. C. van Schagen said: 'We are all mediocrities, honest, dull, thrifty, self-satisfied. . . . The Netherlands consists of millions of pigeon holes.'[17]

The Dutch aver, almost with pride, that they are parsimonious, pragmatic preachers. It is true that many of them are earnest, principled, and even dogmatic and contentious, but they are not so lacking in a sense of humour as they sometimes say they are. Once, when I was lecturing to a group of Foreign Office entrants, one student had put a name tag 'Luns' in front of an empty seat—a very English joke. Neither are they so discourteous as they say: for instance, in cinemas, late-comers will remove their coats in the gangway so that they do not block the view of other people. Many of the Dutch are extremely kind and polite, particularly to the British who are still very popular in the Netherlands. In my own experience, many top people— diplomats, deputies in parliament, members of the nobility, army officers, bankers, professional men, church leaders, university 'dons'—are open-minded, tolerant and courteous. As far as one can generalise about any nation's characteristics, those of the Dutch seem to be paradoxical, a series of conflicting attributes. In any event, it is more difficult to generalise about the Dutch than it is about some other nations; very often those heavy, portly men, brooding over their coffee in the cafés, with their tight-haired, bespectacled wives, turn out to be Americans, not Dutch. There are far fewer recognisable stereotypes than in many other countries, partly because of the great mixture of races and the regional diversity.

Nevertheless, life does not seem so pleasant for many Dutch men and women, particularly the young. Some of them feel the pressure of over-population to such a degree that it verges on a phobia—'you can't get away from people' and 'too many houses' are common complaints. (See Appendixes 1 and 2.) Life is changing but not rapidly enough for the young. Many of them find the country too small to fulfil their ambitions; for others the long, high-pressure years of university study are too difficult. In comparison with many other countries, the way ahead is still too slow, too difficult and too extended. Difficulty in moving upwards was one of the main factors responsible for the biggest emigration in Dutch history shortly after the end of the war. Society is less fixed now, but the rigid stratification by class, by origin, by education and by religion—even though there have been enormous changes in many of these in the last five years— is something that more intelligent and perceptive young people, and some of their elders, find restrictive.

Rank is still one of the most important concepts in Dutch society. A man is expected to live up to the position he holds; it is only when he acts above it—or acts irresponsibly—that he is criticised. Everyone is expected to know and to keep his place. There are few public extremes, but only a middle ideal from which neither those above nor those below are expected to diverge too wildly. These attitudes are deeply traditional; as one writer has said: 'The prudent, bourgeois, parochial way of life has always been highly regarded.'[18]

Social stratification is just as strong among the working classes, too, though the current status symbol may now be an Opel rather than a new bicycle. Because the Netherlands is a small, densely populated country, people are forced to live side by side, so that observation and judgement of others is facilitated.* This is even more so as one ascends the social scale. Combined with the traditional job mobility among the upper class—the pattern of moving easily from university to politics to foundations appeared in the Netherlands very early—it makes it possible for the small class who rule to know each other intimately through many formal and informal contacts. The upper bourgeoisie, men of the right ancestry, education and rank, are still more firmly established than they are in the Anglo-Saxon countries. Their power was sustained until very recently by the distribution of income which was more unequal than in other industrialised countries. In 1955, the top 5 per cent in the Netherlands had 24 per cent of the total income, against 21 per cent in the United States, 20 per cent in England and 17 per cent in Sweden.[19] There have been changes since then, with more of the national income going to the government and to the workers, but wages are still ultimately controlled by the government, as they have been ever since the end of the war. And in

*In the big towns, people rarely draw their curtains at night. This is only partly based upon a traditional openness of life and pride of possession, but just as much upon a desire to observe those outside. Many flats and houses still have a bracketed mirror outside the window so that those sitting by the window can watch passers-by in the street. A Dutchman has told me that fifty years ago as a child he was forced by his mother to sit by the window and tell her whether the men passing by were 'men' or 'gentlemen'.

1965, 5,800 people shared between them over one-quarter of all the private fortunes of over 10,000 guilders.[20] On January 1, 1966, there were 5,764 Dutch millionaires (people with a capital of more than one million guilders).

The class structure of society remains relatively closed, but in other fields—religion, politics and social life in general—vigorous attempts have been made in the last few years to produce a more open society. One attempt to change society, which received much publicity abroad, was that made by the Provo movement. Like other radical movements elsewhere, its composition and its motivations were frequently misunderstood abroad and its activities became inextricably and confusedly mixed with those of other elements.

The movement started, before it got its name, in June 1964, when an anti-smoking magician started to hold a Saturday night series of 'happenings' around a statue in Amsterdam which had been donated by a cigarette manufacturer. These 'happenings' rapidly attracted not only a large number of spectators, but also a smaller number of intellectual sympathisers. The movement's name was borrowed from that used by Wouter Buikhuisen, the writer of a doctoral dissertation at Utrecht University in January 1965, to describe young troublemakers in the streets. The borrowing of the name, with its quite different connotations, may perhaps have been partly responsible for some of the confusion that later arose about the aims, methods and activities of the Provos: for they were not all young by foreign standards, most of them being in their late twenties and one being over sixty; they were not hooligans, but believed in non-violence; and they were not to be found everywhere, but were confined primarily to Amsterdam. The number of full-time Provos did not exceed twenty-five or thirty.[21] Although the Provos never had a uniform philosophy or specific aims, they rapidly became associated with the 'white' plans which attracted world-wide attention—they provided white-painted bicycles for people to use freely for transport about Amsterdam.

This small, intellectual and non-violent protest movement soon became mixed up with the activities of other elements.

Teenage hooligans modelled themselves on the Provos. Teenagers and students joined in the smoke-bomb and firework protests against the wedding of Crown Princess Beatrix to the
German diplomat, Claus von Amsberg, in March 1966. Later
that year, in June, there were more violent demonstrations in
the streets of Amsterdam when non-union building workers
protested against a 2 per cent reduction in their holiday bonus
to cover administrative costs. The turbulent events of that
spring and early summer incited teenagers to riot by starting
fires and breaking windows. The police fired warning shots and
tear-bombs to disperse demonstrators.[22] Outbreaks of trouble
occurred sporadically for four nights. One man died (after two
autopsies, it was established that he died from heart disease);
and eighty-one people, including twenty-eight policemen, were
injured.[23] Although the Provos publicly dissociated themselves
from these riots, many people continued to blame them.

These incidents were much less violent than similar riots by
students, anarchists, left-wing socialists and others which were
soon to occur in many other European countries; but they produced a sense of extreme disquietude in the Netherlands. For
only the sixth time or so in this century, a special meeting of the
lower house was called for an emergency debate. During the
debate there was almost unanimous criticism of the hesitant conduct of the Amsterdam police, and Mr Jan Smallenbroek,
minister of the interior, promised that any new disorders would
be crushed mercilessly.[24] Outside parliament, there was an
equally profound feeling among many radicals that the police
had acted too harshly; and among most people a great sense of
surprise, unease or shock and alarm that such events could happen in the Netherlands at all. The riots provoked much discussion, in parliament, in the press and in academic circles. At
a conference held in December, one speaker, J. E. Ellemers,
affirmed that the riots were not directly related to the Provos,
but to a more general feeling of unease over the behaviour of
the police and the old grievance of non-recognised unions.[25]
This may well have been true. There was never any real attempt
made to achieve a student-worker link-up as there was in

Belgium in the same year in the riots at Louvain University and at Zwartberg pit.[26] The Provos never wanted to leave the boundaries of their own class. In April 1967, for example, when Crown Princess Beatrix gave birth to a son—the first male heir to the throne for a century—the Provos sent her a telegram of congratulations: 'Even if we stand on opposite sides of the fence and differ in opinions, today we sincerely share in your joy.'[27] It was an affirmation of their own sense of belonging and of the national sense of tolerance and fair play. The Provos wanted not so much a radical transformation of the class structure of society, as an adaptation of it to contemporary environmental and educational needs.

Like the new political party which arose in the same year—Democracy '66—they only wanted to demonstrate the need for change, not to affirm irrefutably what these changes should be. They wanted to preserve a democratic openness to new ideas and to new orderings of society, even if this involved their own demise. The challenge to society was more important than the consolidation of their own power. They wanted to avoid the process of institutionalisation, which, in the past, had transformed the living ideals of so many movements into frozen attitudes. Nevertheless, even they did not escape this fate entirely. In June 1966, one of their leaders, Bernhard de Vries, stood for the Amsterdam municipal council. He was elected. A year later he resigned in favour of another Provo leader and with the typical pattern of tolerant accommodation for which Amsterdam has been noted throughout its history, the council allowed a different member to serve annually until the new elections in 1970. In the elections for the Amsterdam municipal council in June 1970, five seats were won by new a group who are in some ways the successors to the Provos—the Kabouters ('gnomes' or 'dwarfs'). They are opposed to war and believe in homeless people occupying empty houses, helping old people and eating pure, natural food. In fact, they have already declared their independence from the state and set up their own alternative ministries: a Ministry of Agriculture to grow food without chemicals; a Ministry of Housing to occupy empty houses; a Ministry of Social Affairs to organise help for old people. To this extent they are more highly organized than the Provos were, but it is doubtful if they will be more durable. But if they eventually disband, their work will have provided, like that of the Provos, another step on which some new organization may climb to new heights as yet unforeseen. Meanwhile, in May 1967, having made their protest, the Provos decided to disband rather than face a lingering decline: they remained disciplined, ordered and respectable to the last.

The consequences of the movement were probably more important than their somewhat limited achievements. For in their open revolt and demonstrations against authority, the establishment and convention, they acted as a catalyst. They showed that the order of society was not fixed immutably forever. They showed that it was not impossible to make effective challenges from the outside—even in the Netherlands.

# 7

# The Churches

In 1954, *verzuiling* still seemed as strong as ever, with members of each bloc sealed off from each other in their own separate self-contained organisations, according to their religious or ideological views.[1] *Verzuiling*, too, has survived partly because it is so institutionalised, and partly because the Dutch are an earnest, cautious, principled people who take their lives, their attitudes and their religion seriously. But it has changed much more than some other aspects of society. It now has little relevance for much of the modern generation and most of those older people who still support it, want it to be used positively and openly to explain and clarify particular points of view rather than in the old negative, closed way, of keeping people divided. Most of the changes that have occurred in *verzuiling* have been brought about from the inside, by people at the top. This is particularly so in one of the major pillars of society—the Catholic Church.

No other Church in Europe has changed its character so rapidly in so few years; it would be necessary to go outside Europe altogether to Latin America to find more extreme transformations. Until a few years ago, the Dutch bishops were among the most authoritarian towards their flock and most obedient to the Vatican in Europe. The Church played a major role in almost every aspect of the lives of the faithful, not only directly, but also through the hundreds of social organisations, which were so numerous that they made 'a book of almost a thousand pages'.[2] Church attendance was very high—some 85 per cent in 1960—and obedience to the Church's doctrine on birth control was more strictly observed than it was, for example, in neighbouring Belgium. It was common for the parish priest to visit a family where the youngest child was three or four years old and to ask the parents pointedly when they were going to have another child; what the Dutch called 'reading the meter'.[3] Relations between the Church and the Catholic party were very close; in fact, some people believed, correctly perhaps, that much party policy was made in those small ornately furnished rooms leading off from the large central hallway of 40 Maliebaan, the austere looking residence of the Dutch primate. As late as 1954, the Dutch bishops issued their celebrated pastoral letter, prohibiting Catholics from joining a Socialist union or listening to Socialist broadcasts—and, by implication, therefore, from voting for the Socialist party—a dictate based on what one priest has described to me as the last manifestation of the 'cattle' mentality.

Since those days, the Dutch Catholic Church has become the most progressive in Europe—in liturgy, doctrine and ecumenical practice. In many churches, even in some parts of the traditional Catholic stronghold of the south, women attend Mass with uncovered heads and the Eucharist wafer is placed in the hand and not directly upon the tongue, though there is still a minority in all churches who receive it in the latter way. In addition, a new catechism has been introduced for adults which has caused considerable controversy.[4] The Dutch bishops have said that the arguments in the present pope's encyclical on birth control, *Humanae Vitae*, should be considered with respect, but that they were not entirely convincing. The bishops have asked for further discussions on a wider basis, to include married people and experts, to find a Christian conception of marriage suitable for our times. They have also said that it was necessary to respect the personal decision of married couples, taken after due reflection, on whether to use the 'pill' or not. They have also supported the idea of priests being allowed to marry and, at the time of writing, were still pleading with the pope for this to be allowed.

Because of these, and other, changes, the Dutch Catholics have been very prominent in the international headlines and on the world's television screens in recent years. Many of these reports have concentrated on the more sensational aspects: the smoking of hashish and the playing of 'beat' music during an experimental service for the young; the 200 married priests who have relinquished their office in the past two years; the rumours —later officially denied by the Vatican—that Professor E. Schillebeeckx, a Dominican father, was to be summoned to Rome for a 'heresy' trial because of his advanced views; and the ecumenical services held by the Shalom (peace) movement, at which bread is broken and wine is poured out, in what looks to some people like an unauthorised celebration of Mass. Some of the changes have caused so much fear and alarm in more conservative Catholic circles abroad that 'in one German diocese the faithful have been asked to pray for the unfortunate Dutch'.[5]

Why have these changes taken place in the Netherlands? Part of the explanation lies in the fact that the Catholics are no longer a minority fighting for full emancipation, but are now the largest religious group in what is still nominally, though not officially, a Protestant country. At the time of the last census in 1960, the number of Catholics exceeded, for the first time, the numbers in the two main Protestant churches combined. (See Appendix 3.) This has given them a new sense of strength and self-confidence. Though there was always a certain official tolerance of Catholic worship even in the republic, this had to

85

be done in secret, the Church itself was proscribed and Catholics were banned from public office. After the Catholic hierarchy was re-established in the middle of the nineteenth century, there was still great discrimination against Catholics which persisted up to the Second World War.

At the beginning of the present century, only 7 per cent of all university students were Catholics. And it was not until 1918 that a Catholic became prime minister, though the party had been one of the major forces in politics for many years before. Many of the top jobs in the public service were held by Protestants, which also applied in some private firms. Even shortly before the last war, so I have been told, one leading economist failed to get a job in the north (which is more Protestant), simply because he was a Catholic. Discrimination was sometimes, as in this case, completely open, the man being asked to state his religion. In other cases it was more concealed, but a man's probable religious faith was often betrayed by his southern accent or by the hand on which he wore his wedding ring.* Once the Catholics had achieved emancipation and had been accepted fully in their own country, there was less need for them to rely upon the identification symbol of Rome.

In itself, however, this is not sufficient to explain the transformation of the Church in the Netherlands. The national character of the Dutch and their history must also be taken into account. Religion was intimately intertwined in the history of the nation from the start and it has played a major role in the lives of the people ever since.† But the Dutch in addition to their religious fervour, also have a sturdy sense of independence, of principle and of knowing what is right. Within each Catholic there has always been a dissenter waiting to burst out, and the achievement of emancipation has enabled them to 'decolonise'

---

*This was, and still is, by no means an infallible guide, particularly in those cases where the same ring is used to symbolise either engagement or marriage. In this case, a man or a woman with a ring on the left hand could be either a married Catholic or an engaged Protestant, and with the ring on the right hand either a married Protestant or an engaged Catholic.

†There is at least one hotel in Amsterdam which is for clergymen only.

themselves from Rome—as one priest has put it to me—and to engage with the Dutch nation instead. There is, indeed, nothing fundamentally new about what is happening now in the Dutch Catholic Church. A remarkable parallel may be found in the history of the Old Catholic Church of the Netherlands, which re-established itself in the eighteenth century and still has just over 10,000 members. It, too, came into conflict with Rome at an earlier period by introducing Dutch into the liturgy, opposing alleged excesses in the worship of the Virgin Mary and assigning to the priest the role of 'servant and shepherd, not of intermediator and ruler'.[6] But it went much further than the Roman Catholics by denying in 1871, the newly proclaimed doctrine of papal infallibility.

But perhaps the most important factor was the need the Catholic Church leaders felt in adapting to the new kind of society in the Netherlands. As the Dutch primate, Cardinal Alfrink, has said: 'There is perhaps no country in the world where the transition from closedness to openness was experienced as rapidly and dramatically as it was in Holland.'[7] This confronted the Catholic hierarchy with a dilemma. It had, to quote the cardinal again, either to

> maintain the strong union and association of the group within itself, even in political and social life, or, send the faithful out into society with an apostolic mission to perform and thereby set yourself open to the influence of all kinds of currents outside of Catholicism.[8]

There were few indications before the present primate took office in 1955 what course he would take. Perhaps the only hint was given in his early days as a student in Rome when his dissertation on the Old Testament was rejected by his teachers as too modernistic, though it was afterwards accepted. Before his appointment as coadjutor to the bishop of Utrecht in 1951, he had been primarily what Catholics call a 'room scholar'—a professor at Nijmegen University and a biblical scholar internationally known for his work on the Old Testament. But soon after he became primate he made it very clear that he intended to choose the open course. He avoided a close involvement in the more introverted aspects of domestic political life by never attending a Catholic party meeting. Instead, he later tried with other churches to reaffirm the Christian point of view on the great international issues of the day. As president of the international organisation, Pax Christi, Alfrink is personally and very deeply involved in the peace movement. The Dutch bishops have taken a firm stand against the proliferation of nuclear weapons, the idea of an independent European nuclear force and the increase in the Dutch defence budget as a result of the Soviet invasion of Czechoslovakia. Since 1967, a peace week has been held jointly by the Dutch churches, with such themes as the United Nations, European conciliation and changing the economic and commercial structure of the Netherlands so that it is more peace-orientated. Though the Church's increasing involvement in international affairs and decreasing commitment in domestic politics has failed to please some circles in the Catholic party, it has already had some influence on general political life in the country.

The Dutch hierarchy felt that the Church had to be adapted to a society which was becoming increasingly open, more democratic and more secular. Even at the time of the last census, ten years ago, about one-fifth of the population were not affiliated to any church, and the numbers are probably much higher now. It is true that some of these 'unchurchly' people would still call themselves Christians, but this is balanced by the fact that many of those who belong to the main Protestant church are only nominal members. Even among the Catholics, there has been a great decline in regular church attendance from about 85 per cent in 1960, to 55 per cent ten years later. It is true that the less authoritarian attitude of the Church has made it possible for members to feel free to choose when they should attend church (a larger number go every three weeks or so); but other factors indicate that the decline in church attendance would probably have happened anyway.

The training of priests has been completely reshaped for the new open society; the walls of the old closed seminaries have been broken down. The number of seminaries has been reduced in four years from sixty-two to six large complexes, based on towns, with the students scattered in small independent groups of fifteen or twenty.[9]

The bishops, under Cardinal Alfrink, have gone further than most communities in trying to democratise the Church and to break down its rigid authoritarian structure, in accordance with the liberalising spirits of the Second Vatican Council which ended in 1965. Shortly afterwards, small discussion groups were started in parishes throughout the country to examine such questions as the authority and the role of the Church in modern times. There are now approximately 15,000 of these groups. In 1968, an experimental Pastoral Council was set up which included seven laymen and three priests from each of the seven dioceses, representatives of other churches and the bishops themselves, in an attempt to find a new method of exercising authority in the modern Church. Meetings are held in public 'at times with almost one hundred journalists present and under television floodlights', but in the words of Cardinal Alfrink 'the moral prestige of the bishops is not harmed, rather it is enhanced'.[10] The bishops retain final authority, but have so far supported the major recommendations of the Pastoral Council, such as its overwhelming vote in favour of married priests, even if this conflicts with the opinions of the pope.

The Catholic Church, completely emancipated, larger now than any other church in the Netherlands, has felt itself free to take the leading role in the growing ecumenical movement. In some cases, the ecumenical movement has been carried to a point which has caused great concern in other countries, particularly in the meetings of the Shalom movement, which includes Catholics, Protestants and Jews, who meet every Friday evening to read theological papers and the Bible and to listen to a discussion type of sermon. Bread is broken and wine is poured out; although some Catholic members have described the meetings as 'a celebration of the Lord's supper' it is not intended as a substitute for Mass, but as an affirmation of 'peace, wellbeing, reconciliation of man with God, of man with his

D

fellow man, of man with himself'.[11] The movement, which was formed in 1963, was first based on The Hague and now meets in a village near Utrecht.

Because the Dutch Catholic Church was so homogeneous and so tightly controlled until very recently, it still contains the most diverse and dissenting groups. And the new democratic structure has encouraged the growth of others, like the Septuagint movement of 1,300 priests, theologians and philosophers which gives vociferous support to married priests. Extreme movements in the Catholic Church are not unknown elsewhere in Europe; there are, for example, sections of the Italian Church with even more advanced views than some of the Dutch. But it is fair to say that no other Catholic Church in Europe has so wholeheartedly tried to democratise its structure, to create such a comprehensive organisation for the expression of dissenting views and, at the same time, give a necessary lead in some of the major issues, for example, world peace.

Will there be a final break with Rome, as some people have suggested? It is possible that if tension with the Vatican increases, some small groups could break away from Rome, as the Old Catholics did at an earlier period, and this would certainly present the Dutch hierarchy with another awkward dilemma. But the hierarchy believes that it is not possible for the Church as a whole to break away, and that, in this modern age, it would be impossible for Rome to excommunicate it.

The Catholics have succeeded in retaining unity so far by not insisting upon uniformity. In contrast, the Protestant churches, through conviction, have had neither uniformity nor unity from the start. Ever since the Protestant church was founded in the Netherlands, it has been subjected to ceaseless divisions and breakaway movements which may be traced back to the origins of the church during the revolt against Spain and the disputes between the latitudinarian Arminians and the more orthodox Gomarists. This conflict between latitudinarianism and dogmatism—which still persists—broke out again in the middle of the seventeenth century with disputes between the pietistic Gijsbert Voetius and John Cocceius over Sunday observance; similar disagreements also occurred in the eighteenth century.[12]

The major divisions in the main Protestant church—the Dutch Reformed (*Nederlands Hervormd*)—occurred in the nineteenth century, when there were two separate breakaway movements by more doctinaire members in 1834 and 1886. Some of these dissident members eventually reunited in 1892 to form the second largest Protestant church, the Reformed (*Gereformeerde Kerken*).* But not all of them did so and some remained in congregations of their own so that, with dissidents from earlier periods, there are now twenty Protestant churches in the Netherlands, divided from each other over doctrine or observance.† To outsiders, some of the beliefs have a certain air of unreality. There is still one sect which adheres firmly to its conviction that, although there was a snake in the Garden of Eden, it did not speak to Eve; and during the disastrous floods of 1953, some small farmers in Zeeland refused to help in rescue operations, but spent the night singing hymns because they believed the floods were the will of God. There are some small sects which are opposed to innoculation, all forms of insurance, vivisection and women in politics.

The basic division, however, is over principle and doctrine.‡ On the whole, the majority of the members of the Dutch Reformed Church believe that the Calvinist confession, with its doctrines of grace and sin, should be adapted to the reality of the present day; while most members of the Reformed Church, and members of the smaller sects even more, think that it should be interpreted literally and strictly applied in daily life. Although the Reformed Church is much smaller than the Dutch

*Both *hervormd* and *gereformeerde* mean 'reformed'. To avoid confusion, the style adopted here is to call the main Protestant church, Dutch Reformed and the smaller, more orthodox church, Reformed.

†Among the various sects are Reformed, Christian Reformed, Old Reformed, Remonstrant, Free Evangelist, Netherlands Protestant Union, etc.

‡The Dutch have a tendency, both in religion and other things, to discuss principles and policies in the minutest detail. The General Synod of the Reformed Church, which meets every two years, lasts for six to eight weeks with ten-hour working days.

Reformed, its members are made of sterner material and are more involved in socio-political life through their connections with their political party, the ARP, the mass media and university education. Until quite recently, many of their members were extremely rigid about Sunday observance; one eighteen-year-old student has told me that as a child she was not allowed to play outside or to catch a bus on Sunday. It is amongst some Reformed Church members that one finds a sense of earnest principle and high endeavour, which is not, however, contrary to popular belief, without its tolerance, kindness and sense of humour.

In contrast, the Dutch Reformed Church seems rather weak and ineffectual, fearing that it may be overwhelmed by the more vigorous Reformed Church and the Catholics in any ecumenical movement, and seemingly powerless to prevent its members from slipping away into non-attendance, indifference and final rejection, as many have done over the past century. One serious financial burden is a legacy from the past—those churches, medieval Gothic outside, but plain and unadorned within—which they took over from the Catholics during the revolt against Spain and still have to maintain with scarcely any subsidy from the state. It is in these churches, which are closed except on Sunday, that services are still held with the congregation sitting in plain wooden chairs in the form of a three-sided square around a raised pulpit. A further problem is that their congregations are ageing more rapidly than the population as a whole. They do not appeal enough to young people.

Both Protestant churches have made some attempt to modernise in the last few years. Women are now allowed to become ministers in both churches. They have also taken part in the growing ecumenical movement, though the Reformed Church has only recently become a full member of the World Council of Churches. (It has had observers at council meetings since 1964.) And among young members of both churches there is a growing desire to press on faster. They hope that the two churches can be reunited again within ten years, but their elders shake their heads in disbelief.

But it is difficult to generalise about the Protestant churches, as each separate congregation has always had a great degree of independence and autonomy, electing its own minister either directly or indirectly. Indeed it would be false to imagine that the changes in the churches and in society as a whole have been total everywhere. Modernisation is far more apparent in the *randstad*, that conurbation of separate, yet nearby, towns—The Hague, Leiden, Haarlem, Amsterdam, Hilversum, Utrecht, Dordrecht, Rotterdam, Schiedam and Delft—where nearly half the total population of the country live. (See Appendix 4.) Even within this densely populated area, there are great variations between the towns: Amsterdam, the capital, is one of the most exciting, progressive and intellectually alive towns in Europe; The Hague, the seat of government, has a certain passionless air; while Rotterdam, the world's largest port, is new, rebuilt and bursting with commercial vigour. Outside the *randstad*, there are even bigger variations. It is one of the many fascinations of the country that, in spite of its small size of 12,906 square miles—about one and a half times the size of Wales or of Massachusetts—there is still so much regional diversity to be found. Less than an hour's drive from the capital there are villages, such as Bunschoten, Spakenburg, Volendam, Marken and Staphorst, in which life is still in some respects medieval. In some of them, traditional costumes may still be worn partly as a bait for tourists; but in Staphorst, the old life of deep faith and rigid prejudices is still lived in great earnestness. (Recently the municipal council there passed a by-law to prevent photographs being taken of women in their traditional costumes without their permission.) Staphorst is still strictly Protestant. On Sundays, some farmers still separate their cockerels from their hens; and many children are not allowed to play outside in the streets. Not many years ago, Dutch women from other parts of the country would be followed in the street by jeering women if they were wearing lipstick. In 1964, a woman accused of committing adultery was dragged from her home at night and paraded through the streets with her paramour in a dung cart. (This has now been made illegal.) But even in Staphorst the old beliefs are being slowly eroded. In March 1971, during a polio epidemic there, most parents defied their pastor and had their children innoculated. Further north again, in the villages on the wind-torn islands of Friesland, men and women, until very recently, sat in separate pews in church.

To the south-west, in the old fishing villages of Zeeland, the religious feelings of earlier times still persist—in spite of all the ecumenical movements in the towns—with old women wearing different decorations on their traditional wide, lace caps, according to whether they are Protestant or Catholic.* And at Maastricht, deep in the Catholic bastion of the south, where the French words start to flow across the frontier from the nearby border with Belgium, there is in the Catholic churches nothing but the expected scene of ritual devotion; the intense, sad, black-clothed women and the old men genuflecting, praying and lighting candles. The desire for modernity, contemporary authenticity and openness does not extend everywhere. It is in such fringe areas as these that the most devout, the most conservative and the most extreme supporters of their own particular faith and points of view may still be found.

---

*Life in Zeeland can be expected to change radically in the next few years as the remote islands are linked to the mainland by modern motorways under the government's plan to reclaim the delta.

# 8

# Mass Media and Culture

IN NO OTHER European country—outside the Communist bloc—do the pillars of society exercise so great a control over the mass media as they do in the Netherlands, particularly in radio and television. The broadcasting structure has no parallel in the world. Programmes are produced not by companies and a public corporation as in Britain, nor by commercial companies as in the United States, but by non-profit-making organisations representing different religious and political views.[1] This unique structure extends back to the start of regular radio transmissions in the mid-1920s, when the government authorised various amateur groups to broadcast programmes of their own. There were five organisations, which either had their own stations or were given a share of broadcasting time: AVRO, a 'neutral' organisation, with strong Liberal overtones; KRO, Catholic; NCRV, othodox Protestant; VPRO, latitudinarian Protestant;

and VARA, Socialist. Thus, all the main pillars of society were represented. When television transmissions commenced in October 1951, these five organisations also took over the chief responsibility for providing programmes on television. They are financed partly by a share of the annual licence fees (75 guilders for a television/radio licence, but nothing for car radios) and also by the dues from members of their associations. Each of the associations has a large membership of many thousands, which have grown considerably in the post-war period. (See Appendix 5.) Increased membership of the associations, however, does not indicate a growth of enthusiasm for the particularist views they represent; viewers become members, automatically and obligatorily, when they take out a subscription to the association's weekly magazine which gives details of forthcoming programmes.* This may seem to be a mere formality, but it is important to the associations in two ways: the size of their membership determines their total amount of broadcasting time; and it also influences the amount of advertising they can attract in their magazines. Apart from that, membership of a particular association is generally, so opponents of the system say, fundamentally meaningless.

Before the last war, the associations had their own studios, but since the war, studio space and technical services have been controlled by two foundations which, in 1969, were amalgamated into one: The Dutch Broadcasting Foundation (Nederlandse Omroep Stichting—NOS). Although the NOS now provides about one-quarter of all programmes, including the main news, and the number of associations has recently been increased by one, the old associations still provide the majority of the programmes. Well over half of Dutch homes have a television set, although the number of hours spent viewing them is less than it is in Britain or the United States.[2]

Since the end of the war, this broadcasting system has been under attack by some politicians who wanted to introduce a national system, by business men who wanted it to become

---

*Only the current day's programmes are published in the press.

commercial and by many intellectuals, journalists and broadcasting employees, who wanted this closed structure to be changed into something more open. By 1965, such a crisis had been reached that the question brought about the downfall of the government. The first post-war prime minister, Willem Schermerhorn, a Socialist, tried to have a national broadcasting organisation set up on the lines of the British Broadcasting Corporation. Although there was some support for this in a number of political parties, all of the associations were opposed, with the exception of the smallest, VPRO. With the help of sympathisers in parliament, the associations continued to oppose all attempts to introduce either a general or a commercial system, fearing that either would diminish their own monopoly. Then, in the summer of 1964, Cornelis Verolme opened a pirate television station on an artificially constructed platform just outside Dutch territorial waters in the North Sea. The programmes, which included advertisements, proved immensely popular with many thousands of viewers in the crowded *randstad*. Nevertheless, a bill was hastily passed in parliament to close the station, which was implemented at the end of the year; but the parties and the associations realised that they could no longer resist growing public demands for some opening up of the system. It proved easier to reach a general decision than to agree on the details. There were disputes in parliament and in the cabinet over whether the established associations should control the advertisements themselves, how much time should be devoted to them and the terms on which new companies might be allowed to enter.[3] Although the Liberal ministers in the coalition government wanted a national system, the Catholic and Protestant ministers were reported to be divided.[4] After endless discussions, no agreement could be reached, and Victor Marijnen's government was forced to resign in February 1965. After a six-weeks' crisis, Joseph Cals, a Catholic, succeeded in forming a new coalition government of Catholics, ARP and Socialists, with two parties in the former coalition, the Liberals and the CHU going into opposition.

In February 1967, a new broadcasting bill was passed by a

large majority. Some concessions were made, but the broadcasting system remained basically intact. Two new associations were licensed. One was TROS, the former pirate station. Although it may provide entertainment, its critics say that, with its deferential, apolitical attitudes, it has done nothing to modify the basic structure of *verzuiling*. The second new association was formed out of the existing AVRO organisation and a new organisation, RTN, which had applied for a licence. The latter was set up by supporters of an independent magazine, *Televizier*, which had tried to break the associations' monopoly on publishing broadcasting programmes. After protracted negotiations, RTN decided to merge with AVRO, thus creating the largest organisation.

At the same time, the associations' share of broadcasting time was slightly reduced, though they still have the vast majority. NOS, which has a government appointed chairman, fills 25 per cent of the time with news, Eurovision programmes, films and features, and up to another 10 per cent is given to smaller political parties, religious sects and secular groups. Commercial advertisements on television were started in 1967 —the same year in which colour television was introduced—but they are limited to a maximum of fifteen minutes a day. They are usually broadcast just before and just after the news. (Commercial advertisements were started on radio, too, in 1968.) A government appointed council supervises the advertisements and has the power to ban any which are contrary to law, public order, truth or good taste. Cigarette advertisements are not allowed. During the first year, a revenue of 54 million guilders from advertisements greatly exceeded expectations.[5] Much of it goes back to the programme associations, so that they now have more money than they had before.

Though the two general associations will probably grow in size, *verzuiling* remains almost as entrenched as it did before. Concessions have been made to business, but very few to the intellectuals and radio and television workers, in what is, after all, their special province. The grip that the old associations still exercise on the most important communications media of the day provokes great despair among many intellectuals. They resent the fact that the choice of cultural programmes, such as plays and concerts, should still be in the hands of the old established religious and political organisations. One leading journalist told me that even the national news was so 'neutral' that it could be called 'castrated'; editorial staff felt extremely 'frustrated'. One intellectual has told me that the associations' background commentaries and documentaries were so biased that you had to put on 'yellow, red or green glasses' to bring them back into a focus of reality. The system perpetuates the tendency for each bloc to preach its own message. According to one leading literary figure, many of the programmes treat viewers 'either as academics or as idiots'.

Some of these criticisms, however, seem a little extreme. After all, television does not suffer from a superfluity of excellence in any country. Some of the Dutch documentaries are of very good quality and the standard of music programmes on both radio and television is especially high. Equally, it is somewhat questionable how far the mass of people want cultural television programmes, either in the old or in the new style; they seem, like many people everywhere, to want entertainment far more. And because the associations' share of broadcasting time is decided by the size of their membership, they cannot be entirely resistant to giving the public something of what it wants. Furthermore, one has the unwelcome suspicion that some critics simply want to exchange one form of authority for another by giving the public what *they* think is right. (The question of real democracy and openness in the mass media is, however, one that no country has yet solved.)

Nevertheless, the critics of the existing system do make some very valid points. The present structure does perpetuate the old closed system. Even the Catholic hierarchy, so open in so many matters, wants to retain *verzuiling* in this field. It is also true, as some critics say, that as a result of the structure itself, all programmes become suspect and lose their integrity and validity; because programmes are provided by the associations, people look for ideological content, and even though none may be present, they often find it. Furthermore, some of the programmes are rather serious and 'stuffy', and do not adequately reflect the ferment of ideas in society as a whole. There have been some recent attempts to make a breakthrough. The practice of religion has been satirised in one programme; and a naked girl has been seen on television screens. Both of these incidents caused minor storms. Though the government does not exercise a direct censorship, it does hold a watching brief, and after many complaints had been received about the satirical programme, it issued a public reprimand.

The breakdown of *verzuiling* has been more rapid in the daily press, which is less institutionalised and more subject to the play of economic forces. Most of the national dailies originally had strong links with a confessional or a political group. For example, the only Dutch newspaper with any real claim to international standing, the *Nieuwe Rotterdamse Courant*, was started by Thorbecke and a group of journalists as a Liberal weekly in 1843, becoming a daily in the following year.[6] Some of the present national dailies started as 'underground' papers during the last war, but still linked with confessional or secular groups: for example, the only Protestant national daily paper *Trouw*; the only Communist, *De Waarheid*; and the Socialist, *Het Parool*. But in recent years there has been a marked swing away from pillarisation in the national press. One analysis shows that the national Catholic newspapers lost circulation between 1955 and 1965, though that of the local and regional papers continued to grow.[7] This change was symbolised dramatically in 1966, when *De Volkskrant* loosened its ties with the Catholics and became a more independent and progressive paper. There have been equally big changes in the Socialist camp. For many years after the war, the Socialist *Het Vrije Volk*, which was owned jointly by the Socialist party and the Socialist trade union, had the biggest circulation. It had, however, an extraordinary clumsy and expensive structure, publishing no less than thirty or forty editions in an attempt to attract Socialist subscribers all over the country.

In the last five years, it has lost its commanding position and in 1967, the Socialist party decided to sell its shares to an insurance company.[8] As society becomes less compartmentalised into separate blocs, readers are turning more and more to the so-called independent daily papers, such as *De Telegraaf*. But as this is in fact a conservative paper supporting ideas of law and order, these changes have also failed to please most intellectuals.

The biggest changes in the press have been brought about by economic factors. As in all other European countries, rising costs of production, newsprint and higher wages have forced many papers to merge or close. Between 1957 and 1967, the number of daily newspapers fell from 115 to 95 and the number of separate newspaper concerns from 60 to 41.[9] This process has been accelerated recently by the introduction of advertisements on radio and television, which eventually caused far more concern to newspaper managements than it did to the broadcasting associations. Newspapers already had to face great competition for advertising revenue from the associations' magazines, which have a total circulation approaching 3 million—almost as high as that of the daily press combined. The daily newspapers claimed that their advertisement revenue fell by 1 per cent in 1967, against an average rise of over 10 per cent per annum in previous years. To compensate them for this loss, the government promised to pay them part of the revenue from television advertisements for a three-year period. During this period, 40 per cent of advertisement revenue, amounting to a total of 56 million guilders, was returned to newspapers. In 1970, the government signed a new agreement under which newspapers will receive 10 million guilders a year for a further three years. The newspapers which have suffered the most loss of advertising revenue will receive proportionately more.

In spite of these difficulties, the Netherlands still has a large number of daily papers for such a small country. Most of them have quite small circulations, being sold only in a province or a locality, and publishing national, international and local news. Of the total sales which approach 4 million, almost half is accounted for by the eleven main national dailies. (See Appendix

6.) Not all of these, however, are likely to survive. Mr W. L. Brugsma, editor-in-chief of the weekly review *Haaguse Post*, told me that the three morning papers were likely to continue increasing their circulations, but there would probably be more mergers among the evening papers, and some of them might become local, instead of national, papers. (In the autumn of 1970 two of the oldest papers, the *Algemeen Handelsblad* and the *Nieuwe Rotterdamse Courant*, merged, though they still appear under their separate titles with a page of different local news.) There could be room in the future for three serious weeklies, instead of the present six.

The Dutch press has a number of special features. Most of the national dailies are published in the evening, because, at one time, the Dutchman liked to spend his evening at home reading the paper. Practically all daily papers—about 95 per cent—are sold on a subscription basis and are delivered direct to the home. Due to the small proportion of news-stand sales, there is no need to have eye-catching headlines; the division into a popular and quality press is less extreme than it is in Britain. And there are no Sunday newspapers. But with the modernisation of society, all of this is slowly beginning to change. The morning papers are now all doing better than the evening papers; streets sales are slowly rising; some papers are making their layouts more striking; and there is even some talk of starting a Sunday newspaper.

By British standards at least, Dutch newspapers are rather staid and respectable. (Conversely, most Dutch people think British papers are highly sensational.) The Dutch press has a much greater sense of responsibility and decorum than some sections of its British counterpart. Journalists' organisations, such as the Federation of Journalists and the Dutch Association of Photographic Journalists, keep a watchful eye on the activities of their members. For example, in 1965, the latter reproved an Amsterdam photographer for abusing the freedom of the press after he had taken photographs of Crown Princess Beatrix and of Claus von Amsberg, thus precipitating the announcement of their engagement.[10] There is a strong tradition in the

Netherlands that there should be no newspaper intrusion into personal life. This is extended to such a degree that newspapers never publish the names of defendants in court cases, though whenever a well-known person is involved his name invariably leaks out. To most Anglo-Saxons this seems to carry the protection of individual liberties too far.* On the other hand, newspapers can be severely critical of governments, institutions and of the public life of individuals. There is no government censorship; the press has been completely free since the revision of the constitution in 1848. And the law of libel is less stringent than it is in Britain.[11]

⊕

In contrast to the mass media, *verzuiling* has never been of much importance in the cultural field, even though the public libraries are still divided into 143 non-denominational, 136 Catholic and 27 Protestant.[12] In the last decade, there has been a cultural explosion in the Netherlands which has made Amsterdam—the intellectual centre of the country—into one of the most exciting, stimulating and intellectually alive capitals in Europe. It has something of the feeling of Paris in the 1930s—an atmosphere of a revolutionary city in what is still in some ways a very bourgeois country—with its American colony, its crowded bars, its animated discussions, its serious chess players crouched over their boards in the Leidesplein, its cafés with their green-topped communal tables and, as might be expected, its earnest commitment to ideas. Proportionately, there now seem to be more pretty, emancipated girls and long-haired boys than in almost any other European capital. These girls are a charming blend of the old and new, sitting at their tables, covered with an imitation Persian rug, in some cosy pavement café, drinking gin or beer and rolling cigarettes while they discuss pop records or

---

*It is, however, interesting evidence of a contrary tendency in England, which brings us somewhat closer to the Dutch position, that names of defendants in juvenile courts cannot be published by the press and that the names of doctors who appear before National Health Service executive councils are not revealed.

philosophy; or in their mini-skirts and maxi-coats riding side-saddle on the rear carrier of their boy friend's bicycle or moped with their feet protruding dangerously into other lanes of traffic. Their attitudes are as free and open, and their discussions as frank as those of girls in London. There has, after all, always been a permissive attitude towards sex in Amsterdam, where prostitution, homosexuality and abortions are all tolerated. There are at least two world-famous homosexual clubs in Amsterdam. Soft-drug taking has also been tolerated in the past in two clubs for young people in Amsterdam, though there could be more of a clamp-down on it after the troubles of the summer of 1970, when many people were injured in riots in the capital, petrol bombs being thrown at police and shops looted. Drug-taking is now officially banned in the Paradiso, in Amsterdam, a psychedelic-painted former church, which no longer echoes to the sound of hymns, but to ultra-modern jazz. (The other club has now changed its name and turned to spiritual meditation.) All of this in a city so beautiful that it attracts millions of tourists every year and now ranks as the fourth European tourist centre after London, Paris and Rome. The old city is divided by rings of concentric canals into ninety small islands connected by more than 650 bridges, with many canals lined by old merchants' houses, built in the Dutch renaissance style with slightly sloping gables, and where there are also many bars and night clubs, and carillons that play *Rule Britannia! Britannia Rule the Waves.*

For such a small country, the cultural impact that the Dutch are now making is quite remarkable. Ballet has a history of only sixteen years in the Netherlands, yet the two companies, the Dutch National Ballet and the Netherlands Dance Theatre, have already achieved a considerable reputation abroad. The latter, which tries to have every dancer of soloist quality, has, as *The Times* ballet critic says, set 'a new style in ballet companies which has now been copied successfully in Britain, America and Europe'.[13] In March 1970, the world première of a ballet, *The Ropes of Time*, by Rudi van Dantzig, joint artistic-director of the other company, the Dutch National Ballet, was held in London.

Rudolf Nureyev was in the leading role, and electronic music was used for the first time in a Royal Ballet production at Covent Garden.

In music, the performances of the Amsterdam Concertgebouw-orkest under its successive conductors, Willem Mengelberg, Eduard van Beinum and Bernard Haitink, have become well known throughout the world. In February 1970, Haitink was awarded the Bruckner Medal of Honour, which has been given in the past to such conductors as Toscanini and Klemperer. The best-known Dutch opera singer is the soprano Gré Brouwenstijn, who has sung in most of the major opera houses throughout the world.

Even more might be done in these spheres, if more theatres were available. Obviously, the amount of money that a small country can devote to cultural affairs is limited; but the opera, ballet and main theatrical company all have to share the Amsterdam Municipal Theatre. Though it has recently been completely modernised, it is still inadequate for their needs. There is a plan to build an opera house some time in the future. In the provincial towns, new theatres have been built or old ones reconstructed since the end of the war, but there still seems to be a shortage of public halls and theatres. In Eindhoven, the electronics firm, Philips, has provided a theatre for the town in addition to the municipal theatre. The big Dutch international companies, which are enormously wealthy, might give more help to the arts in this and other ways.

Of all the arts, the Netherlands is traditionally associated with painting and that great seventeenth-century transition from a predominantly religious to a secular art. In modern times, too, the Dutch have made considerable contributions to painting, even though many of their major artists either lived outside the Netherlands or looked outside it for inspiration, such as Van Gogh* and the abstractionists Willem de Kooning, who emigrated to the United States in 1926, and Piet Mondrian who died in New York in 1944.

*A new museum is now being built next to the Municipal Museum in Amsterdam to house the important Van Gogh collection.

Artists were the first to be affected by the revival of self-confidence in the post-war years. This was epitomised in the creation of the Cobra group in 1948, the name being formed from the initial letters of the capitals of the countries involved—Copenhagen, Brussels and Amsterdam. The paintings of Constant, Karel Appel and Corneille, with their great freedom of expression and free use of colour, had an enormously liberating effect on Dutch painters. Since the end of the war, there has been an enormous outpouring of creative energy, with some very interesting paintings by Martin Engelmann, Co Westerik and sculptures by Carel Visser and many others.[14] Many of these works and even more of those artists from the classic period have been reproduced faithfully and carefully in Dutch art books.*

The nation's literature is less well appreciated abroad. This had always been so. For this neglect there are a number of reasons. German philologists in particular have tended to treat Dutch as a mere dialect of German, like Low German, and most foreigners still believe that there are two separate languages, Dutch and Flemish, the former spoken in the Netherlands and the latter in northern Belgium, when historically and now, in fact, they are one.[15] These two attitudes, combined with a lack of knowledge of the language abroad, have made most foreigners by-pass Dutch literature. But the main reason for this neglect is that Dutch is one of the 'small' languages, spoken by only 18 million Europeans. And as Professor Weevers has perspicaciously observed:

> Even the major literatures of the world are appreciated imperfectly by other nations. Small wonder, therefore, if the poetry of a lesser nation, whose language is little read, may remain virtually unknown abroad, and yet be of high intrinsic worth.[16]

*The Netherlands has always been renowned for its skill in printing. Although Johann Gutenberg of Mainz is now generally accepted as the inventor of printing from moveable type in Europe, there were earlier claims for Laurenz Coster of Haarlem. Printing was established very early in the Netherlands and was consolidated by the work of the Elzevir family in the sixteenth and early seventeenth centuries.

In the post-war years, much has been done to remedy this lack of knowledge. In 1954, the Dutch government set up a completely independent Foundation for the Promotion of the Translation of Dutch Literary Works, which has also been supported by the Belgian government since 1960. The Foundation has already had a considerable success in making foreign readers and publishers more conversant with the Dutch literary scene. (See Appendix 7.) Four years after the Foundation was set up, there appeared the first number of that excellent little review, *Delta*, which is written in English. Its purpose is to cover all aspects of the arts, life and thought in the Netherlands, which it has done with singular success ever since. The man most closely associated with it was a leading Dutch poet, Ed Hoornik, who died in March 1970, at the age of fifty-nine. He was the John Lehmann of the Dutch literary world, discovering and encouraging new writers, particularly poets, many of whose works have been brilliantly translated in *Delta* by James S. Holmes and Hans van Marle.

The Dutch are great readers not only of books in their own language, but also of those in French, German and English. All the main towns have dozens of bookshops, which, because of the great competition, often tend to specialise. There is also a big trade in publishers' remainders. Although Amsterdam is the traditional centre of publishing and printing, with about one-fifth of the national turnover, there are a large number of small publishers all over the country producing a small list of books in which they are really interested. But the same economic factors which have affected newspapers, and the difficulties of small firms in distributing their books, have caused many of them to close or to merge with a larger publisher. In the last two or three years, four or five big publishing groups have started to emerge.* The success of some of these groups has been based on their educational lists.

Like most of their contemporaries elsewhere, many artists and writers in the Netherlands are dissatisfied with the financial

*Some of the big combinations are van Dishoeck of Bussum, Elsevier of Amsterdam, Kluwer of Deventer, and van Goor Zonen of The Hague.

rewards (or lack of them) that they receive for their unremitting work and with the lack of public understanding for their more advanced works. Prosecutions of writers are rare, but they do occur. In 1966, two of the books by Gerard Kornelis van het Reve were criticised in parliament by a Protestant deputy for being 'blasphemous, bestial and even satanic'.[17] This led to his being prosecuted, but he was acquitted. It is evidence of the changing nature of Dutch society that there was much support for him in the press and that after his acquittal a party was held for him in a Catholic church. Both writers and artists have organised protests for bigger financial rewards. At the time of writing, some authors were considering boycotting the annual Writers' Week in support of their demands for royalties from the lending of their books by public libraries.

But the attitude of public authorities is somewhat more accommodating in the Netherlands than it is in many other countries. There is a genuine concern about the financial plight of artists and writers. In April 1965, in an attempt to give culture a central role in the context of modern life, the new Ministry of Cultural Affairs, Recreation and Social Welfare was founded. (Formerly a special department of the Ministry of Education was in charge of cultural affairs.) When the ministry was opened, Mr Joseph Cals, then prime minister, told parliament that the new ministry was not merely an experiment but had 'a definite place in our endeavours to gain a more integrated view of public welfare'. Some novel means of subvention for the arts have already been introduced and many more are being considered. From 1965, a number of artists (nine in 1966) have been given government stipends to enable them to devote themselves entirely to their art; and recently the government introduced a scheme to boost the sales of living Dutch artists by giving the purchaser a government-subsidised 25 per cent rebate on each purchase. Artists who are in temporary financial difficulties can apply to a municipality for a commission and if it is given, the government bears 75 per cent of the cost. It is now being proposed that a fund should be set up to help sculptors with the cost of materials for large-scale pieces of work. And for some time now it has been possible to spend up to 1·5 per cent of the total cost of new government buildings on associated works of art. These schemes are in addition to the more normal methods of subventions, such as prizes, exhibitions and subsidies to various institutions. Indeed, since the end of the war, there has been an enormous increase in the amount of government money spent not only on art, but also on general recreational and welfare facilities. (See Appendix 8.)

# 9

# The Political Parties

A DUTCH FRIEND once told me that he still vividly remembers one occasion before the war when his mother rushed breathlessly into the sitting-room and said that there had been a political landslide: their party had lost three seats at the general election. Yet in the 1967 general election, the Catholic party lost eight seats and a completely new party—Democracy '66—won seven seats. (See Appendix 9.) Even though the total number of seats in the lower house had been raised in 1956 from 100 to 150, it is easy to see why the last election appeared to many Dutchmen to be more in the nature of an earthquake than a landslide. There had not been such a violent swing in the support for any party in the whole of the post-war period; and the only parallel to the success of a newly founded party was the Dutch National Socialist party's gain of four seats in the 1937 election. It appeared to many people that *verzuiling* was beginning to crumble and to collapse. Yet others had their doubts. How significant were these admittedly very big changes in the 1967 elections, when the success of a number of smaller parties reduced the percentage of the valid votes cast for the five largest parties by nearly 9 per cent to 78·8 per cent as compared with 1963?[1]

It is doubly difficult to write about Dutch political parties at the present time. The party system—like much else in the country—is in such 'a process of flux'[2] that it is impossible to give firm indications of what new political combinations may appear. For the last five years, Dutch politicians have been talking about little else, yet few really strong alignments have emerged. There is also a short-term difficulty as there could also just conceivably be a drastic revision of the constitution after the next elections, due to be held in the spring of 1971, which would alter the way in which the prime minister is elected and thus have profound consequences for the whole political framework itself.*

This prevailing uncertainty was the main reason for the results of the provincial elections in March 1970, being awaited so eagerly by politicians of all parties. In themselves, these elections are not important; the provincial councils have few major powers apart from choosing members of the upper house. But as provincial councillors are elected in the same way as parliamentary deputies, the results often give a very good guide to the future composition of the lower house. The main gains in these provincial elections were registered by the Liberals, the Communists and D'66, a party which had not contested them before. The Catholics lost heavily and the right-wing Farmers' party almost disappeared. The group of Combined Christian Parties (CCP) won 6·9 per cent of the vote, while a new left-wing grouping (PAK) won 7·5 per cent.[3]

These results provided no really dramatic changes. D'66 leaders, who had hoped to pass the 10 per cent mark, were very disappointed; the new Christian and left-wing alignments did less well than some of their more fervent supporters had hoped;

*See p. 140 below.

and only the Liberals and the Communists could take much pleasure in the modest increase of their votes. It seemed, therefore to most politicians at the time of writing that the government mixture in 1971 would be the same as before—a coalition of the Catholics, the two major Protestant parties and the Liberals.* Yet the fact that small parties are now gaining a significantly larger share of the total poll shows that there is an increasing lack of confidence in the traditional party system.

Factionalism has always been endemic in the Netherlands; it preceded the institution of proportional representation and was not caused by it. There are always a large number of contesting parties in general elections: in the 1933 election, there were no less than fifty-four and in the 1967 election, there were twenty-three, including a Bachelors' party, which, among other things, wanted a fairer deal for homosexuals.⁴ The system of proportional representation and the low threshold vote makes it possible for parliament to represent shifts in public opinion more swiftly and more formally than the British system does.† Of the twenty-three parties in the 1967 election, eleven were successful in gaining one or more seats. (By 1971, because of splits within these parties, the total had increased to fifteen.)

Thus, many different shades of opinion are represented in parliament ranging from Communists to extreme Protestants, who want to abolish compulsory vaccination and who are opposed to social security schemes, and from Pacifist Socialists to the Poujadist-type Farmers' party. It might be expected that this mixture of opinions would result in some lively debates and clashes of opinion in the house, but as we shall see, this does not happen. But parliament is very important in producing stability by acting as a sounding board for voices in the country and in giving an illusion of involvement and power, even if the reality

*The four government parties won a total of only 74 seats out of 150 in the 1971 elections. This failure to retain their majority was expected, at the time of writing, to result in a long struggle to form a new coalition government.

†The threshold vote needed to capture a single seat has never been higher than 1 per cent of the total vote and since 1956, it has been 0·67 per cent, so that it is comparatively easy for fringe parties to enter the lower house.

is denied. Although the small parties are given proportionately a much greater share of the time than the main parties to express their views in debates, they are never included in government coalitions and are also excluded from most of the summit talks between parties in which policy is really made. No small party—except for the Communists in 1946—has succeeded in obtaining a larger share of the total votes than even the smallest of the big five. This feat was repeated in April, 1971, when D'66 won 11 seats, one more than the CHU. A new, right-wing socialist party, led by Willem Drees, DS'70, won eight seats. The Catholic Peoples party (De Katholieke Volkspartij—KVP), which has been the biggest party for most of the post war years, has lost support steadily since 1963, and in 1971 the Socialists became the largest party with 39 seats against 35 for the Catholics. The KVP has participated in all post-war governments and its predecessor, the Rooms Katholieke Staats partij, was represented in all Cabinets from the end of the First World War. Because it is supported by all classes of the population, it has to adopt a fairly moderate economic and social policy if it is not to lose extremists on either wing.[5]

Undoubtedly one of the main reasons for the Catholic party's recent losses is the severance of the link between the party and the Catholic hierarchy. It was only in 1954, after the Socialists had won the same number of seats as the Catholics in the previous election, that the bishops issued their pastoral letter warning Catholics that if they joined Socialist trade unions or listened to Socialist broadcasts they might be refused the sacrament. The ban on belonging to Socialist trade unions has since been lifted; and in February 1967, the bishop of 's-Hertogenbosch declared publicly that parties based on creed were outmoded.[6]

The party organisation, on the other hand, still retains as tight a grip on the deputies. There is a preferential vote in general elections, but few voters exercise it; most people vote for the party list which is chosen by the party executive. The Catholic party organisation goes much further than some of the others in its formal control over the list. Not only does it reserve one-third of candidacies for 'experts', but every candidate has to sign a pledge that, even if he is elected by preferential vote, he will not take his seat without the permission of the executive.\*[7]

In spite of this strict control, divisions in the party still occur. Before the war, there were a number of left-wing dissidents, and after the war, a right-wing Catholic National party was formed which was opposed to the KVP's colonial policy and to co-operation with the Socialists in government. It gained one seat in 1948, and two in 1952, before its members returned to the main party. In 1967 to 1968, another division in the Catholic party appeared. In November 1967, 'Christian radicals' from the Catholic and the two main Protestant parties held a congress at which they urged that voters should be able to vote for policies and programmes not parties, and that there should be a more progressive policy for the 1971 elections and co-operation with the Socialists in government.[8]

Within a few months, however, much of the impetus had gone out of the revolt, mainly because the dissidents were unable to attract a suitable leader. Three members of the KVP, however, did break away in February 1968, to form a separate parliamentary group known in the country—not, for technical reasons, in parliament—as the Politische Partij Radicalen. They usually vote with the PVDA.

This attempt to break down religious barriers and to form a broadly based progressive party is not the first that has been made in the post-war years. In 1946, a new Labour party (Partij van de Arbeid—PVDA) was formed out of the old Social Democratic Labour party, the Liberal Democratic party, members of wartime resistance groups and progressive Catholics and Protestants. Even though it had to set up a *verzuiling*-type structure in minuscule within the party itself, by creating Catholic, Protestant and 'neutral' working societies, it achieved great success in the decade after the end of the war. One of its leaders, Willem Drees, was prime minister of various coalition governments from 1948 to 1958. In 1956, its percentage of the

---

\*This rule was abolished in June 1970. But in order to take a seat which has fallen vacant between elections, a candidate still needs the permission of the executive.

national vote rose to 32·7, making it the largest party in the lower house. But since then, its share of the national poll has steadily declined.* One reason for this fall has been the breaking away of more radical elements, who were dissatisfied with the more moderate policy that the Socialist party had to adopt to satisfy the broad spectrum of members. In 1957, one group broke away completely to form a new party, the Pacifist Socialist party (De Pacifistisch Socialistische partij), which advocates more nationalisation, opposition to NATO and support for unilateral disarmament. In the 1967 elections it won four seats in the lower house.

Although in the last three years, the Socialist party's programme has veered more to the left, it still has not gone far enough for some radicals who still remain within the party. At the party congress in March 1969, these radicals, the New Left, gained one-third of the seats on the national committee. Their pleas for the congress to endorse a break with NATO did not succeed; but the congress refused to approve the cabinet's plan to spend another 225 million guilders on defence as a result of the Soviet invasion of Czechoslovakia.[9]

There was an even more fundamental division in the Socialist party at a much earlier period when, in 1909, some revolutionary dissidents broke away to form their own Social Democrat party, which was renamed the Communist party of Holland after the Russian Revolution and, in 1935, adopted its present name of the Communist party of the Netherlands (Communistische partij van Nederland).[10] Membership of the Communist Party has never been very high. Even in the boom years for Communists after the end of the last war, there were only 50,000 in the Netherlands against 100,000 in neighbouring Belgium, according to an estimate made by the Soviet journal, *Party Life*. Nevertheless, in 1946, because of their record of resistance to the Nazis and the general European swing towards the left, they gained 10·6 per cent of the national vote. In contrast to neighbouring Belgium, where the Communists were

*In 1959 it was 30·3 per cent; in 1963, 27·99 per cent; and in 1967, 23·5 per cent. In 1971 it rose again to 24·6 per cent.

given a place in all the five short-lived governments that ruled after the end of the war, they were never invited to take part in government in the Netherlands.* In fact, they were purged from the Amsterdam municipal council in 1948, a bill being passed by parliament to enable councils to remove members who had ceased to enjoy popular confidence; and in the same year, their deputies in parliament were excluded from a number of committees, including defence and foreign affairs. They were not allowed back on these committees until 1966.

After 1946, the vote for the Communist party fell steadily, until it reached an all-time low of 2·4 per cent in 1959. This decline was caused mainly by the introduction of the welfare state, which cut the ground from under the Communists' feet, and the Stalinist line adopted by the party chairman, Paul de Groot, who refused to endorse the new liberalising Khrushchev line in 1956.[11] He tried to remain neutral in the Sino-Soviet split believing, rightly, that the party's unity could only be preserved by concentrating on domestic issues. But from 1963 onwards, internal dissensions started to develop and in May 1969, a pro-Peking Marxist-Leninist party was formed in Amsterdam.[12] Since 1963, there has been a slight upsurge in the vote for the Communist party.

Of the other main parties, the biggest is the Liberal party or the People's Party for Freedom and Democracy (De Volkspartij voor Vrijheid en Democratie—VVD), as it has been called since 1948. The Liberal party is the main class-based party in the Netherlands, gaining much of its support from the upper and upper-middle classes. It gained a considerable increase in its support when it was out of office between 1952 and 1959, by its demands for cuts in taxation and more individual freedom and initiative. In 1959, it captured 12·21 per cent of the national vote, though by 1967, this had been reduced to 10·74 per cent.

---

*This does not indicate that there is a greater degree of tolerance among the Belgian establishment than there is in the Netherlands: it is simply that the former's ruling class has a much smaller amount of certainty, confidence and authority. On the other hand, it does give an interesting indication of the limits of Dutch permissiveness at that time.

Though it increased its support in the last provincial elections it lost one seat in the April 1971 elections. To have a Liberal party poster in one's front window still gives some status: it is one sign of having crossed the boundary from the working to the middle class. With rising prosperity, it can be expected to continue to attract new voters, particularly if it does not become ideologically divided.

Before the war, the Liberals were hopelessly divided and in 1967, they lost some support on the left wing to D'66. Some right-wing Liberals have turned to the new Farmers' party, which has gained an increasing share of the national vote since it was formed by Hendrik Koekoek in 1958. Although this party gained its main support among farmers initially, it has a Poujadist-style programme appealing to right-wing elements who want a reduction in employers' social security contributions, a drastic reduction in income tax and a less restricted economy. It now has seven seats in the lower house, but even this minor party is divided. In 1968, four deputies rebelled against Koekoek's leadership; but he claimed that two of them had been expelled anyway.[13] There are also dissidents on the left wing of the Liberal party, particularly among the young, who want a bigger education budget, a later school-leaving age and an increased roads programme, among other things. Out of three recent leaders of the Young Liberals, one is now a Liberal deputy, another is a Socialist deputy and the third is a deputy for the newly formed D'66 party.

The last two of the big five are both Protestant parties—the Anti-Revolutionary party (De Anti-Revolutionnaire partij—ARP) and the Christian Historical Union (De Christelijk-Historische Unie—CHU). The ARP, formed in 1878, was the first modern political party in the Netherlands. Founded in opposition to the spirit of the French revolution, and with equal treatment for denominational schools as an important political demand, it believed that the country should be governed on orthodox Protestant principles. Like the other parties it has been subject to frequent divisions; in fact the CHU was formed in 1908 as a result of defections from the ARP by less orthodox

Protestants at the end of the nineteenth century. This is still the main difference among their supporters today, with the ARP having more voters among the orthodox Reformed churches and the CHU among members of the Dutch Reformed Church. There are other differences, too. The ARP is more doctrinaire in policy, while the CHU is more pragmatic; the ARP finds most of its support in the lower middle and working classes and the CHU in the middle and upper classes; the ARP maintains a tighter party discipline, and its deputies have an even greater fondness for quoting biblical texts in parliamentary debates. There are also minor differences: for example, the CHU believed that the obligation to appear at polling stations to vote in general elections should be continued, while the ARP wanted to abolish it. On the other hand, there is a wide area of agreement between the two parties in their emphasis on the Bible as a source of inspiration for daily life and political action, and their support for small and medium-sized firms. Many Dutchmen find it very difficult to isolate the differences in their policies, though in 1965-7, they took different attitudes to the television dispute. The two parties each gain a fairly steady 8 to 9 per cent of the national vote.

The Protestants have suffered further divisions since the CHU broke away. In 1918, an extremely orthodox group formed the new Political Reformed party (Staatkundig Gereformeerde partij—SGP), which has gained about 2 per cent of the vote since, mainly from electors in remote regions such as Zeeland and Veluwe. Being supporters of a theocratic state, its members want to end all social security, compulsory vaccination and women's involvement in politics. An even smaller Protestant party, the Reformed Political Association (Gereformeerd Politiek Verbond—GPV) has one seat in the lower house. The two main Protestant parties also have dissidents on the left wing who would like to link up with the Catholics in a more broadly based Christian alliance.

The newcomer to the house in 1967 was Democracy '66 (Democraten '66—D'66). Its leader is thirty-eight-year-old Hans van Mierlo, the son of a banker, who has youth, an easy

grace and a charismatic charm which are all somewhat exceptional in Dutch politics. (His supporters compare him to Mayor
Lindsay of New York.) Although many of its members are
bourgeois, party research has shown that a considerable proportion have climbed up from a lower class. It is a very new-style
party; among its members you will find an expected earnestness,
but also an unexpectedly healthy cynicism, which is rather uncommon in the Netherlands. Its main appeal is to intellectuals,
left-wing Liberals and, particularly, the young. (In a mock
election, which was held at the same time as the 1967 general
election, among fifteen to twenty-year-old boys and girls at
schools and colleges as an exercise in civics, D'66 obtained the
highest proportion of the votes—22·9 per cent.[14]) It is the most
individual political party to have appeared in the Netherlands
for years. All the other minor parties have been break-away sects
favouring some modification of the main party's programme to
one extreme or another, whereas D'66 wants something entirely
new, nothing less in fact than a radical restructuring of the
whole of political life and of the constitution. On its first
appearance at the poll in 1967, it received 4·46 per cent of the
valid votes and won seven seats—an astonishing political
victory in the Netherlands.

The policy of D'66 is based upon the premise that the Netherlands has all the general norms of democracy—freedom of
speech, liberty of the subject, humanitarian attitudes, etc.—but
remains fundamentally undemocratic because there is no real
freedom of political choice. It is not the majority of the people
who decide who shall govern, but a small group of the establishment and the party cliques. It wants the prime minister to be
elected by direct popular vote, instead of being chosen after
consultations have taken place between the queen, the party
leaders and other members of the political establishment as hap-
pens now. It believes that this change would allow voters to
express their clear preference for a general pre-election mani-
festo, instead of policy being decided, after the election has been
held, in closed negotiations between members of the inevitable
coalition government. At the same time, it wants to abolish the

present system of proportional representation and to replace it by a district system of voting with three- or four-member constituencies. This, it believes, would intensify relations between the voter and the deputy, abolish some of the fringe parties and allow people to vote for a policy, instead of a party as they do now.

These are the main points in the programme of D'66. It also has a general programme which includes a five-year predictive planning of national resources, modernisation of the educational system (particularly technical education) and more overseas aid. But its general programme is far less important and specific than its plans for constitutional reform. (In fact, its refusal to commit itself more firmly to a specific general programme has alienated some of those who might otherwise support it.) But like the Provos, it wants to demonstrate the need for change, rather than affirm irrefutably what these changes should be. The constitutional changes it proposes are not an end, but only a means of reducing to their proper size, God, authority and the state which, it believes, have been venerated in the Netherlands too long. Moreover, as a believer in grass-roots democracy it does not want to impose its institutional beliefs upon its members; it wants to create action centres rather than a monolithic bloc, and to have full and frank discussions of party manifestos by all supporters as was done in the preparation for the provincial elections in March 1970. It even envisages that if its own programme for reform was carried out, it might be one of the fringe parties to disappear. In its victory, it previses its own defeat.

This is certainly an idealistic programme tempered by Dutch pragmatism and a certain respect for tradition in its retention of a dualistic system of government. But how appropriate is it to the country's present needs?

# 10

---

# System of Government

THE DUTCH system of government is one of the most complex and subtle in the world. It is not based, as in Britain, on a fusion of the executive and the legislature nor, as in the United States, on a strict separation of them, but on a delicate process of balance and bargaining between the two bodies. Ministers are not members of parliament and cannot, therefore, vote in it, though they may speak in either house and regularly do so. Parliament, however, is sovereign and retains the final right of voting a government out of office and of rejecting any bill, though it rarely exercises it, and the right, which is more frequently used, of amending bills. Over the years, both the Dutch parliament and the government have come to respect the limits of their powers and their obligations to each other. If parliament were to exercise its powers to the full, the country would become ungovernable; and if the government and the party leaders were to do so, it would be an oligarchy. In practice, therefore, the role of parliament is in some ways similar to that of the United States senate, to 'advise and consent', or similar to the greater powers of former British monarchs, as they were described by Bagehot, to be consulted, to encourage, to warn—with the final sanction of voting the government out of office.

Parliament is composed of two houses, but it is only the lower house that has any real importance. Members of the upper house, who must be over twenty-five years of age, are elected for a six-year term by the provincial councils. The upper house can only pass or reject bills outright and, therefore, exercises merely a 'blocking' function. Since 1956, there have been seventy-five members in the upper house and twice that number in the lower house. Members of the lower house are elected for a four-year term by all men and women over the age of twenty-one. (The minimum age was reduced from twenty-three to twenty-one in 1966.) Voting is by party list. There is a preferential vote but it is not greatly used. As the whole country forms one constituency, no valid vote is wasted.[1] Until recently attendance at the polling booth was compulsory, though voting was not, as papers could be handed in blank or spoiled. Electors could be fined if they did not appear. However, shortly before the provincial elections in March 1970, this obligation for the voter to appear was abolished, partly because some municipalities no longer enforced it, and partly in reaction against the paternalistic philosophy on which it was based. Nevertheless, a large number of people—nearly 70 per cent—continued to vote at this first 'free' election, though this is expected to fall in future elections approaching the British level of 30–50 per cent at local elections and 70–80 per cent at general elections.

Until very recently, membership of parliament was based, rather as membership of the old London County Council was, upon the idea of public service and the possibility of promotion to a more rewarding job in the political, or some other, sphere outside. In 1958, deputies had a small allowance of 10,000 guilders a year, reimbursement of expenses from 3,000 to 5,500 guilders a year, according to the distance of their home from The Hague, and travelling expenses.² Since then there has been a considerable increase. Deputies' pay, which is prosperity- or wage-linked, was raised in 1969, to 40,000 guilders a year with an additional 7,000 guilders or so expenses.* (It is now 41,000 guilders.) It is too soon to say whether this rise will be successful in producing more young people as candidates, or whether they would be accepted by the party organisations if they appeared. The salaries are probably not high enough in themselves to attract the ambitious, particularly as there is a much smaller possibility than there is in Britain of being pro- moted to ministerial rank (with its prosperity-pegged salary of about 100,000 guilders a year), as some ministers are still drawn from outside the parliamentary ranks. There is, however, a chance of a deputy being appointed burgomaster of a medium- size town, which has both a high standing and a reasonable salary, or of receiving offers from industry, which could some- times double or treble his pay. At the moment, the tradition of public service is still very evident, with many deputies coming from the old ruling élite, whose families have sometimes pro- vided administrators, deputies and ministers for generations, together with an admixture of men with trade union back- grounds. Because the social status of deputies remains high, there are normally a substantial number of people who want to get on the party list, including a fair number of suitable candidates.

As is common in most aspects of Dutch life, there is very little pomp but plenty of earnestness in parliament. A public road runs through the Binnenhof in The Hague, where the meetings of parliament are held. On some public holidays, a fair is held outside, with shooting galleries and stalls selling waffles and nuts —rather as if the car park at the Palace of Westminster was turned into a fairground when parliament is in recess. Though society, in some ways, is still more paternalistic and authori- tarian than it is in Britain, there has always been less show of

*In addition, a deputy can earn up to 5,000 guilders a year from other work, but if he earns more than that, half of what he earns is subtracted from his parliamentary salary, which, however, never falls below 25,000 guilders regardless of how much he earns outside. This rather complex system was designed to be as neutral as possible to deputies doing other work.

authority in the Netherlands. The élite, except perhaps economically, have never oppressed the population too much. Because of this, the Dutch have a dual attitude towards authority, a strange combination of respect and indifference.

The chamber where the lower house meets is small and cosy, with rows of small benches and tables on either side and a central ministerial table, with a telephone for ministers to communicate with officials, though most of the time they use a messenger. Debates tend to be even duller and more unrealistic than they are elsewhere. The Dutch are not great public speakers; most of them can only lecture or preach. (It is not unknown for a minister to have a chart or a blackboard in the house to help elucidate points for deputies: the managerial aspects of government are strong.) What makes the debates even duller than they might otherwise be, is the fact that most speeches are read either from notes or occasionally from a full text. 'Political passion is dissipated at the one extreme in almost theological debate and at the other extreme in petty details.'[3] A full house is even less common than it is in Westminster, very often only fifteen to twenty-five deputies are present at debates. The house, however, does fill up every October for the main budget debates and at other times when topics of major political importance are being debated.

What is often of far greater significance than the debates between parties in public are the disagreements between members of the same party in private. In the country as a whole, parties are weak and becoming weaker, as they also are in many other western countries. The majority of parties rely on membership subscriptions as their main source of revenue, and most of them are financially hard-pressed. In the last few years, membership of all the main parties, apart from the Liberals, has fallen considerably.*

*Figures showing the fall in party membership were published in *Het Vrije Volk* in 1969, and were reprinted in *Le Monde*, September 3, 1969.

|  | 1967 | 1969 |
|---|---|---|
| Catholics | 300,000 | 180,000 |
| Socialists | 130,000 | 105,000 |
| ARP | 95,000 | 86,000 |
| CHU | 45,000 | 35,000 |

But the party machine still has great powers. It chooses candidates and also fills any vacancies caused by death or resignation. By-elections are unknown in the Netherlands. The parliamentary party, even though there is no British system of whips, also exercises considerable power, 'vetting' the speeches of deputies before they are delivered in the house, and occasionally sub-editing them. Questions to ministers are also 'vetted' by some parties in the same way. In the last five years, the authoritarian, paternalistic attitude of party leaderships has diminished somewhat, more in some parties than in others. But basically, the parties still represent the pure, clear voice of uncompromising principle. This has, however, always been difficult to maintain entirely, because within each bloc there have always been and still are ideological or socio-economic differences. The Catholic party, for example, has to represent the views of both employers and employees. Most of the party leaders are involved in a constant struggle to hold their particular combination of conflicting interests together. The right of any individual deputy to vote against his party in the house has always been maintained and it is not unknown for a whole party to vote against a bill proposed by a government in which they are themselves represented. This does not mean that the government will necessarily fall, as it is not entirely dependent on the support of the parties which compose it, but only on a simple majority in the house. Although there are no formal talks between parties and government through the intermediaries of whips, there are plenty of informal consultations.

The dualistic system of government gives greater power to the executive than to parliament, but the latter still has some important sanctions. Parliament retains the right to vote a government out of office, though it is only rarely exercised. (The last occasion was in 1966, when the government of Joseph Cals was voted out of office over the budget.) It can also pass a motion of no confidence in an individual minister, which is usually sufficient to result in his resignation, and this power has been used more frequently. But its main means of control over the executive, apart from these more drastic resorts, is through amendments to bills, which the government very often accepts if there is a strong feeling in the house in favour of them. Recently, however, it has become increasingly common for ministers to threaten to withdraw the whole bill or to resign if unwelcome amendments are proposed. Parliament can also propose amendments to the budget, increasing or decreasing any item, or even adding new items of its own. Opposition amendments are usually voted down by the government parties, but amendments by the government parties are often accepted. Parliament also has the right to institute a full-scale inquiry, at which neither ministers nor civil servants are obliged to appear, though the former usually do. This weapon is rarely used. In the post-war period, a parliamentary inquiry was held to investigate the policy of the government-in-exile during the war. Another means of control is provided by questions to ministers, though the majority of these are answered in writing.

The multi-party system, with its intense ideologies and dissensions within parties, could be a great source of instability. And, indeed, when a government has to be formed after an election, the need to balance conflicting interests and points of view, leads to protracted delays as in other countries, such as neighbouring Belgium, also with a multi-party system. The post-war record was established in 1956, when it took 117 days to form a new government under the Socialist leader, Willem Drees. But the resemblance to many other countries with a multi-party system ends there. For once a government has been formed, it tends to be both stable and relatively strong. Since the end of the war, there have been twelve administrations and five of these have been headed by the same man—Drees. (See Appendix 10.) This paradoxical situation results mainly from the separation of powers of the executive and the legislature, which has its roots deep in Dutch history.

During the Dutch republic, government was primarily federal and oligarchic. This system was destroyed at the end of the eighteenth century by the French, who imposed a strong centralised government, which was continued by William I after his return in 1813. Ministers were considered to be literally the king's servants, and parliament was nothing more than a representative body to voice the opinions of the limited class who were allowed to vote. But just as the regents had repeatedly re-established their power against the stadtholder at an earlier period, so did the liberals under Thorbecke establish the powers of the new middle classes against the king, bringing about a revision of the constitution in 1848, which provided for full ministerial responsibility. Cabinet governments replaced autocratic royal control. There was no thought in the minds of the liberals then that parliament should be anything but a representative body in the old sense. Governments did not resign when an election was held, but remained in office until they were voted out by the new parliament. As Thorbecke said: 'Parliament's business is not to appoint or dismiss ministers, but only to judge their proposals.'[4] It was not for another twenty years that parliament established the principle that the government was dependent on its support by repeatedly voting against the budget between 1866 and 1868. Parliament obtained its powers only after those of the government were firmly established.

This concept of the primacy of government has persisted. It is still conceived that it is the main task of parliament to advise and warn. There have been very few private members' bills, even though this right exists and parliament controls its own timetable. (The right has been exercised more frequently in recent years.) Motions of confidence are unknown; it is assumed that the government has the confidence of the house until it is defeated on a vote. As we have already seen, ministers cannot be members of either house.* The separation of government and parliament is confirmed and emphasised by the tradition that ministers need not be drawn from the parliamentary ranks. Of the 338 ministers who held office between 1848 and 1958, only just over one-third—119—had had previous parliamentary experience.[5] (The proportion in the present de Jong government is about half and half, but the prime

*The only exception is when a deputy is appointed a minister after a general election; he is then given a three months' period of grace to allow him to decide which function he wishes to exercise.

minister, one vice-premier and the ministers of foreign affairs, education and defence, among others, have had no previous parliamentary experience.)

The Dutch have a pragmatic, even technocratic, view of government. In the same period of 110 years, the main previous occupations of ministers were in the professions, the higher civil service and before 1929, in the armed forces, and since 1945 particularly, in engineering in the widest sense.[6] As might be expected, women were admitted to ministerial office somewhat later than in some other Western countries. The first junior minister was Dr Anna de Waal, who became state secretary for education in 1950, and the first minister was Dr M. A. M. Klompé, appointed minister of social welfare in 1956.[7] Even those members of parliament who are chosen for ministerial office tend to change character, for what might be suitable attitudes on the floor of the house are inappropriate in the cabinet room, where some consensus has to be found among, what still are basically, greatly conflicting points of view. It might be thought that the selection of so many ministers from outside parliament would result in a static oligarchy. But the need to represent a broad spectrum of conflicting interest in the government, a sense of great probity in public life, the lack of nepotism and the traditional openness of the ruling classes to newcomers, prevent this development.*

The ability to compromise at the top has been particularly evident since the end of the war. Although all five main parties have never been in coalition together, the Catholic party has been in every coalition and between 1948 and 1952, the Liberals and Socialists served together in a coalition government with other parties. The two main Protestant parties have also been represented in many administrations. At this level, agreement has been hammered out on many post-war issues such as the

---

*As in all countries with a coalition government, there is a tendency for some ministers to hold office for many years. But men like Drees or Luns can only do so because of a genuine and general belief that there is no more suitable candidate for the post. Lengthy tenure of office has obvious advantages and disadvantages.

need for planning and the welfare state. But on other issues, such as the sharing out of the national income, the Liberals and the Socialists are still bitterly, and increasingly, divided, with the Catholics taking up a position between the other two.[8] In the 1967 election, prominent places were given in most party programmes to the issues of less taxation or more government spending; more social security or more personal responsibility; the conditions for the continental shelf gas and oil production; and more council houses or a less restricted building market.[9] But if the country is to remain stable and if the government is to accept its responsibilities. there has to be compromise at the top. The government must continue. That is why as Professor Daalder says, 'There can be such great disagreement over politics and yet, in some ways, alarmingly little over policy.'[10]

This delicate balancing of conflicting forces has produced stable, honest and relatively efficient government, but has it provided real democracy? The answer of D'66 would be 'No'. The Dutch voter has even less choice than in some other democracies as he has to vote for a party list instead of a government programme, and even those general policies for which the party traditionally stands may be compromised when its members enter a coalition government. Furthermore, new coalitions can be formed without any reference to the voter by means of an election, as happened in 1965 when the Liberals and the CHU left the government over the television issue and the Socialists came in to replace them. These are certainly grave defects; but is the British system of 'in-and-out' government, strong party whips, manifestos which often lose their meaning after the election, more fundamentally democratic than the Dutch system of consensus government, towards which, in any case, Britain in the post-war years has increasingly moved? Moreover, the D'66 proposals could provoke greater instability by shutting off the safety valves of fringe parties, while the destruction of the system of proportional representation might create far more severe regional problems. (There would, for example, be a bloc of southern Catholic deputies.)

The system itself, with its balance of opposing forces, not

only in formal government but also in very powerful bodies outside, such as the Social-Economic Council, does provide relatively stable and efficient government—but at a price. It is based more on consensus politics at the top than upon accord at the bottom. Because of this, many of the real decisions are taken across green-covered tables in private, or even at a less formal level.* Furthermore, some of the old parties, as in many other western democracies, have become increasingly out of touch with the real aspirations and needs of their supporters.

But it is convincing evidence of the continuing ability of both government and parliament to react swiftly to new proposals and to changes in society that there should have been so much political activity and new thought in the last three or four years.† One of the first acts of the Piet de Jong government after the 1967 election was to set up an all-party advisory state commission to report on modifying the political structure and the electoral system. In 1969, the seventeen-man commission recommended, by a majority of one, that there should be two votes in a general election—one for a party and one for a man, and that if any one man obtained a clear majority of the votes, the queen would ask him to form a government. (There would be no second ballot.) People's votes are already influenced by the party leader as well as the party.‡ But it is unlikely that any one man would have commanded the necessary widespread support to get a majority of the votes. And it seems unlikely that the recommendation will be accepted, as party opposition to it has hardened since it was made and it would necessitate a

---

*This is becoming increasingly common in all western democracies, and the Netherlands, with its much longer experience of consensus politics than almost any other country, does this extremely well, and to a great extent, fairly.

†The general public, on the other hand, has been somewhat less stirred. Its attitudes reflect a traditional deference—satisfaction with the working of government as a whole—and a more modern disillusion—there are too many leaders, anyway.

‡The clearest example in recent times was the ARP gain of two seats in the 1967 elections, which was primarily a tribute to the successful premiership of Jelle Zijlstra, even though he was no longer on the party list. He is now governor of the Bank of the Netherlands.

revision of the constitution which is difficult, though not impossible, to effect.*

Meanwhile, some of the parties, too, have been trying to create new alignments. For many years the ARP has been advocating a merger with the CHU. Although they have presented joint lists at local elections in the predominantly Catholic south, hopes of a full merger seem to be as far away as ever. In the last three or four years, there have also been proposals to form a CDU-style party as exists in many other continental countries. During the last eighteen months, the Group of 18 was set up containing six representatives from each of the three confessional parties, Catholics, ARP and CHU, in an attempt to draft joint electoral programmes. The group has agreed provisionally to joint operations at the 1971 elections, but the CCP results in the 1970 provincial elections did not give much confidence to doubters. Among many Protestants there was a clear reaction against the idea and the smaller, more orthodox Protestant parties, who are not involved in this scheme, all did well. Many leaders in the ARP are against the idea, some of them fearing that the party would lose its own identity and others not wishing to see an intensification of the religious-secular polarisation of society. The Catholic party is on the whole more in favour of the scheme, though the Catholic Church itself, with its current policy of non-involvement in the intrigues of domestic political life, has remained mute on the question of a possible CDU party. There are again no signs that a progressive grouping of the left is likely to appear in any strength at the 1971 elections. In both cases, the more progress that is made, the more important do the old divisive issues become. There is also, quite naturally, a power conflict between leaders. What seems to be a more likely pattern in the immediate future, particularly in the Netherlands, is that some parties will institute parallel programmes rather than full-scale mergers. (In March 1971, it was reported that the Socialists, D'66 and some left-wing Catholics had agreed to present a joint programme for the general elections in the following months.)

*See p. 140 below.

In the long term, however, it does seem much more likely that new political groupings will emerge. There is a great difference between the pre-war and the post-1954 situation. Before the war, *verzuiling* was still so firmly established throughout society that it created an inbuilt stability in the political system. Voters remained ultimately committed to the main parties, though they might stray from time to time, as they alone held out the hope of further emancipation for their particular bloc. Equally, the parties could always bring most of voters back to heel by playing on their fears that disunity in their own camp would allow the rivals to benefit. Now that emancipation has reached its present advanced state, these fears are no longer so intense.

# I I

---

# Crown and Constitution

THE NETHERLANDS is that rare example of a country which after centuries of republican rule has settled down happily under a monarch. But neither categorisation of the form of government is strictly exact: under the republic, the country was often searching for a monarch, and under the monarchy, it was searching in the early years for some of those freedoms that it had enjoyed in the republic. The result has been that it has ended up with its own special form of parliamentary democracy and a monarch whose powers are still to a certain degree greater than they are, for instance, in Britain.

Owing to the vagaries of birth, women have been rulers or regents in the Netherlands since 1890. When the last king, William III, died, his daughter Wilhelmina was only ten years old, so that her mother, Queen Emma, acted as regent until Wilhelmina ascended the throne in 1898. The climax of her fifty-year reign, and her greatest popularity, came towards the end of it, when her regular broadcasts to the Dutch people from her wartime exile in England became a symbol of the nation's resistance. Shortly after she returned to the Netherlands following the liberation, she developed pneumonia, and it was not long before she decided to abdicate in favour of her daughter. Juliana was inaugurated as queen on September 6, 1948, in Amsterdam. Wilhelmina, who insisted on being called Princess Wilhelmina after her abdication, retired to the seclusion of her palace Het Loo, where she spent the last fourteen years of her life occupied with her memoirs and the study of religion. She died in 1962.

In Queen Juliana's reign, the monarchy has been severely tested; first over her own involvement with a faith-healer and then over the marriages of two of her four daughters. It is a good indication of the underlying strength of the monarchy that it should emerge through all three crises with its reputation scarcely diminished, and also of the inner strength of Queen Juliana and her husband Prince Bernhard, and of their good relationship, that they, too, should have survived these unexpected personal ordeals and yet remained personally unscathed.

The faith-healer episode created, in some ways, more of a sensation outside the Netherlands than it did inside. Indeed, most of the Dutch press, with its strong tradition of non-intrusion into personal lives, was very critical of what it called the 'sensationalism' of much of the foreign press. The story circulated by some foreign newspapers in 1956, was that Princess Marijke,* the queen's youngest daughter, was blind and that Queen Juliana had consulted a faith-healer to help cure her. They also reported that this had precipitated a constitutional crisis and had created such a great rift between Queen Juliana and her husband that the queen was contemplating a divorce and abdication. All these reports were denied by both the government and the royal family. At the queen's request, three elder

*Since April, 1963, the princess, at her own request, has been called by her second name Christina, which will be used from this point onwards.

statesmen were asked to inquire into the whole affair. Meanwhile, it was officially stated that Princess Christina was not blind, but had been born with a clouding of the lenses of both eyes and doctors had been able to restore the sight of one eye as much as possible.

Two months or so later, the Commission of Three issued its report. It stated that the queen had severed all relationships with the faith-healer; that the queen would no longer attend religious services at Het Loo (her mother's home), where the faith-healer had been present; and that the integrity of the faith-healer herself was not in question. Also, there had never been any question of Queen Juliana abdicating. A few months later, three palace officials were dismissed. Some of the more unpleasant and hurtful features of this case could have been avoided if the palace officials had had a better understanding of the foreign press. By the time the third incident occurred, press relations had been greatly improved.

As far as many Dutchmen were concerned, the faith-healer affair was more a cause for criticism of the foreign press than of their own royal family, but the following two incidents stirred up more Dutch than foreign passion, because two shibboleths—one very old and the other much more recent—were involved. The first, though it was never publicly acknowledged, involved the relationship of the monarchy and the established church.

The Dutch monarchy dates back only to 1813, but it is the most important symbol of patriotism and unity because of its links with the House of Orange, the creators and defenders of the republic against Catholic Spain.* Although there is no provision in the constitution that the monarch shall be a Protestant, all of them have been members of the Dutch Reformed Church. In 1964, Princess Irene, who was then second in succession to the throne, was received into the Catholic Church, shortly before her engagement to Prince Carlos Hugo of Bourbon-Parma, son of the Carlist pretender to the Spanish throne.

---

*Article 10 of the constitution states: 'The Crown of the Netherlands is and shall remain vested in His Majesty William Frederick, Prince of Orange-Nassau, to be possessed by him and his legitimate descendants.'

After prolonged discussions between the royal family and the government, it was announced that the princess would not seek parliamentary approval for her marriage (thus renouncing her right of succession) and that she would live outside the Netherlands after her marriage. It was officially maintained then, as it still is, that the reason she did not seek parliament's approval was because of her future husband's involvement in Spanish politics. This was probably a subsidiary reason; but the main reason, as some Dutchmen now admit, was politicians' fears that the possibility of having a Catholic queen could have aroused and inflamed old religious conflicts and prejudices. Certainly, it might have done so among some of the older generation; but many young people, even strict Protestants, have told me that they would have no objections to a Catholic queen.

The last of the three royal crises was the most prolonged and the most violent, because it involved the Dutch attitude towards the Germans. To many Dutchmen, the memory of the German occupation is still raw and recent. In June 1965, the queen announced in a television and radio broadcast that her eldest daughter, Crown Princess Beatrix, who is first in line to the throne, was going to marry a German diplomat, Claus von Amsberg, who had not only served with the Wehrmacht, but had also been a member of the Hitler youth movement. The announcement of this engagement caused a storm of protest, particularly among the Jews, former resistance members, Socialists and the young. There was further dismay when it was discovered that, against all tradition, the wedding would take place in Amsterdam; a decision that some patriotic Dutchmen still deplore to this day.* It was reported that Beatrix had chosen to be married in the most left-wing and anti-German city in the country in the belief that, if her wedding was accepted there, it would be accepted in every part of the country. There were many letters of protest in the newspapers and orange swastikas were daubed on the walls of the royal

*The tradition is that the monarch is married at The Hague, inaugurated as monarch in Amsterdam and buried at Delft.

palace in Amsterdam. But, in all of this, there was little personal animosity against Princess Beatrix. Indeed, there was almost as great a storm of protest when it leaked out that one politician had said that Beatrix's wilfulness 'would have to be curbed'. This opinion had been expressed in a letter written by Mr G. M. Nederhorst, then parliamentary leader of the Socialist party, a copy of which had fallen into the possession of a newspaper, which then published it. Although he protested that his opinions had been purely personal, he was criticised by most other party leaders.[1] The Dutch have little sympathy for personal intrusion of this kind.

Meanwhile, there had been a great improvement in the royal family's relations with the press and shortly after the announcement of their engagement, Princess Beatrix and her future husband gave a press conference for about sixty Dutch and foreign journalists. Their frank answers to questions and the couple's obvious sincerity and affection created a favourable impression. When one journalist asked Princess Beatrix what she thought about all the protests, she said that she welcomed them. 'It is much healthier,' she said, 'for people to speak their minds than to bottle up their feelings.'[2] Such democratic sentiments strike just the right note in the Netherlands. In November, a government bill approving the marriage was passed by 132 votes to nine and the wedding took place in March 1966. Although national protests had been quelled, there was still some local opposition. Almost half of Amsterdam's municipal councillors refused to attend the wedding.[3] And along the processional route, about a thousand young people threw fireworks and smoke-bombs: nineteen people were arrested.

Since his marriage, the popularity of Prince Claus, now known as prince of the Netherlands, has increased enormously. The succession to the throne has been assured by the three sons of the marriage—Willem Alexander born in 1967, Johan Friso born in 1968, and Constantijn born in 1969—so that some time in the future there could be a king of the Netherlands again. On the whole there is very little republican feeling in the Netherlands. A poll held by the weekly review *Elseviers Week Blad*, in

1969, showed that only 10 per cent wanted a republic; and of these, 70 per cent thought that the queen did her job well or very well.[4] There are occasional protests by young people against the monarchy: at the opening of the new session of parliament in September 1968, for example, about fifty young people along the route waved banners and shouted 'Long live the Republic'. There is also a certain amount of disenchantment with the monarchy among some intellectuals, caused not so much by any passionate desire to set up a republic, but more because they see the monarchy as one symbol of the old, closed, established order. But, there are some who hope that the monarchy will be retained because of its unifying force. As Dr Brugsma has pointed out: 'Only the monarchy can lead those social groups or classes, that now fear to be equalised out of existence, into a modern, open society (and ultimately into a united Europe, in which monarchs would liberate themselves).'[5] There could only be a dramatic increase in republican feeling, one southern Liberal told me, if Princess Beatrix did not do her job well when she ascended the throne, but he did not think this was likely to happen.

The tradition of a 'democratic' monarchy is now fairly well established. This unpretentiousness is symbolised by the fact that the monarch is not crowned, but inaugurated at a simple ceremony, attended by both houses of parliament, in the new church adjacent to the royal palace in Amsterdam, where the monarch swears an oath on the constitution.* The present queen lives in Soestdijk Palace, about twenty miles from Amsterdam. Originally the hunting lodge of the Orange family, it has had two wings added, but still remains essentially a modest building, painted white and with shuttered windows.

---

*Article 53 of the constitution prescribes the following oath: I swear to the Netherlands people that I will always observe and uphold the constitution. I swear that I will defend and preserve, with all my power, the independence and territory of the state; that I shall protect the general and particular liberty and the rights of all and each of my subjects, and will employ for the maintenance and promotion of the general and particular welfare, all the means which the laws place at my disposal, as a good king should do.

So help me, God Almighty! (That I promise!)

The lawns and much of the grounds are open to public view from the road. Indeed, on the queen's birthday a local celebration is held on the palace lawns, with bands, pony races and troupes of people in regional costume. While the four princesses were growing up, many of their friends and visitors came from the neighbourhood. All four princesses cycled every day to local schools—New Baarn primary and Baarn grammar school. The queen also rides a bicycle (as did Wilhelmina in her younger days) and buys some of her clothes ready-made. Some of the credit for this democratisation and easy friendliness must go to Prince Bernhard. Princess Beatrix lives in her own small palace near her mother.

In spite of this easy and informal way of life, Queen Juliana is the best-paid monarch in the world with a state allowance of 4,750,000 guilders a year.* In addition, she has a large private fortune. However, according to Professor D. Simons, chairman of the government committee set up to study the queen's finances before she was granted a 90 per cent pay rise in 1968, she is by no means the richest woman in the world, as is popularly believed, or even the richest woman in the Netherlands.[6]

Because of the multi-party system, Queen Juliana's involvement in politics is probably greater than that of the British queen. After a general election, the monarch sees the presidents (chairmen) of both houses of parliament, the leaders of all parliamentary political groups and the vice-president of the Council of State.* If an obvious leader emerges, the queen appoints him *formateur* of a government, but if no obvious candidate presents himself, she will appoint an *informateur* to

---

*From the beginning of 1971 her salary was reduced to about 850,000 guilders and the income of the royal family was made liable to income tax. But most of the expenses of maintenance of households, official receptions, state visits, etc., will now be paid for by the state.

*The Council of State, of which the monarch is titular president, is composed of up to twenty members. At one time it had great importance as the monarch's closest advisor, but now its role has been much reduced, though it still sees all bills before they are submitted to parliament. Since 1964 it has achieved a new and different importance as the highest appeal court in administrative cases.

sound out opinion, and, sometimes, if he fails, a second *informateur*, as was done in 1963. These private consultations between the monarch and the party leaders are another aspect of government to which D'66 is opposed. The proposal for a directly elected prime minister would obviously reduce the monarch's powers considerably.

⊗

The constitution of the Netherlands guarantees all the classic freedoms.[7] Articles 171 to 173, for example, guarantee freedom from wrongful arrest, the privacy of homes and the secrecy of the post, while Article 101 provides for religious liberty. Unlike Belgium, where there has been only relatively minor changes in the constitution, the Dutch constitution has been amended many times, though it is equally difficult to do so.[8] A bill to change the constitution must first be passed by both houses of parliament and then receive the royal assent. Parliament is then dissolved and a new lower house elected. The bill must then be passed again by a two-thirds majority in each house before it receives the final royal assent. The constitution was last revised in 1963.

There is a formal link between the national and local governments in so far as members of the upper house of parliament are elected by members of the eleven provincial councils, who are themselves directly elected by the proportional representation system for a four-year term. In each province there is a queen's commissioner who acts as chairman of the provincial council. But the powers of provincial councils are limited and most local government affairs come under the control of the 965 municipalities: annual estimates for the municipalities as a whole are about 4,000 million guilders against 240 million guilders for the provinces.[9]

With the municipalities, there is again a formal link with the national government, which appoints the salaried burgomasters for a six-year term of office. There is keen competition for the appointment as burgomaster of a large municipality, not only for the salary, but also for the high prestige of the job. The burgomaster is not only appointed by the government, but can also be dismissed as happened in the case of Gijsbert van Hall in 1967, following the Amsterdam riots of the previous year. It might be thought that burgomasters would become the 'tools' of the national government, but this is not so. The burgomaster has his own responsibilities, his own prestige and powers and not only defends his own little empire vigorously, but is even expected by the government to do so. Dismissals by the government are extremely rare. It is not unknown for a burgomaster to be a member of the upper house or even of the lower house, where he readily criticises the government that appointed him.[10] The Dutch make less of a distinction between administrators and members of the government than the British. It is also possible for civil servants to be members of parliament; while they are serving as deputies, their pay is made up, they are placed on the non-active list, but can resume their job later.

The system of government in the municipalities is very similar to the national system. The council is directly elected for a four-year period, but real executive power rests with the burgomaster and a corporation of aldermen who are elected by the council from its own members. The composition of the corporation is not usually based on the majority system, but reflects the party proportions in the council as a whole as closely as possible. The burgomaster and aldermen make the majority of policy decisions which are then presented to the council for its consideration. The council retains ultimate control by its powers over the local budget, the right to pass all by-laws and acts in a similar role to parliament 'as the representative of the people against the government'.[11] In the same way as the national system, it 'has provided high quality local government and has been reasonably responsible to public wishes'.[12]

The municipalities vary greatly in size from Amsterdam with its population of over 1 million, to a few municipalities, which originated in the Middle Ages, where the population is no more than a thousand. During the last few years, there have been a number of amalgamations of smaller municipalities, but these are sometimes opposed because people remain very jealous of their rights and local autonomy. A law passed in 1950, made it possible for municipalities to co-operate in the provision of certain services, and in some cases, such as housing, special acts of parliament have been passed to make co-operation compulsory. In 1964, a supra-municipal authority for Rotterdam and twenty-three other municipalities was established by act of parliament. There has been discussion of a similar larger-Amsterdam scheme for several years. Some of the municipalities, such as Amsterdam, have their own ombudsman, and there have also been proposals that a national ombudsman should be appointed.*

One hundred and twenty-two of the larger municipalities have their own police forces which come under the direct control of the burgomaster, who is personally responsible for maintaining law and order. The combined strength of these forces is 14,500. Smaller municipalities are catered for by the national police corps, with a total of 6,000 men. The corps come under the authority of the minister of justice. Its members are also used for some national tasks, such as patrolling the motorways.

Prosecutions are not brought by the police but only by the department of public prosecutions, which has a staff of public prosecutors throughout the country. The department has a considerable degree of independence and is not compelled to prosecute (with one or two exceptions) if it knows of an offence. There is no trial by jury in the Netherlands and all cases are heard by professional judges who are appointed nominally for life, but, in fact, retire at seventy. There are sixty-two cantonal courts (*kantongerecht*) which deal with minor civil and criminal cases. Almost all felonies, major civil cases, divorce and bankruptcy cases are dealt with in nineteen district courts (*arrondissementrechtbank*). They also act as appeal courts from the decisions of the cantonal courts. There are five courts of appeal (*gerechtshof*) to hear appeals from the district courts and a

*The Liberals, who were among the first to suggest the idea, have now moved more towards an independent, Scandinavian-type ombudsman, rather than the British parliamentary model.

supreme court (*De Hoge Raad der Nederlanden*), which does not re-try cases, but sees mainly that the law is applied uniformly in sentencing. In addition to the courts of justice, there are many administrative tribunals covering social and insurance legislation and other regulations in the economic and social spheres.

At the time of writing, the whole of the civil code of law was being revised and brought up to date. Some of the changes have already been made, such as that mentioned earlier which reduced the age of marriage without parental consent from thirty to twenty-one. The minimum age for criminal responsibility is twelve. Great efforts are made to segregate various types of offenders. There are special prisons for young offenders between the ages of eighteen and twenty-three and separate houses of detention for those who receive a sentence of less than two months, or for those awaiting trial in custody. People who are found guilty of driving a car while drunk are invariably sentenced to imprisonment or to a term of detention. Many of the sentences given by courts are short, for periods of less than a month, and as an experiment many of these offenders are being allowed to serve their sentences at the week-ends.[13]

# Education

THE DUTCH take most things seriously and education more seriously than almost anything else. Young children are treated with great indulgence by their parents (some people say that they are spoilt). But after they have attended school for a few years, they are expected to work and to study hard, because certification is more universal and more rigidly defined and prescribed for jobs of all kinds than in many other countries. Like other institutions in the Netherlands, the whole of the educational system is being totally renovated. The post-primary educational system has already been altered by a law which came into effect in the autumn of 1968 (known as the 'mammoth' law because it covered so many aspects) and university and primary education are also due for revision some time in the future.

The most novel feature of the Dutch educational system is

that about 70 per cent of children attend 'private' schools, while only 30 per cent go to state schools, most of which are run by the municipalities.¹ The former, however, are not 'private' in the English sense, but are run by, or linked to, religious denominations, mainly Catholic, Protestant and Reformed. *Verzuiling* became firmly entrenched in the educational system after 1920, when it became possible to grant 100 per cent subsidies to 'private' schools. It is based on the belief that parents should have the right of free choice in education with, as Article 208 of the constitution lays down, 'every person's religious views being duly respected'. Until very recently, it meant that not only was there denominational religious instruction in 'private' schools, but that the teaching of some history was also 'slanted', particularly over such issues as the Dutch revolt against Catholic Spain, that the ambience of many schools was based upon a particular view of life, and that children were separated from each other at an early age according to the religious persuasion of their parents.² As most kindergarten education is organised by religious bodies and there are also Protestant and Catholic universities, it is still possible to be educated from the age of four to nearly thirty in institutions which are run by people with one's own religious views. With the increasing modernisation of society, *verzuiling* is less important than it once was, but it does tend to perpetuate divisions which might be less marked if the denominational hold over education did not exist.

Compulsory education was not introduced into the Netherlands until 1900, and even now it is compulsory for only eight years. The school-leaving age is fifteen.* But the provision of education is not so scanty as it might sound. Nearly 90 per cent of all children attend infant schools which take children from the age of four. Though many mothers complain about the accommodation in infant schools and crèches as being far too scarce, the provision of pre-primary education is at least as extensive as it is in England. Between the ages of six and seven,

*In 1969 a law was passed providing for nine years of compulsory education. It is hoped to put it into effect within the next few years.

children go on to a primary school. As private schools in the English sense, and boarding schools are almost unknown, primary schools are far more democratic than they are in England, particularly in the country. All the queen's four daughters went to local schools. At the age of twelve, children go on to a secondary school of varying kinds. Education at state schools is co-educational as it is in much of the 'private' sector, except in technical schools. Although the school-leaving age is officially fifteen, more children stay on to the age of sixteen than in England and Wales. (See Appendix 11.)

In recent years, there has also been an increasing democrati sation at the high school level. Although some statistics show that England has two-and-a-half times as many working-class pupils in school of this level, the real differences are very much less if allowances are made for the different methods of classifying social class.[3] There are no tuition fees for education in the Netherlands during the period of compulsory education, though textbooks are not provided. After fifteen years of age, there is a small parental contribution at state schools, based on a means test. There is a maximum contribution of 200 guilders a year. Even at the best 'private' high school in Amsterdam, parental contributions do not exceed £100 ($240) a year. At the age of nineteen, nearly a quarter of all boys are still having some form of full-time education.

The schools set very high standards, particularly at the high school level. Lessons usually start at 8 or 8.30 a.m. and continue until midday when there is a break of about an hour. As very few schools have canteens, most children bring sandwiches. (This is less deprivatory than it may sound, as they would be eating more or less the same thing at home. On the other hand, many schools fail to provide adequate accommodation where children can eat their lunch.) Lessons are resumed in the afternoon, for a varying period, as schools exercise a greater control over the length of the school day than they do in England. The average number of hours for lessons in high schools is thirty-three a week, with at least three hours' homework a night during the final two years. Although there are no annual examinations as there are in England, progress is recorded regularly on report cards (usually every quarter), with marks ranging from 1 to 10, though 1 and 2, and 9 and 10, are rarely given. The last report in each year decides whether a child will move into a higher class; a number are usually kept down for a year. 'The process of selection does not stop at first admittance but goes on from day to day; those who do not live up to the school's standards will fail and will eventually drop out.'[4]

Until recently, the educational system was directed less to teaching children how to live or how to behave, but more to gaining a certificate. There was great emphasis on learning facts. The granting of certificates is administered nationally and the standards are the same for all pupils, whether they come from 'private' or state schools. Here again, there was a very high standard, leading to a bigger drop-out problem than in many other European countries: from 1961 to 1965, the proportion of those who failed to complete their course and to gain a certificate at a high school or its equivalent was 44 per cent.[5]

In the autumn of 1968, a start was made on altering the whole system of secondary education, which will be completed by the mid-seventies. The old system had grown haphazardly over the past century. Pre-university education was provided at a gymnasium with a six-year course, which was divided into a classical side with Greek and Latin and optional Hebrew and a scientific curriculum, after four years. The *Hogereburgerschool* (HBS) had a five- or six-year course which divided after three years into a modern languages and scientific side. Some pupils also went on to university. There was also a secondary school for girls which provided a general five-year high school type of education.

General secondary education was given at what the Dutch describe as an advanced primary school, but which was far in advance of most English secondary modern schools with compulsory English, French and German and many other subjects. This course lasted three or four years. There was also a complementary primary school, with a minimum two-year course, similar to an English secondary modern school, including

147

world history for all, and handicrafts for boys and needlework for girls. In addition, there were a large number of vocational and technical schools, some of which were entered direct from primary school and others after a period of more general education. Before the new 'mammoth' law came into effect, the proportion of pupils at pre-university schools was about 20 per cent; at general secondary schools, 40 per cent; and in elementary technical schools, 40 per cent.

The new 'mammoth' law has tried to cure some of the defects of the old system by making it easier to transfer from one school to another, providing more general education as a basis for future higher or vocational studies, allowing pupils to take a wider range of optional subjects and rationalising the structure of the educational system as a whole. The Dutch have not tried to impose a uniform pattern of comprehensive education, but have left options open for individual authorities controlling schools to amalgamate them if they wish. On the other hand, it has been made easier to transfer between schools by introducing a transitional year between the ages of twelve and thirteen when pupils follow a common syllabus as much as possible, so that transfers can be made at an early age to avoid a drop-out problem later. Selection for different schools may be based on psychological tests and trial classes rather than examinations. To cater for individual aptitudes, there are four private-study periods a week during the transitional year and a greater range of optional subjects later.

But it is already clear to some educationists that the transitional year not only places an extra strain on pupils and parents, but is also too short a period in which to decide a child's future and to assess his abilities. What a number of teachers and educationists would prefer is a middle school from the age of twelve to fifteen. Already ten groups of schools are planning to extend the transitional period by another two years 'working on the basis of non-streamed classes covering the pre-university, continued general and vocational sectors'.[6] But the general development of comprehensive, middle school education, even if it were wanted, would, so one official of the Ministry of

Education and Sciences told me, be difficult to introduce generally at the present time because of the lack of accommodation,
high costs and shortage of teachers.

Indeed, the new system retains an element of selection at
twelve years or older as there will generally be one common
syllabus for children at pre-university, higher and intermediate
secondary schools, and another at the lower levels. The distinctions between the various levels have been retained. At the
pre-university level the curriculum of the old-style gymnasium,
where all pupils were taught Greek and Latin, has been brought
up to date, with more emphasis now on mathematics, social and
natural sciences. The HBS is being abolished. In its place, there
will be a new athenaeum, with mathematics and science, or
economics and social science as its main subjects. At the same
level, there is a new lyceum, which combines the courses of the
other two schools. Other school courses are divided into higher,
intermediate and lower levels. Higher secondary education
lasts for five years and can be followed by vocational or technical
education at a higher level; intermediate education lasts for
three or four years and usually leads on to some form of
secondary vocational training; lower-level education lasts one
or two years at elementary technical schools or at separate
schools and it is followed by further technical training or by an
apprenticeship to a firm.[7]

In theory the system makes it possible to progress vertically
by a series of certificated steps from one level to another, but in
practice it will be most difficult for any but a few exceptional
pupils to start at the lowest and reach the highest levels. As one
writer has said:

. . . The sheep are separated from the goats at the age of
twelve. Those who go on to the lower technical school, to
say nothing of the general intermediate school, are almost
fated to become labourers and to continue as such . . .[8]

Nevertheless, the new system is in many ways an improvement
on the old and its does leave more options open for individual
school authorities to take initiatives.

The Dutch spend a higher proportion of their national income on education than many other countries. Between 1950 and 1967, expenditure increased tenfold to more than one-quarter of the national budget.[9] It is now well over one-quarter. (See Appendix 12.) One of the reasons for this high expenditure is the maintenance of the separate state and 'private' sectors. Though this may be politically necessary, it is always expensive, as Belgium also found in 1958, when it introduced its 'Schools Pact' to provide both state and 'private' schools.[10] In the Netherlands, the three types of school—state, Catholic and Protestant—can usually be found in a town with 50,000 or more inhabitants. Previously, the minister of education had to recognize the need for the existence of a new 'private' school before he granted it a subsidy.[11] Under the new act, a greater degree of planning has been introduced as the minister of education and sciences will draw up every year 'a school plan showing the (public and private) post-primary education schools which will be eligible for state support in the three calendar years following the drawing up of the plan'.[12] In making a decision he will be guided by the demand for the type of school and the flow of pupils anticipated at the end of the three-year period. Closer liaison between the state and the 'private' authorities has been achieved by establishing a plan procedure committee on which all bodies are represented.[13] This is an important step towards achieving greater co-ordination of efforts in education, even though *verzuiling* itself is still retained.

*Verzuiling* is also present in the higher education system. Of the thirteen universities and higher education institutions, one is Reformed and two are Catholic. The Free University of Amsterdam was founded in 1880, the Catholic University of Nijmegen in 1923, and the Tilburg School of Economics, Social Sciences and Law in 1927. They receive subsidies of up to 95 per cent of their costs. They were founded originally to act as intellectual bastions for members of their respective faiths and to counter religious discrimination in university appointments, but they have become increasingly open in recent years. Although the statutes of the Free University still prohibit the appointment of Catholic professors, there are a number o Catholic lecturers; and at Nijmegen there are both Protestant and Jewish professors.[14] At the Free University about 10 per cent of the students are Catholic. The Rector Magnificus* of the university, Professor W. F. de Gaay Fortman, has told me that about half of the remainder entered because of their religious sympathies and the others because it was a small university where personal contacts with professors are more possible than in some of the larger state universities.

Apart from any other factors, these confessional distinctions would have been difficult to maintain in the face of the growing demand for university education common to all countries. The student population in the Netherlands more than doubled between 1959 and 1967. (See Appendix 13.) This has created problems, as in all countries, of staff-student relations, increased costs and accommodation. The Municipal University of Amsterdam—the only municipal university in the country—which is crammed in among the central canals of the capital, is overflowing into seventeenth-century burghers' houses, while the Free University, more fortunately situated on the outskirts, is building a completely new complex, with its own clinic and teaching hospital. At Utrecht, the university is moving to a new site out of the town with well-planned tall buildings connected by roads named after other European universities, such as Oxford and the Sorbonne. Two new institutions of higher education were opened in the sixties: the Twente College of Technology in 1961, and the Rotterdam Medical School in 1966.† Nevertheless, there is still severe overcrowding.

In principle, all universities are 'open' in so far as any Dutchman who pays the prescribed fees may attend lectures; but in practice admission to a university is secured by passing the final examination at a pre-university school, which allows students to take the university examination. As in many other

---

*Chairman of the Senate.

†A full university of which there are six—Leiden, Utrecht, Groningen, Amsterdam Municipal and Free and Nijmegen—must have at least three faculties, of which one must be medicine or mathematics and science.

continental countries, the life of a Dutch student is harder, more protracted and more isolated than that of his English equivalent. Only the Twente College of Technology provides accommodation for students on the campus; all other students have to live at home, in rented rooms or in student hostels. Contact with professors, and even with senior lecturers, is very limited, particularly at the larger universities. Although more use is now being made of seminars, most instruction, especially in the more popular subjects, is still given in the form of lectures. There are no liberal arts courses as in the United States but, like the older universities in England, a 'schools' system with specialisation in one discipline from the start. Higher education is very technologically or career-orientated, with engineering, mathematics and science as the most popular subjects for men, and languages for women.[15] Unlike Anglo-Saxon countries, there is no first degree taken after a period of three or four years' study. There is an intermediate, *kandidaats* examination, which is taken after two to four years, but it gives no status outside the university. The full university course continues for five or six years in most subjects, though in practice it is usually much longer before the student takes his final examination for a *doctoraal* diploma.* The possession of the diploma gives the right to use the title of *doctorandus*, *meester* or *ingenieur*, according to the faculty in which it was taken.

The whole system of higher education was originally designed to produce an intellectual élite and in this it was most effective: Dutchmen have been awarded eight Nobel prizes.† But it was far less suitable for the modern age of mass study. Though the length of the course could be extended, as the student has the right to choose when he would take his examination, there is a limit to persistence. The high standards demanded led to a serious drop-out problem and some embittering failures at the end. This is still the case, particularly among girls. About

---

*The Dutch doctorate is awarded as a result of research undertaken after gaining a *doctoraal* diploma. This can take another two or three years, at least. The *doctoraal* diploma is approximately equivalent to a British M.A.

†Four for physics, two for medicine, one for chemistry and one for peace.

one-quarter of all girls fail to continue their studies after passing their intermediate examination. This is particularly serious as the total number of female students is still too small, though the number has grown considerably since the war. There is now about one female student to every four male students.

There has also been a large increase in the number of working-class youths at universities. There are varying estimates from 8 to 11 per cent, though different methods of assessing social class make exact comparisons with other countries difficult. Almost one-third of students were receiving grants in 1966–7, a much smaller proportion than in England. The grants are based on parents' income, with a maximum grant of 4,200 guilders a year. Gifted students receive a grant outright. But average students, unless they are going into teaching, receive a 60 per cent grant and the remainder in the form of an interest-free loan. Two years after the student finishes his course, he has to repay the loan over a maximum period of four years.

Before the war, the student population was 'an isolated, more or less privileged caste, little interested in politics and almost without contact with society'.[16] Clubs for upper-class students and denominational associations still exist, but they are much less important features of university life than they were. In spite of the influx of new kinds of students from different social backgrounds, the students still remain in general more disciplined, more serious and more career-minded than many of their European counterparts. (Revolt, of a quieter and more disciplined kind tends to start later in the Netherlands, and it more often originates within an organisation than outside it.) Nevertheless, there has been among Dutch students the same requests for more participation in the running of universities, but these have taken a more muted form than elsewhere, though extremism now seems to be increasing. (In May, 1970, one of the institutes of Amsterdam Municipal University was taken over by students and renamed the Karl Marx Institute.) Almost a year after the massive student protests in France, there were a series of sit-ins and occupations in Dutch universities.

In April 1969, about fifty students occupied the senate board-room at Tilburg, but left again about a week later when they were promised that talks on student representation would start. A few days after that, about five hundred students at the Municipal University of Amsterdam occupied the main administrative centre, the Maagdenhuis (which was a girls' orphanage in the eighteenth century). They were ejected by the police and three leaders were sentenced to terms of imprisonment ranging from two to six weeks.[17] Practically the whole of the press and the majority of the political parties condemned the students' actions. Many of their fellow students were also opposed and at some universities, such as Leiden, there has been a certain backlash movement among students in protest against revolt. There were also minor incidents elsewhere. As a body, Dutch students tend to remain somewhat conservative and jealous of their privileges. When it was proposed in parliament that it should be possible to advise students whose work was unsatisfactory to leave the university, there was such a storm of student protest that the idea was dropped.[18]

Under a new draft bill for the reform of university administration, students will have a larger share in the running of universities. It is proposed that new university councils should be set up with up to one-quarter of the members drawn from students. Although the minister would retain some final controls, the councils would have large powers in preparing the budget, drafting development plans and making internal rules and regulations.[19] This does not, however, go far enough to satisfy the more radical students.

# 13

# Social Welfare

THE DUTCH have a long tradition of civic care for the needy. As one eighteenth-century visitor noted: 'One thing the Dutch are much to be commended for, that is, their care of the poor ... After the gates of their towns are shut in the evening, whoever they are opened to, pay something, which is applied to the poor.'[1] But a start was not made on providing a modern-style social security system until the beginning of this century, with the passing of social insurance and industrial accidents insurance acts in 1901. As in other western European countries, there has been an enormous development in both the range and the cost of social welfare schemes since the end of the last war, though there are still great variations in the extent, financing and benefits of social security even amongst members of the European Economic Community (EEC).

The proportionate expenditure on social security is considerably higher in the Netherlands than it is in Britain (though exact comparisons are difficult to make) and the highest of any in the EEC countries: in 1966, it was 16·3 per cent of the gross national product.[2] In all the EEC countries, social security is based far more on the insurance principle, in that contributions from employers and employees are high, while the state's contribution from general taxation is low. (In the last few years, Britain has moved somewhat closer to the continental system both in obtaining a greater amount of money from employers and employees and also in increasing some benefits and linking them to wages.) In the Netherlands, the contribution by the state is the lowest in the EEC and the contribution from employees is the highest: almost half of the total finance comes from employees.[3] (See Appendixes 14 and 15.)

Social security in the Netherlands has some distinctive features.[4] (See Appendix 15.) Unlike the other EEC countries (and also now Britain), the Netherlands has no contributory scheme for graduated old-age pensions, but only a compulsory, flat-rate scheme which provides a basic pension at the age of sixty-five, amounting to 5,725 guilders a year for married couples and 4,032 guilders a year for single persons.* There are, however, a wide range of supplementary contributory pension schemes (of which some are compulsory), that have been set up so far in eighty-four different branches of industry. Including civil servants, members of the forces and other government employees, about two-thirds of the working population are covered by some form of supplementary scheme. (The General Assistance Act entitles all citizens in need of financial assistance to benefits, if necessary, in addition to the basic pension.)

All employees get family allowances from the first child onwards, which are paid to the husband, not the wife. They may

---

*The Dutch, however, allow members of extreme Protestant sects, who object to all forms of insurance on conscientious grounds, to pay an equivalent amount in extra income tax instead. If they wished to do so, they could still claim a pension which is available to all. This typical example of Dutch pragmatism satisfies both the conscientious objector and the state.

be continued until the age of twenty-seven if the 'child' is still in full-time education. There are also small 'prosperity-pegged' pensions of between 1,284 guilders and 2,484 guilders a year for orphans, which normally cease at the age of sixteen, but may again be continued to the age of twenty-seven in the same circumstances. There are widows' pensions, as well. Sickness benefits for employees amount to 80 per cent of their wages (as it is for unemployment) for a period of a year; after that they are eligible for long-term benefits under the Working Incapacity Act of 1967, which provides benefits of up to 80 per cent of wages according to the degree of disability and the amount of nursing required.

The health service has one feature in common with that in Britain, insofar as doctors are paid a capitation fee for each patient; but in most other ways it is quite different. First, it does not cover the whole of the population; non-employed or self-employed people with annual incomes over a periodically-adjusted level (14,850 guilders as from July 1970) are excluded. About 70 per cent of the whole population are covered by the scheme. Secondly, voluntary bodies continue to play a major part in the health services, with the Ministry of Social Affairs and Public Health playing a guiding and inspectoral role. 'The system of conditional State subsidies still forms the silver bridle with which the Ministry guides health care.'[5]

Three-quarters of the country's 265 hospitals are run by private organisations, many of them with a denominational basis.[6] Similarly, much of the district nursing is organised by the cross organisations—the Green Cross (neutral), the White-Yellow Cross (Catholic) and the Orange-Green Cross (Protestant). (The Red Cross has only a limited public health function in the Netherlands in peace time.) These cross organisations came into existence at the end of the nineteenth century and the beginning of the present century to provide better public health facilities, such as pure drinking water and to nurse people in their own homes. The two denominational organisations were established in the belief that it was better for the sick to be nursed by someone of their own faith. Their total membership is still large.\* But the denominational aspect is now less important than it was; the associations tend to specialise, to a certain extent, in particular health problems or illnesses, and there is close co-operation between them in other aspects of their work. Between them, they employ over 3,000 trained nurses. In the larger towns there are separate municipal health services, but even there the cross organisations continue to play some part. In the new towns of the polders there are medical centres with doctors, psychiatrists and nurses providing a comprehensive medical service.

Some well-qualified critics complain about this complicated structure—'the famous crazy quilt of Dutch preventive medical organisation—which directly opposes any attempt to inquire into its efficiency, which defies co-ordination and evaluation, and therefore renders future planning very difficult indeed.'[7] Nevertheless, the public health service appears to work well; the country has one of the lowest death rates and highest birth rates in the world. (See Appendix 16.) Though such figures give only a crude indication of the efficiency of the health service, they do provide some indication of its merits, particularly as the Netherlands is one of the most densely populated countries in the world.

In fact, in many of the welfare spheres in which the Netherlands has made some notable achievements—mental health, the physically handicapped, problem families, and the elderly and immigration—voluntary agencies continue to play a role. This is particularly so in one of the sectors in which the Dutch excel; the treatment and care of mental health patients. Of the thirty-nine mental hospitals, thirty-one are 'private' or denominational. Increasingly the emphasis has shifted in recent years from institutional treatment to outside care. Some of the hospitals have schemes for boarding out patients in nearby homes.[8] There are also three 'half-way houses', with a total of 100 beds, in which patients may stay while they re-adapt to normal life. One of the major features, which has attracted considerable

---

\*In 1966, the Green Cross had about 1·5 million members, the White-Yellow Cross over 750,000 and the Orange-Green Cross, 300,000 members.

attention abroad, is the system of sheltered workshops, which cater for both the physically handicapped and the mentally sick. In 1968, approximately 40,000 manual and white-collar workers were employed in the 180 workshops scattered throughout the country. The emphasis is on leading a normal life as far as possible. A worker can receive up to 95 per cent of the wages he would earn in open industry outside.[9] Because of his disabilities, he is not expected to produce so much as outside workers and his wages are heavily subsidised by the state. Sheltered workshops produce a variety of goods ranging from furniture to handbags, while parts of television sets, typewriters and other products are manufactured under contract for private industry.

Just as the workshops provide an opportunity for handicapped people to work together, so does the village of Het Dorp near Arnhem provide a chance for the physically handicapped to live together in an experimental community with automatically opening doors and a centrally heated, covered main street. The village accommodates approximately 400 single people living in their own separate home, each with its own bathroom and bed-sitting room. Attached to each block of ten dwellings there is a resident trained attendant. Here again the emphasis is on leading a normal life as far as possible. Residents work in a central workshop or in the town of Arnhem and each block of ten dwellings has two guest-rooms, so that the community does not become isolated.[10]

Another very interesting social welfare project, in this case for problem families, has been set up by nine municipalities at Hardenberg, Overijssel. Called the Family Re-adaptation Centre, it consists of a number of three or four bedroomed homes, a nursery school, a kindergarten and a youth club. Families who have been recommended for admission are invited to look around the centre first, before their application is considered. The families live a normal life, but there is intensive care from a social worker and periodic consultations with psychiatrists. The family stay in the centre for at least two years, and the municipality from which they came has to guarantee that it will provide an adequate house when the family return. The centre receives an 80 per cent subsidy from the Ministry of Cultural Affairs, Recreation and Social Welfare.[11]

A branch of this ministry is also responsible for the general supervision of the care of the elderly. (Nearly 10 per cent of the population is over sixty-five.) Again, there is great stress on leading a normal life as much as possible. As Dr Goedmakers, head of the ministry's department of old people's welfare and specialised work, put it:

> It has always been felt that the problems of the elderly should, in principle, be approached in the same way as those of other adults—that is to say, as those of responsible citizens who should themselves decide how they wish to order their lives.[12]

There is a meals-on-wheels service; domestic help is provided; and there are service centres on old people's estates or in districts where there are large concentrations of pensioners. Most people do not continue working after the age of sixty-five, but for those who do, the basic pension is not reduced, though their total earnings are liable to income tax. A number of special workshops for the elderly have been established. One was opened by Philips in 1959 at Eindhoven, where they could work three hours a day in the morning or the afternoon. The scheme has been a great success. By 1965, there were nearly 300 people working there. The scheme is not subsidised and in that year their wages, which were paid out of the profits made, were 1·80 guilders for every hour worked.

In the care of the elderly there is also great emphasis on voluntary agencies. Of the 1,200 old people's homes, only 10 per cent are run by local authorities, and the rest by denominational or philanthropic agencies.[13] In many cases, old people's flats and houses are built near a home so that they can share in the use of its services. Since the war, 455 old people's homes and 30,000 ground floor flats and houses, especially designed for old people, have been built, while another 155 homes have been enlarged and modernised.[14]

One of the greatest post-war achievements of the Dutch has been their successful immigration policy. In the last twenty-five years, there has been an enormous migratory movement—the greatest in the country's history. Approximately 400,000 people have left the Netherlands, while approximately 300,000 immigrants have come to live there. Since 1961, the number of immigrants has usually exceeded the number of emigrants. (See Appendix 17.) Most of the immigrants in the post-war period have come from Indonesia. There were five phases, with the peak periods occurring soon after the capitulation of Japan and the transfer of sovereignty to Indonesia in 1949.[15] There were three main categories: Dutch settlers, officials and employees; Eurasians; and Indonesians.

The Dutch have handled this vast influx of immigrants (which amounts to about 2·5 per cent of the population) with outstanding success. Most of the native-born Dutchmen and the highly educated Eurasians and Indonesians presented few problems, but these were not the majority. Over the years the Dutch created a complex, but very humane, procedure for dealing with immigrants. On arrival at Schipol airport, the immigrants are taken to a reception centre, where they are medically examined and issued with a year's supply of clothes, free of charge, if they cannot afford to pay for them. Those who cannot arrange temporary accommodation for themselves are offered the chance to stay in contract boarding houses at a cost of 4·90 guilders per person a day, a fee which is again waived if they have no money. Five per cent of all homes built under the Housing Act are reserved for immigrants, which reveals a particular generosity and tolerance in view of the great housing shortage. In addition, the immigrants can obtain credit from the local authority to furnish their home if they have no capital. They are helped to find work by the employment exchange and there is a large network of voluntary agencies which also provide care for them.[16]

Because of this sensible policy of planning and control, and particularly the dispersal of immigrants to different parts of the country, the creation of ghettos has been avoided and most

Indonesian and Eurasian immigrants have been firmly integrated into the local community. Discrimination against them is almost unknown. Intermarriage with Dutch girls is fairly common. Educated Indonesians and Eurasians are to be found in the highest positions and even the less educated are not restricted to more menial jobs. Unlike Britain, where immigrants seem to have more than their fair share of menial work, you will see only the occasional Indonesian or Eurasian bus driver. And you will find very few traffic wardens, Dutch, Indonesian or Eurasian; the Netherlands is far too busy producing more essential and profitable services and goods to deploy much of its labour force on that! Overall, coloured immigrants have very little about which to complain. As one, who is now a highly placed civil servant told me: 'The Dutch as a whole behaved worse in the Indies than the British did in India, but they treated us far more fairly when we came to the Netherlands.'

It is no detraction from this remarkable achievement to say that the Dutch were helped by a number of factors. The immigrants were from a wide range of social classes, including some who had been educated in the Netherlands and had held high positions in the East Indies; most of the immigrants, in the early days, spoke Dutch; and the Eurasians, in particular, were intensely patriotic and wished to be integrated. But even with those groups who did not, the Dutch policy has been fairly successful.

Indonesians who were incapable of being integrated because of their age, have been housed in special old people's homes, where native food is served, native costumes worn and native customs maintained.

A group which did not want to be integrated was the Ambonese, from the South Moluccas, who provided the bulk of native troops in the colonial army in the East Indies. They fought with the Dutch against the Indonesian 'rebels' in 1947 and 1948. Two years later, after Indonesia had acquired its sovereignty, there was an abortive revolt in Amboina when the South Moluccas was proclaimed a free republic. Following the failure of the revolt, over 12,000 Ambonese left for the Netherlands; and there are now about 27,000 in all. At first, the Ambonese were housed in camps, but the majority now live in non-integrated housing estates of their own, scattered over fifty municipalities. Most of the Ambonese do not want to return to Indonesia, though in 1968, a few hundred did so; and most of them are resentful that the Dutch, whom they served so faithfully for many centuries, did not give them aid in their struggle for independence. It was this feeling that resulted in the short-lived take-over of the Indonesian Embassy in The Hague by Ambonese in August 1970. The Ambonese belong to neither world.

Although the Dutch have been generally successful in coping with these special problems, it is impossible to say if they would have been so successful in dealing with a large influx of black immigrants or of foreign workers. Both categories exist, but in small numbers. As the inhabitants of Surinam are Dutch citizens by law, and, therefore, free to enter or to leave the Netherlands as they wish, there is no exact knowledge of their numbers, but it was estimated that there were just over 13,000 in the Netherlands in 1966.[17] With these black immigrants 'there is very decided discrimination on the labour market and in the housing sector'.[18] There is also at least one restaurant in Amsterdam, so I have been told, which will not admit black people. But the problem, partly because of the small numbers involved, is not acute, though the growing number of foreign workers might conceivably cause more social stress in the future. Foreign workers are not integrated in the way that the Indonesians are. In Utrecht, for example, as in many other continental cities, they have made the railway station their club—waiting for friends to come and dreaming of the day they can go. Some students, in particular, are very critical of the way in which foreign workers are treated. The government does what it can by trying to prepare the local population to welcome them by means of propaganda and also by trying to prepare the migrant workers for the different attitudes and living conditions they will find. Wherever possible, this preparation is done by an organisation with the same religious, and preferably, the same political affiliations as the worker.[19]

Dutch governments have adopted an equally positive attitude towards emigration. From the 1950s, the government has sponsored emigration by providing, in accordance with the means of the emigrant, a contribution towards the fare, the expense of of the journey and living expenses for the first few days after arrival. Most of the emigrants have gone to the United States and emigration was at a peak in 1952. The main causes were the difficulties in rebuilding the country and the rigid controls that this entailed, the structural unemployment in agriculture and over-population. Not all of them left to seek a new life, but more to preserve, as much as possible, the old. As B. P. Hofstede wisely remarks. 'The Dutch who emigrated were really the ones who stayed at home, and those who remained behind were the emigrants.'[20] Similarly, many of the immigrants, with their Dutch flags and their pictures of the queen, had come to take up a life that many of them had only ever lived in their dreams before. They wanted to become more Dutch than the Dutch themselves. The post-war migration, as in many other countries, has involved a great levelling-out of loyalties.

# 14

## The Economy

MANY TOURISTS who visit the Netherlands, quite naturally, go in search of tulips, windmills, clogs, old fishing villages and seventeenth-century burghers' houses which, with many other attractions of a different sort, may still be found there. Very often therefore, they observe only incidentally that the Netherlands has become one of the highly industrialised nations of western Europe. They would be even more astonished if they discovered the true extent of the extraordinary transformation of the economy in the post-war years. Among many other products, the Netherlands makes its own airliners and will soon produce its first jet. It also makes its own cars. It has produced three of the world's major international companies, Royal Dutch Shell, Unilever and Philips; and has the world's largest port, Rotterdam. And it has only 8 per cent of its labour force working on the land, the lowest proportion in the EEC, apart from Belgium.

Yet, in some ways, it is not surprising that there should be such a gap between reality and myth, because the Netherlands only recently became industrialised. Even in 1939, the country was still primarily engaged in agriculture, international trade and shipping, on which many of the industries that did exist, such as food processing and shipbuilding, were dependent. The major part of the transformation has been effected since 1945, and this, in its turn, has changed the face of the country and the structure of society. In the last twenty-five years, no other country in western Europe has made such great changes in its economic and social structures with so little internal friction and with such beneficial results. This industrialisation has been the prime cause of all the major post-war changes in so many other fields.

How has this transformation been achieved? It has been brought about by a combination of many factors of which the psychological ones are by no means the least. After the war, probably no other country in western Europe, with the exception of Germany, felt itself to be, and indeed, was, in such a bad plight. The Dutch had not experienced a war for over a century and had lost proportionately more than many other countries in western Europe. A large part of Rotterdam and part of The Hague had been destroyed; the islands in the southwest had been flooded; thousands of resistance workers had been shot; and many people, who were reduced to eating tulip bulbs, had died of starvation.[1] The official estimate of total war damage was 25,000 million guilders.[2] But the loss of Indonesia in 1949 was even more devastating. Before the war, it provided about one-seventh of the national income. Its loss added despair to desperation and many Dutchmen emigrated. Those who remained had no choice but to build a completely new country. Their losses gave them strength.

Even immediately after the end of the war, there was a general consensus among responsible people that drastic measures had to be taken if the country were going to re-establish itself. Like other western European countries, the Netherlands received great economic benefits in the immediate post-war years from Marshall Aid and the absence of German competition. It is doubtful, however, if these would have been enough in themselves to achieve the economic transformation, which in many ways is more remarkable than the German 'miracle', if the government had not taken firm action. This was made possible by the traditional expectation in the Netherlands that the government (whether it does so or not) should govern honestly, wisely and, if circumstances demand it, even harshly. This the government did. In collaboration with the unions and the employers, the government imposed a severe wage-freeze, which enabled the country's exports to be more competitive. Until 1959, wages were, at first, raised only to maintain their 1945 purchasing power and later in accordance with general rises in productivity. Since then, there has been a gradual, but not total, freeing of wages. Since the early 1960s, the government has also taken other fiscal and monetary measures to keep the economy in good shape. Attempts have been made to finance government spending from taxation revenue and funds available on the capital market, and to keep the quantity of money in circulation at a norm of 30 per cent of the national income.[3] The severe restrictions on wages and public spending and a restrictive monetary policy provided a context in which it was believed that private enterprise could operate most profitably and efficiently.

Some early hopes that the government could, as it were, hold the ring for private enterprise have not been entirely fulfilled. Even before the last war, it was forced to become the only shareholder in the railways and most of the mines; it also has a controlling financial interest in the national airline, KLM, and a 40 per cent stake in the exploitation of natural gas. The government has tried to avoid direct involvement in industry as much as possible. Although it owns over half of the capital of KLM, it is still run as a private enterprise. Occasionally when the government has become directly involved, as in the case of a rolling mill and tinplate factory at Ijmuiden, it has later sold the enterprise to private industry. The state has conceived its role as one of stimulating companies in preference to owning them.

But increasingly in recent years, it has been forced to take a more active part by way of guarantees, subsidies and investment allowances, both to help in the development of 'grey' areas with high unemployment rates and also to attract foreign investment which is offered such advantages by other countries, particularly neighbouring Belgium. In addition, the state or public authorities run the main public utilities, such as electricity and gas distribution, the post, telegraph and telephones, and maintains and improves the sea channels to ports.[4]

In the decade from 1955 to 1965, there was a rapid sustained industrial expansion, with only brief fluctuations caused mainly by overspending and monetary tightness. Industrial production rose on average by more than 6 per cent a year and the gross national product by 4·5 per cent. (See Appendix 18.) The growth rate between 1965 and 1968 was 4·9 per cent a year and industrial production was running at the highest level in the EEC.[5] On the other hand, in spite of controls, the Netherlands has been less successful in holding down prices, which rose by the highest amount (4·5 per cent) in the EEC between 1965 and 1968.[6] Indeed, one long-term survey shows that the Netherlands had the fourth highest rise in consumer prices among industrial countries between 1958 and mid-1969 after Denmark, Japan and France.[7] Inflationary pressures are still a grave problem—with prices for private consumption up by 7 per cent and for houses, 11 per cent in 1969—though this is also a problem in many other industrial countries. Among the main causes of these increases were rises in import prices, the change to the added value tax, wage increases of between 10 and 11 per cent in the year and the high rate of interest.[8]

Since April 1969, there has been a system of price controls which replaced the general price policy which existed previously. There is an obligation to lower prices when external circumstances are favourable and the possibility of raising them when they are not. Some people—restaurant owners and driving schools among others—have been prosecuted and fined, and the number of inspectors has been increased. But as in other countries, it has been found very difficult to control prices, as manufacturers can evade controls by introducing new products or altering the size or composition of an existing one. Price rises could push up wages to a level at which exports become uncompetitive, but so far the Netherlands has been remarkably successful in increasing the level of exports. (See Appendices 19 and 20.) Before the war, about one-third of earnings came from invisible exports, but these have now diminished to about half that proportion, mainly owing to the loss of Indonesia. Germany is now the biggest trading partner, as it was for imports before the war. (See Appendix 21.) If the competitiveness of exports can be maintained and inflation can be checked, the country's immediate prosperity seems assured. But the government in the queen's speech of September 1970, announced that the balance of payments for 1970 is expected to be more unfavourable than anticipated, with a deficit of 700 million guilders. The government announced a number of measures to curb inflation, including a cut of 140 million guilders in government spending and an increase in income tax. But these are current problems throughout the western world. The long-term picture is brighter. Indeed, as one recent survey has said:

> With the biggest port in the world, a high rate of industrial expansion, a relatively modern agricultural sector, large reserves of natural gas and a modern motorway and communications network second to none, Holland's future economic prosperity appears assured.[9]

Some of this buoyancy seems to be reflected in the Ministry of Economic Affairs, which with its gay, striped awnings over the windows, its pleasant, smiling 'commissionaires' and handsome stairways looks more like a prosperous bourgeois hotel than a ministry.

## Industry

There is a great diversity and number of small firms in the Netherlands, particularly in the old central heart of Amsterdam where they still manage to thrive in tiny workshops in the old burghers' houses along the narrow cobbled streets by the concentric ring of canals. (See Appendix 22.) But the real underlying strength of the economy rests in half a dozen large companies: the big three, Philips, Unilever and Royal Dutch Shell; the synthetic fibres combines AKU (Algemene Kunstzijde Unie); and the mining, chemical and pharmaceutical combines of Staatsmijnen/DSM and AKZO. Between them they employ over 20,000 people in research and development. About 12 per cent of Dutchmen of working age are employed by the big three, who also provided about one-third of all exports and all investments in the country in 1966.[10] In 1956, the total sales of Royal Dutch Shell were bigger than the national income of the Netherlands.[11] The activities and the headquarters of these three big companies are dispersed throughout the world, but one of them, Philips, still dominates the town of Eindhoven in the south, which was largely its own creation.

To any visitor, it is obvious from the moment he arrives at the railway station with its television-style train indicator screens—made by Philips, of course—that Eindhoven is Philips and Philips is Eindhoven. The enormous figure of Jesus which towers above the spire of the main church in this predominantly Catholic town is illuminated at night—by Philips lamps, again. One of the two theatres and the main hotel are owned by the company, and many other hotels are full of Philips' employees from all parts of the world. In restaurants there is endless talk of sales and in bars lengthy anecdotes about computers, which always seem to have the same pay-off line: 'I am God.' Philips now employ approximately 40,000 people in the town out of a total population of 183,000. Thirty years ago, before other industry was attracted to the town also, the company presence was even more dominant, so one old Philips employee told me.

Since 1891, when Gerard and Anton Philips set up in business with a staff of ten to make electric lamps, the company has grown into a vast international concern with over a quarter of a million employees in sixty different countries. It produces a large range of electrical and electronic goods and has just entered the computer field. Just under half of the shares still remain in Dutch hands.* Partly because of this, perhaps, it still retains its national character more than the other members of the big three, though a deliberate attempt is made in all the countries where it operates to create a 'home-grown image'.[12] In Eindhoven, there is still great stress on paternalism, a characteristic feature of Dutch (and Japanese) industry. Philips was well in advance of the state in providing social welfare benefits, ranging from sewing and cookery classes to free medical treatment and pensions. There is also great emphasis on company loyalty. At the managerial level particularly, it is not unusual to find men who have served their whole working lives with the company. Co-operation is one of the keynotes of the company's success, not only between management and unions, but also among the workers themselves. Two or three years ago, an attempt was made to break down the rigid assembly line process by creating small teams of three or four workers, responsible for making one component, such as a tuner in a television set, right from the beginning to the final testing.

The other two large firms were both formed by mergers with British companies. Royal Dutch Shell was formed in 1907, by a merger of the Royal Dutch Petroleum Company and the 'Shell' Transport and Trading Company. These parent companies now have a substantial holding in the proportion of 60–40 respectively in the wide range of Royal Dutch Shell companies. Unilever was formed in 1929, by a merger of the British firm of Lever Brothers and the Margarine Unie, which itself had been established two years previously by a combination of the Dutch firms of Jurgens and van den Bergh. Thus, long before multinational companies became at all common, the Netherlands was participating in three of the biggest in the world. It was the smallest country in the world with such large companies.

These firms influence the Dutch economy in many obvious, and less immediately apparent, ways. As we have seen, they

*At the end of 1967, the company's shares were distributed among the Netherlands, 43 per cent; United States, 17 per cent; Switzerland, 20 per cent; France 11 per cent; Britain 3 per cent; Germany 3 per cent; and Belgium and Austria together, 3 per cent.

are responsible for much of the research and development, exports and investment. It is sometimes thought that they exercise a great political influence, too. Obviously, no Dutch government could afford to ignore the existence of these giant companies on its soil. 'The Dutch government, to the oil industry, acts as a very friendly neutral.'[13] Conversely, the government can sometimes play a bigger international role than it would do otherwise, as in the oil supply crisis after the Six-Day War in 1967.[14] But the companies' much wider, international interests and responsibilities make it impossible for them to give precedence to Dutch interests. It is just possible, that all other things being equal, this could happen, but it is unlikely. Their relationship is largely one of mutual reciprocity; neither side, and particularly the government, can entirely neglect the fact of the other's existence.

The companies, particularly Royal Dutch Shell, also play an important part in lessening the brain drain by providing a cadre of retired men who can later inject the benefits of their international business experience into the Dutch economy. It is the ambition of many young Dutchmen to work for one of these firms, where they often acquire a social polish and an international outlook that their formal education sometimes fails to provide. Because of the opportunities for travel and career advancement offered by these companies, there is less emigration of highly skilled men than there might be otherwise; these companies offer more than adequate opportunities for the commercially ambitious to fulfil themselves. Employees of Royal Dutch Shell who work abroad are pensioned at the age of fifty-five, when they are sometimes offered important posts at home, which makes a career with the oil company doubly attractive.

The biggest industries are still the food, drink and tobacco processing industries (based upon the country's traditional role as an agricultural country and an importer of overseas products) and the engineering industry, which in 1969 had a turnover of over 20,000 million guilders each; these industries are also the biggest exporters. (See Appendixes 23 and 24.) But industry is no longer restricted to these traditional spheres. One of the major growth points is in chemicals, particularly in the area of Rotterdam-Europoort, where many oil refineries are sited. Although a steel industry was not started until 1917, Hoogovens (Koninklijke Nederlandse Hoogovens en Staalfabrieken), if its proposed merger with the German firm of Hoesch goes through, will have the second largest output in the EEC.[15] For such a comparatively small country, it is somewhat surprising to find both a thriving native aircraft and car industry. Five hundred of the Fokker F-27 Friendship airliners have been sold all over the world and an F-28 Fellowship jet passenger aircraft is now in production. A similar success has attended the small workmanlike DAF car, with its automatic gears; in 1967, a large new factory was opened in Limburg in the south. There are are also many other firms, such as C & A, which have made some international mark.[16]

As in many other industrialised countries, some industries, such as textiles and shipbuilding, have been having a difficult time recently and there have been many mergers. The process of rationalisation has resulted in other mergers in many spheres, including metal, insurance, banking and brewing.[17] In the two years from July 1965 to July 1967 there were, according to Mr P. J. J. Mertens, the Catholic union leader, 131 mergers in industry.[18] In common with the rest of western Europe, there has been an appreciable growth of foreign investment. (See Appendix 25.) But mainly because of its international companies, the Netherlands still has quite large investments overseas; it is one of the few nations to have a bigger investment in the United States than the latter has in it. In 1967, the United States' direct investment in the Netherlands amounted to $917 million while the Netherlands investment in the United States was about $1,400 million.[19]

## Communications

Industry is well served by one of the finest communication networks in Europe, in which, as one might expect, sea and inland waterway transport plays a major part. Its favourable geographical situation has enabled the Netherlands to continue in its traditional role of carriers, not so much now perhaps for the world, as for the EEC. Twenty-seven per cent of all goods brought into the EEC in 1965 were handled by Dutch ports, the vast majority by Rotterdam-Europoort, the largest port in the world.[20] It now handles over 140 million tons of goods every year. Deep-dredged channels in the North Sea allow it to be used by ships of up to 250,000 tons and there are plans to accommodate ships of twice that size. With its twenty-mile long complex of wharfs, warehouses, refineries and factories, it has become the biggest industrial site in the Netherlands.

The other major port, Amsterdam, has also been improved recently. In June 1967, a new enlarged harbour entrance was opened at Ijmuiden and the canal connecting it with the North Sea was widened so that it could be reached by ships of up to 80,000 tons. An oil refinery is also being built in the Amsterdam area. But as an industrial port complex, Rotterdam is a long way ahead of the capital and it is likely to remain so. By the end of the 1950s, Rotterdam was operating roll-on/roll-off service and at about the same time started to handle containerised freight. There are now five container berths and plans are in hand to build a completely new container centre, downstream, capable of handling container vessels of up to 100,000 tons, hovercraft, hydrofoils and ferries.

The increase in the use of containers for general transport and pipelines for oil have posed something of a long-term threat to the canal network, the most extensive in the EEC. But inland waterways still have certain advantages, particularly for such a country as the Netherlands, and the recent development of push boats which can handle a string of barges, has made them more competitive. The railways, which up until the present have handled mainly passenger traffic, have benefited slightly from the growth in container traffic, but have continued to show a loss since 1964.

The large number of canals and rivers and the nature of the subsoil presents certain road building problems in the Netherlands, but it has a reasonably impressive network, with about four hundred miles of motorway. As most of the country is flat, these could be built straight, but they are deliberately 'kinked' in places to keep drivers awake. So far, little has been done about building throughways in many main towns, partly because of a desire to preserve historic city centres and partly because so many people used public transport or bicycles in towns. With rising prosperity, however, car ownership has increased considerably in the last few years, and this has led to disputes in many towns over whether some canals should be filled in and used as roads. In Amersfoort—an extremely attractive town which is not so well known to tourists as it might be— a compromise has been effected by making half of the outer dike into a road, but leaving the inner one intact. (This is the kind of dispute about which the Dutch can become passionate. A politician once told me that much time at one of his meetings had been taken up with the question whether he preferred tunnels or bridges. He found this rather trivial; but such issues may be more fundamental than they appear to be.)

The major airport, Schiphol, which is built, like many other places, below sea-level on the bed of what was at one time a lake, is situated about seven miles from Amsterdam. It is one of the most modern airports in the world, having been rebuilt in 1967. It has berths for twenty-five aircraft, most of them grouped around a three-pointed star so that planes can be entered direct from the terminal building through covered passages. It now handles over 3 million passengers a year, but has been planned so that it can be considerably expanded. It is also the main headquarters of the national airline, KLM (Koninklijke Luchtvaart Maatschappij), which was founded in October 1919 and is probably the oldest airline in the world still operating under its original name. A new administrative headquarters for the company is being built two or three miles away from the airport. KLM operates a world-wide service and is equipped mainly with Douglas jets and has six Boeing 747s on order for 1971.

## Natural Gas

Much of the industrial development has been concentrated in the west, leaving problems of structural unemployment in the mainly agricultural area of the north, the textile region of Twente in the north-east and the coal-mining district of Limburg in the south. Then in 1962, the country had an enormous stroke of good luck, when large deposits of natural gas were found at Slochteren in the northern province of Groningen. It transpired to be one of the biggest fields in the world with known reserves of 1,650,000 million cubic metres. The state has a 40 per cent direct share in the exploitation of the gas, which was discovered by a subsidiary of Royal Dutch Shell and Esso.

There have been some accusations that the government favoured established oil interests by not pressing for the gas to be sold at the cheapest possible price so that it would provide real competition with fuel oil. There may be something in this argument, but as one acknowledged authority on this subject has said: 'The Dutch government is treating this gas bonanza as a rich windfall, but one that in the history of the country may be counted as short-lived.'[21] If first reports are correct, the north has just had a second stroke of equal good fortune with the discovery in 1969 of valuable deposits of potassium and magnesium chloride, within twenty-five miles of the gasfield.[22]

The discovery of gas has opened up completely new posibilities for planning, development and industrialisation in the north, upon which the government and private industry have been quick to seize. Already a chemical works and an aluminium smelting plant have been opened in the area, and the government plans to expand the existing port of Delfzijl, build an entirely new port area on the river Ems near the German border and transform the triangle between these two ports and Groningen into a considerable industrial area, probably by the late seventies. The sales of gas abroad are already showing in the balance of payments and by 1975, it is planned to sell half the output abroad and to use the other half at home, which will supply about one-quarter of the country's total energy needs.

The state mines which has a share in its exploitation, has been able to use some of its profit to help the declining coal-mining regions in Limburg in the south.* In co-operation with Royal Dutch Shell the state mines are building an oil refinery there and DAF have opened a plant, as well.

## Housing

Although the west of the country has so far received the major share of benefits from rapid industrialisation, it has not been without its problems of a different kind—particularly those relating to over-population, pollution and housing. In December 1967, there was still an official shortage of approximately 55,000 homes, mainly in the most densely populated part of the country.[23]

Since the end of the war, over 1·5 million new homes have been built. (See Appendix 26.) In 1967, the number completed was the highest per 1,000 inhabitants of any EEC country and about 25 per cent higher proportionately than in Britain.[24] But the Dutch policy of strict rent controls, subsidies and stringent rationing of permits for private building, which has been practised since the end of the war, has failed to provide enough new homes and has left the problem of the 320,000 sub-standard houses—almost one in ten of all houses—largely untouched.[25]

In parts of many old towns, such as Utrecht and Amsterdam, there are some poor houses and even in modern towns, such as Rotterdam, there are, by the railway line, depressing rows of sub-standard houses with small backyards and tin baths hanging on the wall. But the small size of the country has fortunately prevented the growth of large slum areas such as those to be found in the vast conurbations of Tokyo, New York and London.

Most Dutch people rent their houses. Only about one-third of the population are owner-occupiers and of these many are

*Within a few years all coal mining will cease and the pits will be closed. Production in 1969 amounted to just over 5·5 million tons, of which nearly 40 per cent was produced by the state mines.

farmers and farm workers. There is very little difference between the proportion of professional and middle-class people and manual workers owning their own homes.[26] It is quite common to find senior civil servants and professional men of all kinds living in rented houses. In the Netherlands, there has been a long tradition of building houses for rent ever since the first non-profit-making house building corporations were formed in the middle of the nineteenth century, Since the end of the war, it has been extremely difficult to get a licence to build a private house, unless it was being built for letting. Furthermore, the cost of new houses is high: a three or four bedroomed house, with a study, might cost something in the region of £17,000 ($40,800) or more, even on the edge of a main population centre.

There is not the English passion for the conversion of old cottages and windmills into middle-class houses.* Some old farmhouses have been bought and let to tenants or converted into restaurants, but most people prefer to buy a new home, if they can get one. This is understandable as, on the whole, traditional country architecture in the Netherlands is not particularly interesting. Most of the fine houses are in the towns, and many of these, particularly in the capital, have been taken over by business or by public corporations or are preserved as museums.

Since the end of the war, therefore, most houses and flats have been built for renting and 84 per cent of them have been subsidised—a far higher proportion than in Britain and a level approached among EEC countries only by France.[27] Rents have been controlled by the Ministry of Housing and Physical Planning. In an effort to establish some parity in rents of pre-war and post-war houses, the rents of the former were increased more than threefold between 1950 and 1966, and since then there has been a general increase in rents of about 4 or 5 per cent a year to help cover the cost of the initial subsidy. The rents of houses

---

*On the other hand, the conversions and appointments of some public buildings are particularly good, such as, for example, the new offices of the cabinet of the vice-president in an old building in The Hague.

still vary considerably according to size and whether they have central heating and other shared services or not, but the cheapest would be about 100 guilders a month.

New houses and flats are of a relatively high standard.[28] Of all houses built in 1968, 70 per cent had central heating.[29] And all houses built since the war have been fitted with a bathroom or a shower, so that now 68 per cent of all houses have one or the other—the highest proportion in the Common Market countries. But serious problems, apart from shortages, still remain, particularly in the older parts of towns, where the narrow houses, with their almost perpendicular staircases, have been divided into small flats. And even with new flats, housewives complain of the lack of cupboard space and inadequate sound-proofing. Since 1965, however, new regulations have been introduced to make adequate sound-proofing of common staircases in blocks of flats and partition walls compulsory.

## Flooding and Land Reclamation

Fear of flooding is one of the things with which the west of the country has had to live throughout history. Much of the Netherlands is situated below sea-level: if there had been no land reclamation and all water-control activities ceased, the main coastline would run from Groningen to Utrecht. Extensive flooding occurred in 1894 and also in 1916, but warnings that even worst floods could occur were ignored. On the night of January 31, 1953, the dykes were breached by a violent north-west gale and an exceptionally high spring-tide. More than half a million acres of Zeeland and South Holland were flooded and 1,835 lives were lost. Only three weeks later the Delta Commission was set up and after discussions lasting several years, work started on one of the most ambitious engineering projects ever undertaken in Europe. It was decided to dam off the sea arms of the delta altogether, apart from the channel leading to the port of Rotterdam and the Western Scheldt, which allows ships to enter the Belgian port of Antwerp.[30] The gaps between the islands are being dammed by sinking concrete caissons and by dumping boulders, imported from Belgium, from trolley cars suspended on overhead cables. The scheme, which will cost an estimated 3,000 million guilders will be completed by 1978. When it is finished, the total length of coastline will have been reduced by several hundred miles; the former inlets of the sea will have turned into freshwater lakes, which will be used to replace part of the supplies from the heavily polluted Rhine; the salinity of the adjoining land will have been greatly reduced, making it more fertile; and these isolated islands will be linked to the mainland by a new motorway running over the tops of the dams and across bridges, bringing these rather backward communities into direct touch with the modern industrial world and also providing a valuable overspill site for Rotterdam's rapidly expanding population.

'Land reclamation is not the purpose of the project; very little, if any, will be gained.'[31] The main purpose is to prevent a repetition of the 1953 disaster. There are, naturally, disadvantages, including the loss of valuable oyster and mussel beds, though it has been planned to move the oysters further north. And there is the cost. Estimates of the expenditure on the scheme compared with the anticipated returns have varied from a negative balance of £46 million to £135 million.[32] But it is extremely difficult to calculate the insurance value and the unanticipated benefits that might result.

In contrast to the delta scheme, the earlier project to dam off the Zuider Zee had land reclamation as one of its main purposes. Work was started on building the 19-mile-long barrier dam, which separates the Zuider Zee from the North Sea, in 1927 and was completed just over five years later. The provinces of North Holland and Friesland are now linked by a road across the top of the dam, with the sea on one side and what was once the Zuider Zee and is now the freshwater lake of Ijsselmeer on the other. Part of the area will remain a lake, but the rest will be pumped dry and converted into agricultural land. The first area of reclaimed land (polder) was ready in 1930, and the last will be finished by 1980. The scheme will enlarge the total area of the country by 7 per cent. The total cost of the latest polder to be reclaimed, Eastern Flevoland, including all building, etc., is officially estimated at approximately 18,000 guilders per hectare (about 2·5 acres).[33]

## *Physical Planning*

The results of long-term schemes are very often different from those originally intended: this has been partly true with the Zuider Zee works. One of the original purposes was to provide extra high-quality agricultural land, which it still does, but this has in many ways become less important than other benefits which were not considered so important at the time. One of its main purposes now is to provide recreational facilities for the increased population of nearby Amsterdam and better road communications for commuters to overspill towns. Amsterdam is in the fortunate position of being the only major city in the world which has the chance to create extra land on its own doorstep. This presents some tremendous opportunities for physical planning, which the Dutch have eagerly seized.[34] They have one of the longest traditions of city planning extending back to the creation of those neat, orderly, space-saving *grachtensteden*, or canal towns, built on land reclaimed from marsh or lake, of which the classic example is Delft.[35] They intend to use this traditional skill and knowledge to create out of the *randstad* what is, in effect, a completely new kind of conurbation.

The horseshoe shaped *randstad* is already one of the most remarkable conurbations in the world with the unique advantage, from the planner's point of view, of its 'polycentric quality'.[36] It is mainly a fortuitous product of political and economic history that the various functions of a modern conurbation should have been broken up between nearby but separate towns, with The Hague as the seat of government, Rotterdam as the main port and heavy industrial centre and Amsterdam as the cultural, financial and light industry centre. The Dutch plan to build on this existing structure in an exceedingly clever way. The overspill population of Rotterdam will be accommodated on some of the nearby islands through the delta scheme. Further north, the polders of the reclaimed Zuider Zee will remain largely agricultural, but lakes with specially 'kinked' edges and sandy beaches to make them appear more natural, will be retained, and woodlands, shrubs and bushes will be planted, to provide recreational facilities for the capital's population. (The only thing the Dutch do not provide are hills.) At the same time, Amsterdam will be linked by a new motorway, via the main polder town of Lelystad, to the new industrial centre of Groningen. The British concept of the green belt, which was suitable for the age before mass motoring developed, has been rejected in favour of linear extension along main roads and wedges of chequer-board fields and countryside in between. If this all seems rather contrived and unnatural (which, of course, it is) it must be remembered that the Dutch with their high density of population are facing now problems which may occur for many other industrial countries soon. According to one British planning expert 'there seems little doubt that for most of the rapidly growing world cities of the present time, the Dutch solution is the right model'.[37]

There are naturally many disadvantages. Originally, it was proposed that the polders as a whole would form a twelfth province, but this plan has now been dropped in favour of making them part of existing neighbouring provinces.[38] In spite of this, it is difficult not to image that a certain local loyalty will arise, and as local rights are jealously protected in the Netherlands, this could cause some dissension between the residents in the polders and those in the big industrial cities on the fringe. Already there have been complaints from the people of Amsterdam because they were not allowed to rent empty houses in polder towns which the latter were keeping in the hope of attracting industry. And with such a large industrial conurbation, the threat of water and air pollution are all increased. The Dutch, however, are very conscious of these problems. Perhaps the biggest long-term danger as a whole is that of over-industrialisation, which is particularly acute as the Dutch plan to reduce the total area of agricultural land even further. By the year 2000, when the population is expected to have increased to 20 million, the amount of land devoted to farming, it is estimated, will have been reduced from three-quarters to about half of the total.[39]

## Agriculture

The necessity to reduce the amount of land used for farming has been caused by increased efficiency and the problem of Common Market surpluses. Agriculture in the Netherlands, with its emphasis on cost-efficiency, intensive capitalisation and the matching of production to consumers' needs, has become highly 'industrialised'. In many ways, the concept of farming and its adaptation to indigenous needs and capabilities is far in advance of that in many other European countries. The basic concept of much of Dutch farming is that of a vast processing industry. Because insufficient land is available to grow much grain economically, vast amounts of grain and animal feeding stuffs are imported from abroad. These are fed to animals and 'processed' into poultry, eggs, meat and dairy products. The high milk-yielding Friesian cow has become one of the most popular milkers in Europe; the milk yield of Dutch cows is the highest in the world.[40] Forty per cent of the milk is processed into dairy products for export, and in all, well over half of all agricultural and horticultural products are processed in some way, which roughly doubles their value.[41] The Dutch have gone a step beyond the Mansholt plan for the EEC of creating larger farm units and judging their viability by the gross product, to the concept of vertical integration, where farms are linked with both processing and distribution firms so that farm output is planned according to marketing possibilities.[42]

Moreover, they have already gone some way towards reorganising their own farms into larger units at a cost, so they claim, considerably lower than that envisaged under EEC plans. About one-tenth of the total agricultural area has already been consolidated, with the agreement of the owners, into larger units with better drainage, water supplies, irrigation and farm buildings—schemes which are heavily subsidised by the government.[43] There is a five-year period of preparation in which all the agricultural, geological, cadastral and socio-economic factors in the region are intensively studied, followed by a further long period of professional attention. There is a government advisory service with a large number of graduates among its officers.[44] The end result of all this agricultural effort can be seen in the neat farms of the polders; the extensive use of glass (about half of the total area in Europe is in the Netherlands); and the modern processing plants in all parts of the country. Many of these plants are run by co-operatives which have played a major part in Dutch farming since the agricultural slump of the 1880s, not only in processing, but also in marketing, purchasing and credit.[45] Over one-quarter of all exports consist of agricultural products: it seems likely that the Netherlands will continue to remain one of the main flower, vegetable and processed foods centres of Europe.

*Labour Force*

Since 1950, the number of people working on the land has been reduced by half; some of them have emigrated, while others have gone to work in the new factories in the growing towns. The decline in the agricultural labour force is one of the reasons —but only one—why the Netherlands, until recently, has not had to induce married women to go on working. In 1968, it still had the lowest proportion of working women of all EEC countries.[46] It is still relatively uncommon to find a married woman with children in full-time employment.

In the last few years, however, as the pace of industrialisation has quickened, there have been some significant changes. In 1966, the Social-Economic Council, the powerful body which advises the government on economic policy, recommended that there should be more nursery accommodation, better tax relief and more part-time work for women.[47] Philips has already set up a special factory for women who want to work part-time.

The growing shortage of labour has also created a need to employ more foreign workers, including a large number of Moroccans and Turks. (See Appendix 27.) The percentage of foreign workers, however, still remains low compared with that in most other industrialised countries of western Europe.

## Wage Control

The Netherlands is one of the few countries which has successfully operated a stringent wage-control policy for most of the post-war period. In 1959, some freedom was restored, when different branches of industry were allowed to give increases related to their own particular rise in production, though the government retained the right to intervene in the last resort. On the whole this policy has been maintained with great uniformity; it was, after all, very much in the interest of employers to support it, particularly as for most of the period there was no acute shortage of labour. Where there was, as in the building industry, employers were willing to run the risk of prosecution (though comparatively few of them ever were prosecuted) by paying wages above the stipulated rate—'black wages' as the Dutch call them. In 1956, when there was still a strict wage control, it was officially estimated that about 3 per cent of all wages were 'black'.[48]

Why were the Dutch so successful in this policy when so many other nations have tried and failed? Partly the reason was that dismissals were also controlled; no employee could be dismissed without the permission of the District Labour Office.[49] There was also a price policy, though this was far more difficult to administer and therefore less effective. But the main underlying reason was the consensus among the 'emigrants who remained', that drastic measures were necessary if they were to succeed in their journey to the newly promised land of industrialisation. In Britain, with its relatively high prosperity by continental standards immediately after the end of the war, most people never really believed governmental exhortations to 'export or die'.

The British did not die, but have endured instead a slow, relative, lingering economic decline. In the Netherlands, on the other hand, there was an intense consciousness of the need to export more and only lingering fears that they might never succeed in doing so. The unions, organised before the war into three main federations, with trained economists on their staffs, were as conscious of this need as anyone. Employers, too, realised much earlier than in Britain, that little progress could be made without the co-operation of the unions.

## The Unions

Like many other institutions the unions are organised on a *verzuiling* basis. The biggest of the three recognised unions is the Socialist Nederlands Verbond van Vakverenigingen (NVV). There is also a smaller Catholic Nederlands Katholiek Vakverbond (NKV) and a Protestant Christelijk Nationaal Vakerbond in Nederland (CNV).* In addition, there are a number of smaller unions, including a very small white-collar union ideologically orientated towards the Liberals. About two per cent of the total union membership is affiliated with Communist-controlled unions.[50]

Co-operation between unions and employers had already started before the war. In 1928, the High Court of Labour was set up, in which they had regular, but informal, consultations. Ten years later, it was decided to make this into a more formal body, but the war intervened. With this background of co-operation, it became possible to set up the Foundation of Labour (Stichting van de Arbeid) immediately after the liberation. Composed of an equal number of representatives from the employers' organisations and the three main unions, it meets regularly for consultations on industrial problems and to advise the government on social and economic questions. To a certain extent it has been superseded by the more powerful

*Membership of the three unions in December 1968 was NVV 556,000; NKV 424,000; and CNV 240,000. These are all federations to which individual unions are affiliated.

Social-Economic Council (Sociaal-Economische Raad), established in 1950. Of its forty-five members, one-third are appointed by the government, one-third by employers' representatives and the remaining one-third by the three large unions in proportion to their memberships.* Because it represents so many established interests and includes government appointees, of whom some are leading economists, its recommendations to the government, particularly when they are unanimous, are usually accepted. It is the pinnacle of consensus politics, but because its meetings are held in secret and its members are appointed by established interests, it is scarcely democratic in the conventional sense. That is why D'66 wants to reform the council by having directly elected members.

*Strikes*

The price that the established unions had to pay for admission to such high-level consultations was to act responsibly and constructively, or, as more militant unionists might say, to keep wages down and to prevent strikes and industrial disputes. The Foundation of Labour and the Social-Economic Council have certainly succeeded in doing that. As P. S. Pels, secretary of the Social-Economic Council wrote in 1966:

> The 'goodwill' of the Labour Foundation, its insight into Dutch wage policy, and the good personal relations between the leaders of the central organisations have, over the years, given the Foundation an authority which has enabled it to prevent potential labour disputes or to settle some that did occur.[51]

Even before the war, however, the Netherlands had a relatively high strike-free record. At Philips, for example, there has not been a strike for sixty years, since the founder of the firm tried to stop his then predominantly Catholic workers from

*The distribution of seats among employers' organisations is industry, four; agriculture, three; shopkeepers, three; trade, two; banking, insurance and transport, one each. On the union side, the NVV has seven seats, the NKV, five seats, and the CNV three seats.

observing religious festivals as a holiday.* In the post-war period, the Netherlands has been able to evade some of the industrial troubles that have afflicted other countries through the general agreement on the need to industrialise; the division of the unions into three main federations; the traditional defer-ence of the older Dutch workman; and the elaborate process of consultation through works councils, with elected members from the factory floor, and between managements and unions direct. There is also a national process of collective bargaining; contracts are legally enforceable. The right to strike—which is still not possessed by government employees, including railway workers—is used only in the last resort. Even then, it is not entirely free from the processes of the law. In a celebrated case in the sixties, a union was brought to court and fined for a strike in the harbours of Rotterdam which the supreme court judged unjustifiable. There is now a draft bill to give unions the legal right to decide on the justifiability of strikes.

The Dutch have one of the lowest strike records in the world. Between 1958 and 1967, the Netherlands lost on average only twenty-one days per thousand workers a year—the lowest in the EEC after Germany.[52] But in the last few years there has been increasing trouble on the labour front, though it has not been as violent or as serious as that in many other countries in western Europe. In June 1966, there were serious riots among building workers in Amsterdam. There were wildcat strikes near Rotter-dam in 1969 against the price rises caused by the introduction of the added value tax; and further strikes in the port of Rotterdam in August 1970. In the early months of 1970, there were a series of wildcat strikes in the 'grey' areas of the north—organised by Communists, say members of the establishment; by professional strikers, say union officials. But the main back-ground causes are continuing unemployment, which has, how-ever, been greatly reduced since the fifties; the effects of mergers; and above all the changing attitudes among the younger generation of workers. Young workers are less willing to be

*This record was broken in September 1970, when some of the Philips employees went on strike for higher pay.

deferential and are more inclined to make comparisons with the benefits that workers are obtaining in other countries. As J. Bosma, president of the Federation of Netherlands Industry, has said: 'The older generation was used to accepting orders. The younger generation on the other hand is less prepared to accept orders without knowing something of their implication.'[53]

There has also been trouble on the wages front. Since 1963, there have been considerable increases in Dutch wages to bring them more into line with those in other EEC countries.* In 1968, employers and unions agreed to base collective bargains on the half-yearly reports of the Social-Economic Council which lays down guidelines for this and other things. But in 1970, wage control was reimposed under Article 8 of a new bill which restored the powers of the government to restrict wage increases in any sector of industry where it might be harmful to the national interest. The Socialist and Catholic unions were not willing to accept this. For some time they have been concerned with fears that they might have been co-operating too much with the establishment. So at the time of writing they have decided to take no further part in helping to compile the half-yearly reports of the Social-Economic Council. (They are still involved in its other work.) At one time, the union leadership, mainly through its involvement in discussions with the establishment, seemed to have lost touch with the rank and file, but some union leaders now, particularly A. H. Kloos, of the Socialist union, who is one of the youngest and the most dynamic, are far more militant than many of their own members. There have been some attempts to bring the three federations closer together. So far there has been little progress, though in 1968, the three federations did demonstrate together for the first time in Utrecht against agovernment proposal for a six-month wage-freeze.[54] The unions are certainly more militant thanthey were.

*From 1963–4 wages rose by 16·8 per cent, and by 10·4 per cent in each of the following two years. Wages rose by about 11 per cent in 1960. The Dutch experience is a clear refutation of the British hypothesis that high wage increases and inflation are necessarily incompatible with economic growth.

*Taxation*

The Netherlands is one of the more highly taxed countries, with, until 1968, particularly high rates of direct taxation. But in 1968, reductions were made on earnings up to 27,000 guilders a year.[55] Much of the benefit, however, was wiped out by a large increase in prices in January 1969, as a result of the replacement of the turnover tax by the added value tax in accordance with general EEC tax harmonisation policy. Prices rose by 3·5 per cent in the first month.[56] The increases were so steep that the government imposed a price-freeze. A wildcat strike at a factory near Rotterdam brought the workers there a 'dearness' allowance of 25 guilders a month, and within a fortnight similar allowances had been made to other workers whose collective wage agreements were still being revised.[57] The minimum wage —which was introduced in 1966 for all employees over twenty-five—was also increased at that time by 2 guilders, to 142 guilders a week.

Tax rates rise to over 70 per cent for those in the £20,000 a year bracket and in addition there is also a small wealth tax of 0·6 per cent.* But there is no capital gains tax and complete freedom of capital movement. The obligatory breaking up of an estate into equal shares for the wife and children and one other share which can be left to anyone, makes it difficult to keep large estates intact. On the other hand, there is a considerable gain in social harmony through the fact that by law neither children nor a wife can be disinherited.

---

*In 1968, the tax payable by a married man without children on a taxable income of more than 165,000 guilders was 95,507 guilders plus 7·05 guilders for every 10 guilders earned in excess of 165,000 guilders.

# 15

# Foreign Policy and Defence

BEFORE THE war, foreign affairs played a relatively minor role in the Netherlands. A deliberate attempt was made to keep out of involvements with other countries, except when crises such as the Luxemburg affair or the outbreak of the First World War made some action necessary.* This policy of non-involvement or isolationism was reflected in the size of the Ministry of Foreign Affairs, which had only eighty-one officials in 1940.¹ The diplomatic service was dominated by members of the old nobility, whose families had in some cases served in the department for generations. Catholics were greatly under-represented. Of the ten foreign ministers from 1900 to 1940, seven belonged to the nobility.² Because of the special nature of Dutch government, members of this ruling élite were able to move effortlessly from one diplomatic post to tenure of the

*See p. 65–6 above.

foreign affairs portfolio and back again. Members of parliament were kept uninformed of what little activity there was on the grounds that they were uninterested, ignorant or that public discussions might disturb the delicacy of secret negotiations.[3] The department was so well imbued with the spirit of conservatism, which was such a characteristic feature of so many aspects of Dutch life in those days, that even by May 1940, the Netherlands had still not recognised the Soviet Union.[4] Since then there have been very considerable changes.

It is true that before the war a few tentative steps were made in concert with some other small European countries to increase economic co-operation. Under the Oslo agreement of 1930, the Netherlands and five other countries consented not to increase existing customs duties between themselves.* In 1931 under the Ouchy agreement, the three present members of Benelux—the Netherlands, Belgium and Luxemburg—decided to reduce their import duties by half in four years. But these premature attempts at regional economic co-operation, which were to become so fashionable in the post-war world, were crushed at that time by Britain and the United States who were opposed to the granting of such discriminatory favours. The Ouchy agreement was never put into effect and the Oslo pact did not last for long. There were also some positive attempts in the Netherlands to make The Hague into a world peace centre, even though this was done to a certain extent in the hope that it would help to protect the country from attacks against its self-imposed isolationism. As Mr Dirk Stikker, foreign secretary from 1948 to 1952, has said of those pre-war years: 'There was but one policy for Holland: to be left in peace. Later on they called this a policy of neutrality.'[5]

The basis of Dutch foreign policy was to maintain good relations with its powerful neighbour Germany and to rely on the non-continental power of Britain to preserve the balance of power in Europe and to protect the sea lanes to the Dutch East Indies. Even when the policy of collective security began to

*The other members of the Oslo pact were Belgium, Luxemburg, Denmark, Norway and Sweden.

break down in the second half of the 1930s, the Netherlands persisted with its hopes that it might still be able to preserve its neutrality as it had done in the First World War. Certainly, the Nazis repeatedly assured the Dutch, right up to the time of their invasion, that they intended to respect Dutch neutrality. Nevertheless, just before the Second World War broke out, the Dutch government ordered the mobilisation of its forces, which it maintained throughout the 'phoney war' to the time of the invasion.[6] The German invasion of the Netherlands began at 4 a.m. on May 10, 1940, and four days later, while surrender negotiations were in progress, German planes bombed Rotterdam, destroying one-eighth of the city.[7]

The invasion completely demolished the century-old policy of neutrality or isolationism, presenting the Dutch with a dilemma which has persisted since. Historically, the enemies of the Netherlands have been first Spain, then England, and finally France. The last German invasion of Dutch territory, before 1940, had occurred at the end of the eighteenth century when Prussian troops under Charles William Frederick, duke of Brunswick—a nephew of Frederick the Great—helped to restore the legitimate stadtholder to power. Relations between the two countries sometimes became strained as they did during the short-lived Luxemburg affair and during the First World War, but on the whole they lived together, if not in harmony, at least in mutual tolerance. Indeed, there were many close connections between them. William of Orange, the founder of the country's independence, was a German prince. Queen Juliana's father (the duke of Mecklenburg) and her husband, Prince Bernhard (prince of Lippe Biesterfeld) were of German extraction. Before the war, many Dutchmen finished their university or technical education in Germany, and there were fairly sizeable pro-German elements, particularly near the border. There were also strong economic links, as the Germans were one of the biggest importers of Dutch goods, particularly agricultural products, and there was a shared interest in traffic on the Rhine. Not least of all, the Dutch relied on German good faith for the continuance of their policy of neutrality.

All of these traditional attachments were swept aside in five short days in May 1940. It is this, perhaps, which has made the Dutch more persistent in their fears, and even hatred, of the Germans than almost any other nation in western Europe, including Britain. For most Dutchmen the destruction of Rotterdam still ranks beside the bombing of Coventry and the destruction of Warsaw in 1944, as the prime examples of Nazi ruthlessness in the Second World War. Many Dutchmen have neither forgotten nor forgiven the virtual elimination of the Jewish community during the occupation. Throughout history, the Netherlands has always been an asylum for refugees of many different kinds, including Jews. Before the war there were 140,000 Jews in the Netherlands. The vast majority were shipped off through the transit camp of Westerbork, in Drenthe, to extermination camps in Germany and Poland from which only a few hundred ever returned.[8] Half of the 20,000 Jews in hiding in the Netherlands during the war were betrayed or discovered. The schoolgirl, Anne Frank, has left a poignant account of her time in hiding in her diary, which has now been translated into over forty languages.* For many older Dutchmen, the memory of the occupation is still raw.

In these circumstances, there was bound to be a certain ambiguity in the Dutch attitude towards the Germans in the post-war world. On the one hand, the Netherlands had a special fear of Germany because of its proximity and the recent experience of Nazi duplicity and terror; on the other hand, it had a special need of Germany as a major trading partner. This was, indeed, a common experience for other western European powers, but the Dutch, with their pre-war German connections, and the sudden, ruthless awakening from the long twilight sleep of the inter-war years, felt it more deeply than almost any other nation. Immediately after the war, the Dutch put their faith in the United Nations as a means of protecting their own security.

*The Frank family's hiding place is preserved as it was in their house at 263 Prinsengracht, Amsterdam. It is now also the headquarters of the Anne Frank Foundation, which exists to foster understanding between all peoples regardless of race, religion or politics.

But when it became obvious that there no longer existed the four-power agreement on which such collective security could be based, they turned to regional alliances instead. The formal turning-point came with the Brussels treaty of March 1948.[9] By the following year, the Dutch had also lost the major part of their overseas empire—Indonesia. Loss of empire was again to be a common experience of the other European colonial powers. What distinguished the Netherlands in this was the early stage at which it occurred. By the beginning of the 1950s, the Dutch, unencumbered by most imperial problems and shaken out of their pre-war isolationism, were free, for the first time for a century, to take an active part in international affairs—as a minor power, but one with a special attitude and characteristics, so that its voice has become of increasing importance in European affairs.

The Netherlands was a founder member of all the important western organisations for which it was eligible: OEEC and OECD, the Council of Europe, NATO, Western European Union and the European Communities. But of all of these, the real cornerstone of post-1950 foreign policy has been membership of NATO. It has been the most dedicated country in western Europe to the Atlantic concept.

The kind of defence pattern and power grouping that might emerge after the end of the war was forecast with remarkable accuracy in a speech made in 1943, by Mr E. N. van Kleffens, who was then minister of foreign affairs in the government-in-exile. He foresaw the power of Russia in the east being balanced by a united western block, consisting of the United States and Canada as the arsenal, Britain as a base, particularly for the air force, and the Netherlands, Belgium and France as a bridgehead in Europe.[10] Though this was a prediction, not a guideline for policy, it was to be largely fulfilled by the end of the 1940s. The Dutch have seen their ultimate guarantee of security as being on the other side of the Atlantic, not only against any possible threat from Russia, but also against any revival of German power. If the United States remained paramount, then even powers such as Britain, Germany and France would be reduced relatively to something nearer the Dutch size. As one writer has said:

> The insistence upon the Netherlands' role in nuclear planning in NATO, the Dutch rejection of all alternatives to the American monopoly over the control of the use of nuclear weapons, and the Dutch support for non-proliferation agreements which reinforce that situation, form a consistent foreign policy aimed at enhancing Dutch influence in NATO.[11]

It is only in the context of a wide alliance that small powers, such as the Netherlands, have a chance to manoeuvre successfully against the larger European powers.

For the same reasons, basically, the Dutch have supported the idea of a wider, looser grouping in Europe. This grouping would be less likely—if Britain and other countries were members—to be dominated by either Germany or France alone or in combination. As Joseph Luns, the Dutch foreign minister, has written:

> We are firmly committed to Atlantic unity which remains the very corner-stone of our foreign policy. We are also committed to the European ideals that have found expression in the treaties of Rome and Paris on which the Common Market was built. If some form of European political co-operation could be found, compatible with these ideals and in no way harmful to the European communities or the Atlantic Alliance, then we should be glad to take part. However, as long as there exist deep differences of views among the Six on the very principles of Atlantic and European co-operation, we should not go further than attempting a loose form of co-operation, preferably with the participation of Great Britain. From what has been said before, it is clear that in our view defence matters should remain where they belong, in NATO.[12]

The primary concern of the Dutch has been to keep Europe as open as possible, so that they have more room for manoeuvre. On the whole they have been more keen on economic than political integration. As the deputy director of the country's most influential paper, the *Nieuwe Rotterdamse Courant*, he has said:

> This does not mean that the idea of a united Europe itself is a fallacy. European economic integration, for one thing, is an entirely rational aim. . . . The fallacy starts when it is believed that the motives for political integration are as rational as those for economic integration.[13]

The limits of Dutch interests were well illustrated in Benelux, which started as a customs union during the war and became effective as an economic union in 1960. It has no supra-national element and little political force.[14]

The Netherlands has been able to adopt a consistent line on these issues because of some special political characteristics. The dualistic system of government gives ministers, particularly successful ones, a great degree of authority. Furthermore, the fact that they are not necessarily drawn from parliamentary ranks has made it possible for one man, Joseph Luns, to be foreign minister for eighteen years. From 1952 to 1956, there were two foreign ministers—Luns and J. W. Beyen—but from 1956, Luns has held the post alone. Educated in the Netherlands, Germany and England, Luns has been one of the most vocal and persistent supporters of British entry into the Common Market.

But it is somewhat doubtful if Dutch foreign policy will remain quite the same in the future. To begin with, Luns has announced that he will not accept office in the next government in 1971.[15] Then the altered situation in Europe, with the emergence of West Germany from political apathy, the diminished status of France, the possibility of Britain and other countries entering an enlarged community and the lessened American interest in purely European affairs, means that the Netherlands will have to adapt to this fluid situation and its aftermath. Finally, there are all the internal changes in the Netherlands itself; what Professor Russell calls the 'politicisation of Dutch foreign policymaking'.[16] The breakdown of authoritarianism, the Dutch Catholic Church's increasing involvement in international issues and retraction from domestic politics, the attitude of fringe parties, such as the Pacifist Socialists and the New Left within the Socialist party itself, and the greater concern among young people, particularly students, with foreign affairs, may well mean that it is no longer possible for a foreign minister to speak as authoritatively as Luns has done in the past. As Professor Russell remarks:

> An increased involvement by the masses in foreign policy will mean a tendency to move away from the United States and NATO, possibly toward neutrality, but clearly toward a more favorable attitude toward the Soviet Union, more interest in disarmament and lessened military appropriation.[17]

These changes are unlikely to come quickly and indeed it appears at a superficial glance that just the opposite is taking place. The Piet de Jong government was successful in appropriating another 225 million guilders for defence after the Soviet invasion of Czechoslovakia: the estimated total defence expenditure for 1970 was 3,893 million guilders out of a total budget of just under 30,000 million guilders. The army is replacing its outmoded British tanks with 415 Leopards purchased from West Germany at a cost of 459 million guilders.[18] The navy is being given several nuclear submarines, designed for a tracker role, not for carrying missiles.[19] And the Dutch are buying 105 Northrop F-5 fighters and reconnaissance planes from Canada at a cost of 601 million guilders.[20] The total strength of the forces is approximately 128,000, with 86,000 in the army, 20,500 in the navy and 21,500 in the air force.

But many of these decisions were made at an earlier period when the effects of 'politicisation' had not been felt. Even so, there have already been some reactions to these new forces. In 1967, the length of conscription was reduced by two months to its present general length of sixteen months in the army (with eighteen months for officers and specialists) and up to the maximum period of twenty-four months in the other two arms of the services. There are now demands that it should be reduced even further, and among the young particularly, demands that conscientious objection should be allowed on political grounds, not only religious as at present. A disarmament department has been set up in the Ministry of Defence to advise on problems connected with the reduction and the control of arms.[21] And in 1969, the Netherlands set up a disaster brigade, consisting of approximately 1,700 men and 300 vehicles, to help in emergencies in the Netherlands or elsewhere. It first went into action during the floods in Tunisia in that year.[22] There is also an increasing emphasis on foreign aid which has risen greatly in the last few years from an estimated 174 million guilders in 1966 to 662 million guilders in 1969.[23] It is hoped to bring the total up to 1 per cent of the national income by 1971. Like other countries in a similar position, such as Norway, the older traditions of small-power isolationism are not so easy to discard.

# 16

## Loss of an Empire

Up to the Second World War, the Dutch East Indies (now Indonesia) was the broad base on which the pyramid of established interests in the Netherlands rested. It produced wealth, opportunities for overseas employment, a shared status as a colonial power with much bigger European countries, and shaped, to a large extent, the directions of Dutch foreign policy. It was the main legacy from the glorious age of Dutch maritime power in the seventeenth century.

The Dutch first sailed to south-east Asia at the end of the sixteenth century in search of spices. In April 1595, four ships under the command of Cornelius de Houtman, set out for south-east Asia. They reached Bantam on the coast of Java just over a year later and visited other islands before they returned to Europe, loaded with a valuable cargo of spices. Only eighty-nine of the 258 men who set out returned, but the profits of the voyage, which took two and a half years, were so great that other merchants were encouraged to form companies to finance further voyages. By 1602, these companies had been united into one—the United East India Company, which was given the exclusive right by the Dutch government to trade with the Indies. In 1619, Jan Pieterszoon Coen, one of the company's first governor-generals, seized Jacarta, which he renamed Batavia, after one of the original tribes which inhabited the Netherlands. Batavia (now renamed Djakarta) became the company's main base in south-east Asia. The Portuguese had arrived in south-east Asia almost a century before the Dutch, but their power was destroyed after the Dutch in 1641 captured from them the strategically important stronghold of Malacca, which dominates the straits between Malaya and Sumatra. By the middle of the seventeenth century, the Dutch controlled 'the shipping lanes from the Bay of Bengal and Ceylon to Japan . . . Cinammon and cloth from India; copper from Japan and spices from the Moluccas; silks from Persia and sugar from China; all were exchanged in Batavia, and only there'.[1]

Initially the Dutch were more interested in trade and the destruction of Portuguese power than in the acquisition of territory. When Ryckloff van Goens wanted to assume sovereignty over Ceylon, he was reproved by the company's court of directors in Amsterdam who told him: 'This would be the work of a great and ambitious king and not one of merchants who only look for profits.'[2] But the search for profit led the Dutch, like other colonial powers, into savage wars of repression and deeper involvement in local affairs. Where the Dutch could not come to some arrangement with a local ruler, they imposed their will by force. Many natives on the Banda islands, in the eastern part of the archipelago, were killed so that the Dutch could obtain a monopoly of the world's supply of nutmeg and mace. They also tried to restrict the growing of cloves to the nearby island of Amboina so that supplies would be restricted and the world price kept high. This involved the destruction of clove plantations in the main Moluccas islands, where the clove grows naturally.[3]

But the policy of attemping to create a world monopoly in the spice trade was ultimately self-defeating. Not only was it most difficult to enforce, but it also encouraged the English and the French to grow cloves, nutmeg and other spices in India and elsewhere. As profits from the spice trade started to fall, the main focus of Dutch interest started to shift from the spice islands in the eastern part of the archipelago to Java in the west. At the beginning of the eighteenth century, the coffee plant was introduced from southern India into Java, in whose fertile soil it flourished.

The local rulers were forced to deliver a tribute to the company in the form of coffee or to sell their crops to the company at low prices. Reluctantly the company was compelled to change its interests. From a group of merchants interested primarily in the carrying trade and the establishment of forts and trading stations, it gradually evolved into a far more land-based concern, involved in the production of agricultural crops and the internal politics of Java. By the middle of the eighteenth century, most of Java was under the control of the company, whose influence was also felt in most other islands of the archipelago. The production of coffee was never so profitable as the spice trade. By the time the French troops invaded the Netherlands in 1795, the company was near bankruptcy and shortly afterwards it was dissolved 'as a result of its staggering losses, its enormous overhead costs, the corruption among its officials, the competition of the English and the outmoded machinery of its commercial monopoly'.[4]

Just as the French created the basis for a modern state in the Netherlands, so did their emissaries, and then the British, sweep away the old system of company rule in the East Indies. From 1808 to 1811, Herman Willem Daendels was governor-general and he created a centralised form of administration and reformed the system of justice. In 1811, the British captured Java and assumed control over the Dutch possessions in south-east Asia. Thomas Stamford Raffles, who was later to found Singapore, was appointed lieutenant-governor. He completed the reforms that Daendels had begun by imposing a centralised form of direct rule, reducing the powers of the local rulers still further and letting land directly to peasant cultivators. After the defeat of Napoleon, the British handed the East Indies back to the Dutch. In 1824, the British and Dutch carved out their respective spheres of influence in south-east Asia in a treaty, under which the Dutch recognised the British claim to the newly founded Singapore and exchanged Malacca for a few British ports in Sumatra.

The East Indies now came under the direct control of the Dutch king, William I. In 1825, a revolt broke out, which was not finally crushed until five years later. It is estimated that 200,000 Javanese died (most of them from starvation and disease) together with 15,000 Dutch soldiers, including 8,000 Europeans. In the same year that the Javanese war ended, the Belgian provinces revolted against the Dutch crown. The combination of these two events brought the Netherlands to the verge of bankruptcy. Solvency was maintained by instituting a forced labour system (*cultuurstelsel*) in Java, under which peasants had to work for one-fifth of the year on growing export crops for the government, as an alternative to paying rent and taxes. This system of direct economic exploitation, which was to be used with similar success by King Leopold III of Belgium in the Congo Free State sixty years later, was highly profitable.[5] Between 1831 and 1877, 823 million guilders, mainly in the form of coffee, sugar and indigo, flowed into the Netherlands; the income from the East Indies amounted to almost one-third of the Dutch budget.[6] This immense influx of wealth helped to pay off Dutch debts and helped to finance the creation of a merchant fleet which soon became the third largest in the world after those of Britain and France. The maritime power of the Netherlands was rebuilt on the profits of forced labour in the East Indies. But it is rather doubtful if the ultimate benefits were all that great as continued reliance on the carrying trade and the cultivation of tropical agricultural products made the Dutch less keen to industrialise at home.

The wealth that flowed in from the Indies helped to create a new, prosperous middle class, particularly in Amsterdam, which not only wanted to curb the autocratic powers of the king at home, but also wanted to open up the exploitation of the Indies to free enterprise. In 1848, the constitution was revised and the king's exclusive right to control the East Indies was terminated. Parliament gradually gained greater power over colonial affairs; in 1854 it gained control over the administration of the East Indies, and ten years later over the budget.[7] Increasing parliamentary control and the pressure from humanitarians, such as E. Douwes Dekker, brought about the end of the forced labour system. In 1860, Dekker, writing under the pseudonym of Multatuli, published an attack on the forced labour system which attracted enormous interest not only in his own country, but also in England and in Germany. He wrote:

> When one has regard to the immense quantity of Javanese products put up for sale in the Netherlands one must at once be convinced of the effectiveness of the policy, though one may not judge it a noble one. For if anyone should ask whether the cultivator of the soil himself receives a reward proportionate to the results, the answer would have to be a negative one. The Government compels him to grow on *his* land what pleases *it*, it punishes him when he sells the crop so produced to anyone but *it*, it fixes the price which it pays him. The cost of transporting to Europe, by a privileged trading company, is high. . . . Profit can be made in no other way than by paying the Javanese exactly enough to keep him from starving, to the end that the productive power of the nation shall not decrease. . . . *Famine?* In rich, fertile, blessed Java, *famine?* Yes, reader. Only a few years ago whole districts were starved out.[8]

Shortly after the publication of Dekker's book, the forced labour system was abolished for all products but sugar and coffee. Coffee crops continued to be produced in this way until the First World War, but the cultivation of sugar by forced labour was terminated in 1870. In the same year, the liberalisation of the economy was increased by a law which allowed companies and private individuals to take out a seventy-five year lease on government lands. At the same time the property rights of Indonesian peasants were protected.

It was in the last quarter of the nineteenth century that the foundations for new prosperity were laid. The main basis was still agricultural—sugar, coffee, tea and tobacco—but organised by private enterprise. A new class of rich Dutch planters was created, but with the slump in world demand for these products at the end of the nineteenth century, many of these estates were taken over by companies based in the Netherlands. In 1883, the rubber tree was introduced into Sumatra. Large-scale production of rubber started in the twentieth century and by the 1920s, the Dutch East Indies was supplying about one-third of the world's output. In 1890, a small company was formed to exploit an oil field in Sumatra; since then, it has developed into the international combine of Royal Dutch Shell. Much of the profits from these enterprises still flowed out to the Netherlands and, increasingly in the twentieth century, to Britain and the United States as they also started to invest in the East Indies.

At the beginning of the twentieth century, the Netherlands, like other imperial powers, somewhat belatedly recognised that the possession of colonies involved not only commercial exploitation but also some obligations to the natives. In 1901, a new Dutch government under the ARP leader Abraham Kuyper came to power determined 'to imbue the whole conduct of the government with the consciousness that the Netherlands had a moral duty to fulfil with respect to the people of these regions'.[9] To launch this 'ethical policy', as it was called, the Dutch government made a grant of 40 million guilders for the improvement of social and economic conditions in Java and Madura. Around the turn of the century, railways were built there; education expanded; village banks set up to prevent money-lenders exploiting the peasant cultivators; and local councils established. But any benefits from this rather belated concern for native welfare were almost cancelled out by the phenomenal growth in the population of Java, which increased from about 3 million in 1800 to 28 million in 1900. (This in itself was some tribute to the Dutch improvement of health services, and the combating of diseases such as beri-beri and the common outbreaks of plague.)

At the same time as the 'ethical policy' was introduced, the Dutch started to extend their control to the outer islands. Bali was finally occupied in 1906 and Celebes in 1910, by which time the whole of the present territory of what is now Indonesia was firmly under Dutch control. This extension of territorial control to most parts of the archipelago helped to create a sense of Indonesian nationhood which certainly did not exist before.

By the outbreak of the First World War, there were a handful of Indonesians and Eurasians who had been educated in the Netherlands. It was among these and among native traders, who wanted to diminish the Chinese grip over trade, that protest movements first arose which were later to develop into full-scale nationalist movements. In 1909, some native traders set up Sarekat Islam, which helped to create nationalist feelings by its anti-Chinese policy and its dedication to the Muslim faith. Ten years later it had grown into a large political party, pledged to independence, with 2·5 million members. In 1915, one of the few Indonesians to receive higher education in the East Indies stayed with the founder of Sarekat Islam while he attended Surabaya high school. The boy was Achmed Sukarno, who was to become the first president of independent Indonesia.[10]

In an attempt to silence these early rumblings of nationalism, the Dutch decided in 1916 to set up a Volksraad (people's council). As half of the members were nominated by the government and the council had no legislative, but only advisory powers, it did little to placate the feelings of the nationalists and only provided a bigger opportunity for them to voice their grievances. In 1922, the Dutch made a greater step towards giving more autonomy to the East Indies by revising their own constitution; the word 'colony' was dropped and the Volksraad was given some legislative power. But by the time the Dutch parliament had produced new constitutional regulations for the Indies in 1925, much of the liberal spirit of the 1922 revision of the constitution had been lost. The Dutch parliament was given greater powers to intervene in disagreements between the governor-general and the Volksraad, and the single electorate was transformed into one based on race, with Europeans, Indonesians and Chinese electing their representatives separately.[11]

Undoubtedly, the reason for this change of heart was the upsurge of Communist activity in the East Indies. Early in the 1920s, the more revolutionary members of Sarekat Islam had broken away to form the Partai Kommunis Indonesia—PKI. There were Communist-inspired strikes in Java in 1926 and in Sumatra in the following year. 'The Dutch suppressed the uprisings with considerable bloodshed and arrested some thirteen thousand Indonesians. Six thousand of them were imprisoned, detained as political prisoners, or deported.'[12] The fate of exile or imprisonment befell many of the future leaders of independent Indonesia, such as Sutan Sjahrir, Mohammed Hatta and Sukarno, who had helped to form the Partai Nasional Indonesia (PNI) in 1927. During the slump of the 1930s, Indonesia, as a producer of primary products, suffered exceedingly; a policy of severe government retrenchment was adopted. Nationalist demands increased after the Netherlands had been occupied by the Germans in May 1940, but the Dutch government-in-exile still refused to make many concessions. Then, in February 1942, the Japanese attacked and Indonesia surrendered three weeks later. Although most Dutchmen and Indonesians did not realise it then, the Netherlands was never again to resume full control over the whole territory of the East Indies. Dutch rule, which had lasted nearly 350 years, was at an end.

What should be the judgement on the Netherlands as a colonial power? Viewed in one way, their association with the East Indies is a sorry record of gross economic exploitation, brutal colonial wars, repression of elementary rights (press censorship was not abolished until 1906) and indifference for most of the 350 years to the social, educational and economic needs of the subject people. Writing of the period from 1750–1858, that brilliant Asian historian K. M. Panikkar says: 'The Dutch alone of the European nations in the East carried out a policy which systematically reduced a whole population to the status of plantation labour, without recognising any moral or legal obligation to them.'[13] Yet is it possible to condemn the Dutch nation as a whole when parliament did not begin to assume control over colonial affairs until the middle of the nineteenth century, and when previously what happened in the East Indies was the responsibility either of the merchants involved in the affairs of the United East India Company or of the king and his personal advisors and servants? In spite of the long association with south-east Asia, the Dutch nation has been responsible for what happened in the East Indies from the middle of the nineteenth century at the earliest—a period of less than a hundred years.

During this time, many mistakes were made and many errors of judgement, commission and omission were perpetrated, but it is both unfair and unhistorical to criticise the Dutch, as is sometimes done, for not acting in ways of which they were incapable—even in their own country. Their actions as an imperial power must be seen in the context of their own contemporary limitations and in relation to those of other colonial powers. When this is done their record does not seem so dreadful.

The Dutch have often been criticised for distributing seats in the Volksraad on a racial basis, for failing to give the Volksraad sufficient powers and for not introducing enough industry into the East Indies. Yet in all of this, the Dutch were simply imposing the same pattern by which they lived at home. The division of the electorate into Chinese, natives and Europeans, which, incidentally, included Eurasians, was the equivalent of pillarisation at home. The powers of the Volksraad were limited not only because it was a colonial body, but also because the Dutch believed in a dualistic form of government, in which the government ruled and parliament represented the voice of the people. There was very little industrialisation in the East Indies (a textile industry was not started until the 1930s); but neither was there very much at home. The Dutch may have been unimaginative, as most colonial powers were, in believing that their attitudes had a universal applicability, but at least they were not being hypocritical.

In the same way, they applied the knowledge that they had

and the skills that they knew to help solve some of the country's problems. For their own profit admittedly, they introduced many new crops—rubber, tea, coffee, etc. They tried to prevent soil erosion by planting nearly a quarter of Java with forests and increased the artificially irrigated area of the island from 450,000 acres in 1895 to 3·5 million acres by 1939.[14] To help solve the problem of over-population in Java, the Dutch introduced in the 1930s a scheme of assisted migration to the 'outer' islands.

This is not meant to be an apologia for the Dutch, but it seems important to remember that many of their measures were based on the genuine, even if misguided, premise that they would be as effective in the Indies as they were at home. But even when these qualifications have been made, there are still grave criticisms which can be made of Dutch rule. Higher education for Indonesians was neglected and even 'the Netherlands-returned *Meester* or *Doctorandus* found little scope for applying his knowledge'.[15] The composition of the Volksraad was such that the Indonesians could never attain a majority. And too much of the enormous wealth of the Indies flowed out of the country into the Netherlands.

Before World War II the Indies were estimated to have supplied 90 per cent of the world's production of quinine, 86 per cent of the world's pepper, 75 per cent of its kapok, 37 per cent of its rubber, 28 per cent of its coconut-palm products, 19 per cent of its tea, and 17 per cent of its tin as well as sugar, coffee, oil and most of the world's cigar wrappers.[16]

This is a great tribute to Dutch skill and efficiency, but the native population received far too small a proportion of the wealth produced. There were great variations in the prices of primary products before the war, but 'at its pre-war trading peak the archipelago provided an income directly or indirectly to one in every seven Dutchmen'.[17] In 1938, Dutch investments in the East Indies amounted to about 4,000 million guilders or 15 per cent of Dutch national wealth.[18]

The Japanese occupation brought the Asian people into the

modern world as the French had done with other European peoples 150 years before. In Indonesia the rapid victory of their troops showed that the Europeans were not invincible; the imprisonment of Europeans and Eurasians in concentration camps showed that they, too, could be humbled. For their own purposes, the Japanese encouraged Indonesian nationalism by releasing political prisoners, including Sukarno, allowing the Indonesian flag to be flown and permitting the use of the syncretic Indonesia language, *Bahasa Indonesia*. In October 1944, the Japanese, conscious that the tide of war was turning, promised independence to Indonesia, hoping thereby to achieve a political victory over their European opponents even if they should themselves suffer a military defeat.

Even at that late stage, independence was still totally unacceptable to many of the Dutch people. The Communists and many Socialists supported it. And among Dutch officials in the East Indies, there had been a liberal element, which as early as 1930 had been formed into an association—Stuw—devoted to the political separation of the two countries.[19] But there were far more who, like Pieter Gerbrandy, the wartime prime minister of the Netherlands, misguidedly but genuinely believed that the loss of the Indies would lead to the 'pauperisation' of the Netherlands. At that time the view seemed more reasonable than it does now. But far more than economic factors were involved. There was also an enormous psychological dependence. With the East Indies still in its possession, the Netherlands, so many people believed, could remain a great maritime power, sharing a common status as a colonial power with much bigger European countries. Without it, the Netherlands would be nothing but a small nation of about ten million people, crowded into a small corner of Europe, which was deficient in most raw materials and constantly threatened by encroachments of the sea. The total abandonment of the Indies was too devastating even to contemplate, particularly at a time when their own homeland was under the jackboot of the Nazis. The most the Dutch would promise, in a broadcast by Queen Wilhelmina in December 1942, was a commonwealth with internal self-government for the Indies.[20] This went somewhat further than the constitutional revision of 1922, but Indonesian leaders could scarcely fail to be aware of the fact that generalised promises were one thing, while specific regulations, such as those of 1925, were another. The Indonesians now had the necessary confidence to seize independence. Their opportunity came with the Japanese capitulation. Two days later, on August 17, 1945, Indonesia was declared independent and a republic was set up with Sukarno as president and Hatta as vice-president.

Initially there was very little that the Dutch—or indeed anyone else—could do to counter this move. For six weeks or so, until the Allied troops arrived, the Japanese remained in control, ordered by the Allies to maintain law and order, which they did, and not to support the republic, which only some of them did not. Originally, it had been thought that the Americans would take over in Indonesia, but at the last minute it was decided that the British South-East Asia Command under Admiral Mountbatten should do so. The British already had commitments in Burma, Malaya and Indo-China; their main body of forces did not arrive in Indonesia until September 29, which gave the republicans a great opportunity to establish themselves.

The Dutch had a political interest in Indonesia, while the British were only militarily involved. Almost inevitably this created a great conflict of interests between the two powers. The British, who were on the verge of handing over much of their Asian empire to the indigenous people could scarcely be expected to help the Dutch in retaining political control over theirs. Furthermore, the war-weary British troops did not want to become involved in further military conflicts, but to settle the final details of Japanese disarmament and to return home. For many Dutchmen, however, the British were there as the 'bailee for Netherlands property' with the duty, as an ally, of returning it intact.[21] They thought that Sukarno, and other Indonesian leaders who had collaborated with the Japanese, should have been arrested. Relations between the British and the Dutch became more strained after General Christison, the commander of the British forces in Java, issued an order in November 1945, prohibiting Dutch forces from landing there.[22] The British wanted to avoid further conflict and bloodshed; but some Dutchmen at the time erroneously saw only a political motivation in this. The British, however, could not, and did not, prevent Dutch forces, made up of ex-prisoners of war, from landing on the outer islands. But by the end of 1945, the Dutch still had only 20,000 troops in Indonesia and until February 1946, the transport of reinforcements from Europe could be blocked by the Allies as Dutch ships remained part of the Allied 'pool'.[23] In April, however, Dutch troops began to replace the British forces who were due to leave Java and Sumatra by November. Under British pressure, talks had already been held between the Dutch and the republicans. In November 1946, a meeting between the Dutch and the republicans at Linggadjati gave *de facto* recognition to the Indonesian republic in Java, Madura and Sumatra. It was agreed that before January 1, 1949, an Indonesian federation consisting of the republic and other states in the archipelago should be set up and that it would be linked to the Dutch crown in a Netherlands-Indonesian union. An uneasy peace followed, with constant military incidents between the republican forces and the Dutch, and with both sides interpreting Linggadjati in their own ways. In the Netherlands itself, there was growing pressure for more decisive action to be taken against the republic. By July 1947, the Dutch had 150,000 troops in the areas outside republican control. In the same month they launched an attack against the republican forces in Java and Sumatra in what was euphemistically called their first 'police' action.

India and Australia brought the matter before the Security Council of the United Nations, who called for an immediate cease-fire. A good offices committee was appointed and a truce was eventually agreed in January 1948, under which the Dutch were allowed to keep the considerable amount of territory that they had captured from the republicans in Java. The Dutch and the Indonesians continued to disagree on the final form of the proposed union and in December 19, 1948, the Dutch launched their second 'police' action. This time the Security Council took a firmer line, calling for a cease-fire, the release of captured republican leaders and the establishment of a United Nations Commission for Indonesia with authority to talk to the republicans. World opinion had shifted decisively against the Dutch. In the United States, there was growing pressure for economic sanctions against the Dutch if they did not carry out the Security Council's resolution.

By November 1949, an agreement had been reached at a Hague Round Table Conference, under which the Dutch agreed to transfer all sovereignty to a federal United States of Indonesia, which would be linked to the Dutch crown in a Netherlands-Indonesian union. Under the union, both countries remained sovereign and independent but agreed to consult one another on matters of common interest. More important for the Dutch than this rather shadowy commonwealth-style association, was the guarantee of security for Dutch investments and Dutch citizens, the acceptance by Indonesia of a debt of 4,300 million guilders and the Dutch retention of Western New Guinea (West Irian). The motives for retaining this territory were a curious compound of obstinacy, hopes of finding more mineral and oil deposits, the possibility of using it as a springboard for some future return to imperial power and genuine humanitarian concern with the stone-age inhabitants. West Irian was to be the main source of contention between the two powers in the following decade.

The Dutch themselves were only partly responsible for the loss of Indonesia. It was true that their policy was confused; they could never really decide whether to try to restore full colonial rule, to allow a gradual development towards self-government, or to come to terms with the republic and get out as quickly as they could. This confusion was caused by differences between the attitudes of the Dutch government, the Dutch parliament and their representatives in Indonesia. The Catholic Party, which was in all three Dutch coalition governments during the Indonesian crisis, was divided on this issue. Furthermore Dr R. J. van Mook, lieutenant governor-general in Indonesia until November 1948, had been a member of the pre-war Stuw movement. His liberal views did not coincide with those of many of the politicians at home. But the biggest factor in the loss of Indonesia was international pressures, particularly from Britain and the United States. For over a year, the British were in physical control and throughout the whole crisis the United States could wield a powerful weapon through the threat of economic sanctions. Both powers were committed to ending old-style colonial rule in Asia. With hindsight it is possible to see that they were right: the Netherlands would ultimately have been no more able to retain control in Indonesia than a much bigger European power was able to do in Indo-China. But the Dutch felt little gratitude towards Britain or the United States at the time.

The loss of Indonesia was a traumatic experience for the Netherlands. More than any other event, it marked a real dividing line between the old and the new, between those who could accept the loss and those who could not—who chose to emigrate. Many Dutchmen still believe that the crucial event influencing their post-war development was the German occupation and the new-found sense of unity that they discovered then. This is probably true, though some recent Dutch research has revealed that they were neither so united nor so determined in their resistance as they would like to believe.[24] But to the outsider, at least, the loss of Indonesia seems just as significant in opening the way to the whole range of changed attitudes in the post-war period. With the loss of the major part of the empire, the Dutch had to change. They had no choice. And in retrospect it can be seen that they were fortunate in losing Indonesia as early as they did, rather than fighting two protracted colonial wars like the French, or like the British trailing clouds of past imperial splendour for far too long. By 1950, the Dutch could start afresh. They had been liberated themselves.

The tidying-up operation in Indonesia took some time. Relations between Indonesia and the Dutch gradually deteriorated after the Hague conference: the main source of friction was

West Irian. It had been agreed at the conference that the political status of the territory should be decided by the two countries in the following year. But the Dutch refused to relinquish control; and the Indonesians persisted in their claims that it was part of Indonesia, claims that became more strident, as growing internal troubles in Indonesia gave such a chauvinistic issue increasing political usefulness. In April 1956, the Indonesians abrogated the Netherlands-Indonesian union. In August of the same year, they repudiated their debt to the Netherlands, which then totalled 4,081 million guilders.[25] In December 1957, the Indonesians announced that most Dutch nationals would be expelled in stages. Over 33,000 arrived in the Netherlands between December 1957 and August 1958.[26] Dutch businesses, banks, mines and railways were taken over and many of them were nationalised. The final breach came when the Indonesians severed diplomatic relations with the Netherlands in August 1960. In 1962, President Sukarno started talking of taking West Irian by force. After a number of military incidents, secret talks were held between the Dutch and the Indonesians in Washington and in May 1963, the Indonesians occupied the territory, promising that the native people would be given a choice between independence and incorporation into Indonesia by 1969.

Diplomatic relations between the two countries were resumed in 1963, but relations with the Netherlands, as with the rest of the western world, did not begin to improve greatly until after the fall of Sukarno in 1966–7, and his replacement by General (now President) Suharto. In July 1968, the Dutch and Indonesian foreign ministers, Joseph Luns and Adam Malik, signed economic and cultural agreements in Djakarta. A year later, the West Irian question was finally settled when just over 1,000 representatives of the estimated 800,000 primitive inhabitants of West Irian decided unanimously by the Act of Free Choice, supervised by the United Nations, to remain in Indonesia. The improvement in the countries' relations were crowned by the visit of Prince Bernhard in March 1970—the first royal visit ever to Indonesia. It is possible that the queen may go there in 1971.

Although the Dutch failed to establish a lasting union with Indonesia, they succeeded in doing so with the two smaller territories of Surinam and the Dutch Antilles, though it is somewhat problematic how durable this will prove to be. Surinam is a densely forested country of 55,000 square miles, with a population of approximately 150,000, sandwiched between Guyana and French Guiana on the north-eastern coast of South America. It was first colonised in 1650 by the English, who exchanged it with the Dutch for New Amsterdam (New York) in 1667. Its most important produce is bauxite, used in making aluminium, of which some 4 million tons is produced annually, but there are also iron ore and manganese deposits and oil has recently been discovered, too. A start has also been made on exploiting the vast timber resources of the territory.

The Dutch Antilles consist of two groups of three islands each in the Caribbean, about five hundred miles apart. One group, Aruba, Curaçao and Bonaire, are in the Windward Islands off the coast of Venezuela; and the other, St Eustatius, Saba and the southern part of St Maarten, are in the Leeward Islands. (The northern part of St Maarten belongs to France.) Their total area is 403 square miles, with a population of over 200,000, many of whom live in Willemstad, the capital of Curaçao, which is the largest and the most important island. The main industry is oil refining. 'The refineries of Shell at Curaçao and Esso at Aruba, processing Venezuelan oil, make these Dutch islands one of the most important export refining centres of the world.'[27] But there have recently been riots among the workers in Curaçao where the situation at the time of writing, remains tense. Tourism is rapidly becoming an important second industry.

In December 1954, the Netherlands, Surinam and the Dutch Antilles, were linked together in a single kingdom under the House of Orange by a new charter. It gives each territory full autonomy in its domestic affairs, but provides for consultation on defence and foreign policy which affects the kingdom as a whole. Whenever the council of ministers in The Hague is discussing these matters of common concern, ministers plenipotentiary, appointed by the governments of the two Caribbean territories, are brought into the discussions with full voting powers. There is an elaborate system of safeguards to ensure that they shall not be simply outvoted by the 'home' government.[28]

But there are pressures both within the overseas territories, and the Netherlands itself, for greater independence. The overseas governments want to increase the native representation in the armed forces (a start has already been made on this); and also to increase the native representation in Dutch embassies to deal with affairs affecting themselves. With their increasing prosperity, self-confidence, and the generally prevailing spirit of national independence throughout the world, it seems unlikely that the union will be much more durable in the long-term than that with Indonesia.

# 17

# Prospect and Retrospect

BEFORE THE war and for some years after it, Dutch society was one of the most rigid and authoritarian in Europe. People were divided from each other not only by class and rank, but also by religion and ideology. Employers were in a stronger position than in most other European countries; the government was dominated by men whose families had sometimes exercised power for generations; the religious leaders, particularly the Catholics, maintained great authority over their flocks through the schools, the unions and the mass media; higher education was still the preserve mainly of the upper and the middle classes; the professors dominated their own little world of authoritarian remoteness; ordinary people were so subject to the *diktat* of officialdom that they were not even allowed to choose the forenames of their own children unless the names were on one of the officially acceptable lists. It must also be said that, in contrast, there was no oppression, the rule of law was maintained, there were great traditions of paternalism and tolerance and fewer displays of power and ostentatious wealth than there were in many other European countries.

There were not, so one deputy has told me, two nations as in Victorian England—but twenty. This rigidity is no longer characteristic of the Netherlands today. Industrialisation has allowed a modern nation to emerge from the long twilight sleep of the pre-war years. Now, every attitude is being questioned and re-examined; many institutions are in a process of change. There is all the *élan* and intellectual excitement of a society where change has been compressed into a few brief years. The turning-point came between 1963 and 1966 with the massive increase in wages, the opening up of the Catholic Church, the emergence of the Provo movement, the start of the new political party D'66 and the riots in Amsterdam. Authority came under attack on many fronts.

Society, which was once so closed and so rigid, is now more open and in a state of flux. This process of change has gone much too fast for some people and much too slow for others. The difference is not to be explained only in terms of generations or the contrasting attitudes of insiders and outsiders. As in many other western democracies, the clash is at once wider, more complex and more significant than that. The twentieth-century technological revolution which has impinged on all modern, industrial countries in a similar way, has produced a ferment of confused questionings and intellectual gropings towards some new way of life. As the old patterns seem to lose their applicability to contemporary society, new alignments start to form between those who wish to preserve the security of the old closed system and those who wish to found a new, and more open, society. Representatives of all generations can be found in either camp, and, equally, supporters of the closed and of the open society in all institutions. The challenge is very often greater from within the institution than it is from the outside. This is particularly so in the Netherlands where the ruling élite has always contained and sometimes accommodated its interior rebels. What distinguishes the Netherlands in all of this is the complex nature of the challenge, and until very recently, its comparative lack of violence—two factors deeply woven into the country's history—and the rapidity with which these changes have been made. This is a continuing process and society is still in such a state of flux that it is difficult to make firm judgements about the course of future events—except to say that even bigger changes are predictable.

Nevertheless, it can be said that in the last few years, the Dutch have suddenly awakened to the fact that they are a nation which has something to contribute again. Success has come to them in many spheres, both great and small: the emergence of Rotterdam as the world's major port; the Shocking Blue's record, *Venus*, at the top of the American hit parade; the European Commission's interest in producing a half-yearly report on the same lines as that of the Social-Economic Council; the 2–1 win by Feyenoord, of Rotterdam, over Celtic in the European Cup Final in May 1970. Increased travel to other countries, the growth of international conferences, closer co-operation with the five other powers in the EEC, have made the Dutch realise that they are no longer backward. As Mr C. Overdijking told me at the Ministry of Cultural Affairs, Recreation and Social Welfare—an eighteen-storey building in Rijswijk near The Hague—'every year we have more and more foreign visitors; even the Swedes come here to study some aspects of our social services'. The Dutch are keen for foreigners to know about their society and to appreciate how it has been rebuilt and restructured since the war. There is no image that they, so rightly, resent, as that of a land of wooden clogs and tulips.

The extent and depth of this new self-confidence must not be exaggerated. The Dutch know they are only a small power. There is still a highly tentative quality about many of their experiments and attitudes. For example, in one store window in January 1970, there was a display of women's fashions: London says 'mini'; Paris says 'midi'; New York says 'maxi'. There was a fourth display stand, which was empty but for the question—

'What does Amsterdam say?' They had not left themselves much choice. But the Dutch do have confidence now that things can be changed.

In the past, the Dutch have relied upon institutionalised manipulation to retain control. But that is no longer appropriate to the open age. Violence is increasing. On the queen's birthday, May 1, 1970, there were riots involving approximately 1,000 young people in Amsterdam in which ten people were injured.[1] There were further riots in the capital four days later, on Liberation Day, when 136 people were arrested. And during the long hot summer of 1970, there were repeated disturbances in Amsterdam and in other large cities—caused, in the official view, to a large extent by Dutch and foreign agitators with Maoist training.

Within some organisations, such as the Catholic Church, there are increasing pressures for even bigger changes. These pressures are even more extreme from the outside—from the new Kabouter group, which has replaced the Provo movement in Amsterdam, and from the Maoists, anarchists and Red Socialists in the capital—even though, within these groups themselves, there is often little cohesion of thought or unity of purpose. But much of the pressure also comes from the non-aligned, intelligent drop-outs, who, as some of them have told me, have no desire to affirm, but only to be 'clowns', so that they can retain their sense of humour in what seems to them to be an increasingly humourless and crazy world. For them, the Provos disbanding when they did was an act of 'beauty', as was also the dismissal of the burgomaster of Amsterdam. Such parties as D'66, they consider to be old-fashioned and of little interest.

So far, the authorities have treated all these manifestations of new attitudes and thought with considerable tolerance. At the Pop Festival in Rotterdam in June 1970, one Dutch observer told me, so much 'hash' was smoked that mosquitoes dropped dead from the sky, yet the police did not interfere. But indications that there might be some change in the authorities' attitudes were contained in the queen's speech from the throne in September 1970, when a warning was given that the Dutch government would take drastic measures against all groups trying to force their views on others in an irresponsible way.[2] Perhaps the real battle in the Netherlands will come when the outstanding problem of social class is tackled. Meanwhile, it will be interesting to see if the Dutch are able to retain their tolerance and accommodation in the face of these new challenges and an earlier epoch's kindness in a modern industrial age. There is one writer who hopes and believes that they will. The Dutch, as a whole, remain a very loveable people, even if they sometimes doubt it themselves.

# Appendixes*

Density of Population

| Country | Inhabitants per km² |
|---|---|
| Netherlands (1967) | 379 |
| France | 90 |
| West Germany | 232 |
| Italy | 172 |
| Belgium | 312 |
| United Kingdom | 224 |
| Sweden | 17 |
| Norway | 12 |
| Denmark | 111 |

*Source: Statistical Yearbook, U.N., 1966.*

* Except where stated otherwise, the figures have been supplied by the Ministry of Economic Affairs.

2

Area: 33,385 square kilometres = 12,890 square miles
Population

| Year | Number of inhabitants × 1,000 | Indices (1953 = 100) | Under 5 years old | By age groups 5–14 years old | 15–64 years old | Older than 64 years |
|---|---|---|---|---|---|---|
| | | | | | in % | |
| 1930 | 7,832 | 75·4 | 10·5 | 20·1 | 63·2 | 6·2 |
| 1940 | 8,834 | 84·6 | 9·5 | 18·4 | 65·1 | 7·0 |
| 1950 | 10,027 | 96·1 | 12·0 | 17·4 | 62·8 | 7·8 |
| 1960 | 11,417 | 109·4 | 10·1 | 19·9 | 61·1 | 8·9 |
| 1961 | 11,556 | 110·7 | 10·0 | 19·4 | 61·4 | 9·2 |
| 1962 | 11,721 | 112·3 | 10·0 | 19·4 | 61·4 | 9·2 |
| 1963 | 11,890 | 113·9 | 10·0 | 18·9 | 61·8 | 9·3 |
| 1964 | 12,049 | 115·3 | 10·0 | 18·6 | 62·0 | 9·4 |
| 1965 | 12,212 | 116·9 | 10·0 | 18·4 | 62·1 | 9·5 |
| 1966 | 12,377 | 118·6 | 9·9 | 18·3 | 62·2 | 9·6 |
| 1967 | 12,535 | 120·1 | 9·7 | 18·3 | 62·3 | 9·7 |
| 1968 | 12,661 | 121·3 | 9·5 | 18·2 | 62·4 | 9·9 |
| 1969 | 12,798 | 122·6 | — | — | — | — |

3
Religious Affiliation, in percentages

| | |
|---|---|
| Catholic | 40·43 |
| Nederlands Hervormd (Dutch Reformed) | 28·27 |
| Gereformeerd (Reformed) | 9·32 |
| Lutheran | 0·59 |
| Mennonite | 0·55 |
| Remonstrant | 0·34 |
| Jewish | 0·13 |
| Others | 2·03 |
| None | 18·34 |

*Source:* 1960 Census.

(Recent public opinion polls show that the percentage with no religion is now higher and these figures indicate only church membership not active participation.)

4
Distribution of Population

| Region | Inhabitants × 1,000 | in % | Area km² | in % | Inhabitants km² |
|---|---|---|---|---|---|
| Northern and Eastern Netherlands (Groningen, Friesland, Drenthe, Overijssel, Gelderland, Isselmeer Polders) | 3,740 | 30 | 17,686 | 53·0 | 212 |
| Western and Central Netherlands (Holland and Utrecht) | 5,907 | 47 | 6,857 | 20·5 | 862 |
| Southern Netherlands (Zeeland, Brabant, Limburg) | 3,009 | 23 | 8,847 | 26·5 | 340 |

5
Membership of Broadcasting Organisations (in thousands)

| | 1947 | 1967 |
|---|---|---|
| AVRO/RTN (Algemene Vereniging Radio Omroep, Stichting Radio Televisie Nederland) | 86 | 700 |
| KRO (Katholieke Radio Omroep) | 85 | 563 |
| NCRV (Nederlandse Christelijke Radio Vereniging) | 101 | 470 |
| VARA (Omroepvereniging Vara) | 101 | 465 |
| VPRO (Vrijzinnig Protestantse Radio Omroep) | 46 | 130 |
| TROS (Televisie en Radio Omroep Stichting) | — | 182 |

*Source:* Schaafsma, op. cit.

6

National Dailies. (All published in Amsterdam, unless otherwise stated.
Circulation figures for January 1969.)

|  | Circulation | Political leaning |
| --- | --- | --- |
| Algemeen Handelsblad | 65,139 | liberal |
| De Courant Nieuws van de Dag | 175,090 | independent |
| Trouw | 110,950 | protestant |
| De Tijd | 100,760 | catholic |
| Het Parool | 100,600 | socialist |
| De Telegraaf | 466,391 | independent |
| De Volkskrant | 211,900 | catholic |
| Het Vrije Volk (Rotterdam) | 294,030 | socialist |
| De Waarheid | not available | communist |
| Algemeen Dagblad (Rotterdam) | 294,590 | independent |
| Nieuwe Rotterdamse Courant* (Rotterdam) | 59,970 | liberal |

Information supplied by Instituut voor Perswetenschap, Amsterdam.

*Now merged with Algemeen Handelsblad.

7
Modern Literature
A quarterly bulletin, in English, dealing with modern Dutch literature is
issued by the Foundation for the Promotion of the Translation of Dutch
Literary Works, Herengracht 400, Amsterdam-C. Two of the bulletins deal
extensively with the works of two authors, giving translated extracts from
their works, while the other two bulletins consist of brief notices of a large
number of recent works. Recent translations from the Dutch include:
Manfred Wolf, *Change of Scene*. Contemporary Dutch and Flemish poems in
   English translations. Two Windows Press, San Francisco 1969.
Adriaan Morriën, *The Use of a Wall Mirror*, Two Windows Press, San
   Francisco 1970.
Remco Campert, *In the Year of the Strike*, poems, Rapp and Whitting, London
   1968, and *The Gangster Girl*, Hart-Davis, London 1968.
Ward Ruyslinck, *The Deadbeats*, Peter Owen, London 1968.
Heere Heeresma, *A Day at the Beach*, Ross, London 1967.
Jan Wolkers, *A Rose of Flesh*, Secker and Warburg, London 1967.

8

Government Subsidies for Recreation and Culture (in guilders)

|  | 1946 | 1956 | 1966 |
|---|---|---|---|
| Open air recreation | — | 158,500 | 18,000,000 |
| Physical training and sports | 75,000 | 835,200 | 3,047,700 |
| Adult education | 274,000 | 930,000 | 6,983,300 |
| Libraries | 400,000 | 988,740 | 14,798,200 |
| Practice of the arts by amateurs | — | 172,500 | 1,681,600 |
| Youth work | 934,625 | 6,071,500 | 18,855,950 |
| Community, village and district centres | — | 1,320,000 | 3,790,000 |

*Source:* Ministry of Cultural Affairs, Recreation and Social Welfare.

9

Distribution of Seats in the Lower Chamber since 1946

|  | 1946 | 1948 | 1952 | 1956* | 1959 | 1963 | 1967 |
|---|---|---|---|---|---|---|---|
| Catholic People's Party (KVP) | 32 | 32 | 30 | 33 | 49 | 49 | 50 | 42 |
| Labour Party (PVDA) Socialists | 29 | 27 | 30 | 34 | 50 | 48 | 43 | 37 |
| People's Party for Freedom and Democracy (VVD) Liberals | 6 | 8 | 9 | 9 | 13 | 19 | 16 | 17 |
| Anti-Revolutionary Party (ARP) | 13 | 13 | 12 | 10 | 15 | 14 | 13 | 15 |
| Christian-Historical Union (CHU) | 8 | 9 | 9 | 8 | 13 | 12 | 13 | 12 |
| Democracy '66 | — | — | — | — | — | — | — | 7 |
| Communist Party (CPN) | 10 | 8 | 6 | 4 | 7 | 3 | 4 | 5 |
| State Reformed Party (SGP) | 2 | 2 | 2 | 2 | 3 | 3 | 3 | 3 |
| Pacifist-Socialist Party (PSP) | — | — | — | — | — | 2 | 4 | 4 |
| Farmers' Party | — | — | — | — | — | — | 3 | 7 |
| Catholic National Party (*right-wing Catholic*) | — | 1 | 2 | — | — | — | — | — |
| Reformed Political Association | — | — | — | — | — | — | 1 | 1 |
| Total | 100 | 100 | 100 | 100 | 150 | 150 | 150 | 150 |

* In pursuance of the 1956 amendment to the Constitution, the number of seats was increased from 100 to 150; the distribution of seats was adjusted proportionately.

*Source: Digest of the Kingdom of the Netherlands.*

10

Cabinets since 1945

| | |
|---|---|
| 1945–1946 | Schermerhorn—Drees Administration (Socialists and KVP) |
| 1946–1948 | Beel Administration (KVP and PVDA) |
| 1948–1951 | Second Drees Administration (KVP, PVDA, CHU and VVD) |
| 1951–1952 | Third Drees Administration (KVP, PVDA, CHU and VVD) |
| 1952–1956 | Fourth Drees Administration (PVDA, KVP, ARP and CHU) |
| 1956–1958 | Fifth Drees Administration (PVDA, KVP, ARP and CHU) |
| 1958–1959 | Beel Interim Administration (KVP, ARP and CHU) |
| 1959–1963 | De Quay Administration (KVP, VVD, ARP and CHU) |
| 1963–1965 | Marijnen Administration (KVP, VVD, ARP and CHU) |
| 1965–1966 | Cals Administration (KVP, PVDA and ARP) |
| 1966–1967 | Zijlstra Administration (KVP and ARP) |
| 1967– | Piet de Jong (KVP, VVD, ARP and CHU) |

*Source: Digest of the Kingdom of the Netherlands.*

11

Percentage of Dutch Youth Continuing Full Time Education after Completing Primary School in 1964–5

| Age (yrs) | Boys | Girls | Total |
|---|---|---|---|
| 15 | 76·3 | 56·5 | 66·5 |
| 16 | 64·2 | 37·1 | 51·0 |
| 17 | 50·7 | 23·5 | 37·4 |
| 18 | 37·1 | 14·0 | 25·8 |
| 19 | 23·7 | 8·3 | 16·2 |
| 20–25 | 9·7 | 2·8 | 6·3 |

12

Budget 1970 (million guilders)

| | |
|---|---|
| *Total expenditure* | 29,397 |
| of which: | |
| education, sciences, culture and recreation | 8,439 |
| defence | 3,893 |
| social benefits and public health | 3,346 |
| traffic and waterworks | 3,270 |
| housing | 2,540 |
| other purposes | 5,666 |
| unpaid interest and redemption of public debt | 2,243 |

*Source:* Netherlands Central Bureau of Statistics.

13
Growth of the Student Population

| | 1937/38 | 1950/51 | 1959 | 1967/68 |
|---|---|---|---|---|
| State University, Leiden | 2,384 | 4,250 | 4,842 | 9,579 |
| State University, Groningen | 921 | 2,117 | 2,796 | 7,509 |
| State University, Utrecht | 2,670 | 5,287 | 5,730 | 12,100 |
| University of Amsterdam | 2,438 | 6,952 | 6,594 | 14,034 |
| Free University, Amsterdam | 611 | 1,443 | 2,621 | 6,343 |
| Catholic University, Nijmegen | 446 | 1,088 | 2,459 | 7,134 |
| Delft University of Technology | 1,838 | 5,615 | 6,104 | 9,000 |
| Agricultural University, Wageningen | 409 | 1,047 | 917 | 2,296 |
| Netherlands School of Economics, Rotterdam | 566 | 1,157 | 1,556 | 3,855 |
| Tilburg School of Economics, Social Sciences and Law | 222 | 780 | 758 | 2,349 |
| Eindhoven University of Technology | — | — | 513 | 2,793 |
| Twente University of Technology | — | — | — | 854 |
| Rotterdam Medical Faculty | — | — | — | 451 |
| Total | 12,505 | 29,736 | 34,890 | 78,306 |

*Source:* Thomassen, op. cit.

14
Social Security contributions in million guilders*

| | Employers' contribution | | | Family contributions | | | Government contributions | | |
|---|---|---|---|---|---|---|---|---|---|
| | 1965 | 1966 | 1967 | 1965 | 1966 | 1967 | 1965 | 1966 | 1967 |
| Accident insurance | 251·4 | 262·1 | 135·0 | — | — | — | 15·8 | 17·9 | 9·25 |
| Disability | 13·8 | 1·9 | — | 0·5 | — | — | 6·0 | 6·8 | 6·8 |
| Disability pensions (Interim) | 290·0 | 492·8 | 266·0 | — | — | — | 93·0 | 99·0 | 55·25 |
| Government contribution towards deficit in the Disability Pensions (Interim) Fund | | | | | | | — | — | 58·55 |
| Sickness benefit insurance | 618·3 | 891·0 | 1,210·0 | 221·0 | 223·0 | 290·0 | — | — | — |
| Working incapacity insurance | — | — | 448·5 | — | — | 97·5 | — | — | — |
| Redundancy pay and unemployment benefits insurance | 103·0 | 102·8 | 117·0 | 103·7 | 103·9 | 117·0 | 89·0 | 82·0 | 94·0 |
| Health Fund insurance | 453·1 | 540·2 | 709·0 | 840·7 | 997·8 | 1,173·0 | 73·6 | 83·2 | 104·3 |
| Children's allowances insurance | 1,147·7 | 1,389·4 | 1,510·0 | 93·4 | 103·8 | 120·0 | 8·1 | 9·2 | 10·0 |
| General old age pensions insurance | — | — | — | 2,905·4 | 3,180·2 | 3,476·0 | 180·0 | 183·0 | 194·0 |
| General widows' and orphans' pensions insurance | — | — | — | 500·5 | 548·3 | 553·0 | 5·0 | 3·6 | 3·0 |
| Total | 2,878·2 | 3,680·2 | 4,395·5 | 4,665·2 | 5,157·0 | 5,826·5 | 407·5 | 485·6 | 583·15 |

* Provisional figures.

*Source: Digest of the Kingdom of the Netherlands.*

15

Social Security Payments, as a Percentage of Wages paid by Employer and Employee, on July 1, 1970

| *National Insurance* | *Employer* | *Employee* | *Maximum Assessable Income* |
|---|---|---|---|
| General Old Age Pensions Act | — | 9·9 | 17,450 guilders per year |
| General Widows' and Orphans' Pensions Act | — | 1·5 | " |
| General Special Sickness Expenses Insurance Act | 1·25 | — | " |
| General Children's Allowance Act | 2·15 | — | " |
| | | | *Maximum Assessable Daily Wage (for a five-day week)* |
| *Employees' Insurance* | | | |
| Sickness Insurance Act* | 5·5 | 1 | 89 guilders |
| Incapacity to Work Act | 4 | 1·3 | 89 guilders |
| Compulsory Health Insurance Act (only for wages not exceeding 14,850 guilders a year) | 3·75 | 3·75 | 48 guilders |
| Unemployment Insurance Act | 0·5 | 0·5 | 89 guilders |
| Children's Allowance Act for Wage Earners | 3·3 | — | 17,450 guilders a year |

\* Percentages are averages, as there is no uniformity for all branches of industry.

*Source:* Ministry of Social Affairs.

16

| 1966, per 1,000 inhabitants | Death rate | Birth rate | Excess of births over deaths |
|---|---|---|---|
| Britain | 11·7 | 17·7 | 6·0 |
| United States | 9·5 | 18·5 | 9·0 |
| France | 10·7 | 17·5 | 6·8 |
| Sweden | 10·0 | 15·8 | 5·8 |
| Netherlands | 8·1 | 19·2 | 11·1 |

*Source:* Muntendam, op. cit.

17
External Migration

| | 1960 | 1964 | 1965 | 1966 | 1967 | 1968 |
|---|---|---|---|---|---|---|
| Immigrants | 45,410 | 67,079 | 76,572 | 81,842 | 55,784 | 64,775 |
| of whom from: | | | | | | |
| Indonesia | 5,324 | 3,809 | 5,278 | 3,941 | 2,286 | 1,748 |
| Europe | 15,860 | 35,130 | 43,510 | 45,193 | 29,333 | 36,167 |
| Emigrants | 58,230 | 53,419 | 57,808 | 61,892 | 67,383 | 58,701 |
| of whom to: | | | | | | |
| America | 22,060 | 11,607 | 11,586 | 14,016 | 14,423 | 13,305 |
| Oceania | 9,950 | 4,549 | 4,223 | 4,005 | 3,911 | 4,283 |
| Emigration surplus (−) | −12,820 | +13,660 | +18,764 | +19,950 | −11,596 | +6,074 |
| Immigration surplus (+) in % of net population increase in the year concerned | −9·2 | +8·0 | +11·4 | +12·6 | −7·4 | +4·8 |

18

National Income and National Product in millions of guilders

| Year | In current prices | National Income (net market prices) Indices col. 1 (1963=100) | National Income (net market prices) In prices 1963 | Indices col. 3 (1963=100) | National Product (gross market prices) Current prices | National Product (gross market prices) Indices col. 5 (1963=100) |
|------|------|------|------|------|------|------|
| 1958 | 32,407 | 68 | 38,010 | 78 | 35,930 | 68 |
| 1960 | 38,823 | 81 | 43,320 | 89 | 42,732 | 81 |
| 1961 | 41,082 | 86 | 44,670 | 92 | 45,288 | 86 |
| 1962 | 43,972 | 92 | 46,230 | 96 | 48,517 | 92 |
| 1963 | 47,918 | 100 | 47,920 | 100 | 52,858 | 100 |
| 1964 | 56,695 | 118 | 52,370 | 109 | 62,154 | 118 |
| 1965 | 63,227 | 132 | 54,940 | 116 | 69,237 | 131 |
| 1966 | 68,230 | 142 | 55,800 | 117 | 74,810 | 141 |
| 1967 | 75,070 | 157 | 58,900 | 125 | 82,270 | 156 |
| 1968* | 82,280 | 172 | 64,013 | 133 | 89,980 | 170 |
| 1969* | 90,540 | 189 | 66,609 | 139 | 98,810 | 187 |

\* Estimation Central Planning Office.

Nat. Income, gross market prices = Nat. Income, net market prices + depreciation by enterprises and government; Nat. Income, net market prices = Nat. Income, net factor-costs + indirect taxes minus subsidies.

19

Balance of Payments on Transaction Basis (current account)
(According to the Balance of Payments Manual of the IMF)
in millions of guilders

|  | 1962 Credit | 1962 Debit | 1963 Credit | 1963 Debit | 1964 Credit | 1964 Debit | 1965 Credit | 1965 Debit |
|---|---|---|---|---|---|---|---|---|
| *Merchandise fob:* | | | | | | | | |
| Export and imports fob | 15·871 | 16·942 | 17·115 | 18·850 | 19·708 | 22·440 | 21·809 | 23·846 |
| Transactions abroad (net) | 134 | | 130 | | 132 | | 247 | |
| Foreign travel | 692 | 628 | 770 | 775 | 874 | 958 | 993 | 1·134 |
| Transportation Insurance | 1·867 | 806 | 2·074 | 1·053 | 2·496 | 1·318 | 2·583 | 1·331 |
| (saldo) | | 47 | | 24 | | 29 | | 14 |
| Investment income | 1·395 | 1·001 | 1·683 | 1·038 | 1·863 | 1·125 | 2·016 | 1·297 |
| Government, not included elsewhere | 81 | 433 | 213 | 359 | 109 | 407 | 162 | 431 |
| Miscellaneous | 1·478 | 1·015 | 1·607 | 1·131 | 1·727 | 1·330 | 1·864 | 1·563 |
| Total current account | 21·518 | 20·872 | 23·592 | 23·230 | 26·909 | 27·607 | 29·674 | 29·616 |
| Net current account (−=deficit) | 646 | | 362 | | −698 | | 58 | |

20
Foreign Trade and Services Foreign Trade

|  | *1938* | *1949* | *1953* | *1959* | *1966* | *1967* | *1968* |
|---|---|---|---|---|---|---|---|
| Imports (million guilders) | 1,416 | 5,332 | 9,026 | 14,967 | 29,024 | 30,182 | 33,639 |
| Imports in % of national income (net market prices) | 26·3 | 34·6 | 41·3 | 43·1 | 42·5 | 40·2 | 40·9 |
| Exports (million guilders) | 1,043 | 3,851 | 8,180 | 13,705 | 24,443 | 26,381 | 30,197 |
| Exports in % of national income (net market prices) | 19 | 25 | 37·5 | 39·4 | 35·8 | 35·1 | 36·7 |
| Imports covered by exports in % | 73 | 72·2 | 90·6 | 91·6 | 84·2 | 87·4 | 89·8 |
| Volume index-figures (1963=100) |  |  |  |  |  |  |  |
| Imports | 32 | 48 | 40 | 69 | 130 | 136 | 156 |
| Exports | 27 | 24 | 46 | 76 | 132 | 143 | 166 |
| Price index-figures (1963=100) |  |  |  |  |  |  |  |
| Imports | 21 | 84 | 104 | 102 | 104 | 103 | 100 |
| Exports | 23 | 88 | 100 | 101 | 104 | 103 | 102 |

21

Imports from and Exports to Principal Countries (in millions of guilders)

| | | | | *Imports* | | | |
| --- | --- | --- | --- | --- | --- | --- | --- |
| | *1938* | *1959* | *1964* | *1965* | *1966* | *1967* | *1968* |
| West Germany | 301* | 3,098 | 6,199 | 6,392 | 7,211 | 7,670 | 8,876 |
| Belgium and Luxemburg | 162 | 2,717 | 4,911 | 5,299 | 5,508 | 5,567 | 6,046 |
| United States | 153 | 1,651 | 2,813 | 2,768 | 3,295 | 3,208 | 3,671 |
| United Kingdom | 115 | 1,132 | 1,829 | 1,758 | 1,770 | 1,674 | 1,844 |
| France | 65 | 532 | 1,366 | 1,659 | 1,746 | 1,920 | 2,183 |
| Italy | 13 | 272 | 812 | 1,076 | 1,216 | 1,299 | 1,524 |
| Sweden | 30 | 431 | 710 | 742 | 752 | 706 | 786 |
| Indonesia | 102 | 272 | 344 | 400 | 353 | 355 | 216 |
| Argentina | 64 | 277 | 313 | 313 | 286 | 348 | 298 |
| Kuwait | — | 512 | 359 | 314 | 385 | 507 | 696 |
| Other countries | 411 | 4,043 | 5,883 | 6,289 | 6,502 | 6,928 | 7,499 |
| Total | 1,416 | 14,967 | 25,539 | 27,010 | 29,024 | 30,182 | 33,639 |

| | | | | *Exports* | | | |
| --- | --- | --- | --- | --- | --- | --- | --- |
| | *1938* | *1959* | *1964* | *1965* | *1966* | *1967* | *1968* |
| West Germany | 154* | 2,964 | 5,661 | 6,428 | 6,576 | 6,885 | 8,393 |
| Belgium and Luxemburg | 106 | 2,009 | 3,207 | 3,438 | 3,685 | 3,886 | 4,319 |
| United Kingdom | 235 | 1,470 | 1,923 | 2,011 | 2,009 | 2,330 | 2,579 |
| France | 60 | 726 | 1,865 | 1,955 | 2,185 | 2,423 | 3,180 |
| Italy | 12 | 370 | 971 | 1,071 | 1,128 | 1,296 | 1,451 |
| United States | 37 | 786 | 812 | 882 | 1,112 | 1,241 | 1,579 |
| Sweden | 36 | 574 | 668 | 753 | 762 | 761 | 836 |
| Denmark | 8 | 345 | 408 | 445 | 426 | 374 | 422 |
| Switzerland | 21 | 323 | 474 | 512 | 526 | 575 | 619 |
| Norway | 16 | 301 | 301 | 311 | 333 | 338 | 300 |
| Other countries | 348 | 3,835 | 4,735 | 5,338 | 5,701 | 6,272 | 6,519 |
| Total | 1,043 | 13,703 | 21,025 | 23,144 | 24,443 | 26,381 | 30,197 |

* All Germany.

22

Size of Industrial Enterprises by Number of Persons Employed in 1966

| Size class | Number of enterprises | Persons employed | Persons employed in % |
|---|---|---|---|
| 10–24 persons | 4·381 | 65·462 | 5·7 |
| 25–49 persons | 2·681 | 92·862 | 8·1 |
| 50–99 persons | 1·661 | 114·689 | 10·1 |
| 100–199 persons | 852 | 117·937 | 10·3 |
| 200–499 persons | 534 | 161·345 | 14·2 |
| 500–999 persons | 178 | 121·476 | 10·7 |
| 1,000 and more | 131 | 465·414 | 40·9 |
| Total | 10·418 | 1,139·185 | 100 |

23

Number of Persons Employed and Turnover in Industry,* per Major
Group of Industry, 1969

| | *Persons†* *employed* | | *Sales (excl. sales tax),* *million guilders* | | | |
| | *Total* ✕ 1,000 | *In %* *of total* | *Domestic* | *Foreign* | *Total* | *In %* *of total* |
|---|---|---|---|---|---|---|
| ɪ Earthenware, glass, lime, bricks | 48·1 | 4 | 1,904 | 348 | 2,252 | 3 |
| ɪɪɪ Printing and allied industries | 50·4 | 4 | 1,792 | 177 | 1,969 | 3 |
| v Chemical industry | 97·8 | 9 | 5,738 | 5,795 | 11,533 | 15 |
| vɪ Wood, straw | 45·8 | 4 | 1,740 | 176 | 1,915 | 3 |
| vɪɪa Clothing | 62·5 | 6 | 1,710 | 325 | 2,036 | 3 |
| vɪɪb Cleaning | 12·8 | 1 | 233 | — | 233 | 0 |
| ɪx Leather, rubber | 33·7 | 3 | 944 | 475 | 1,419 | 2 |
| x Mining | 25·1 | 3 | 1,082 | 681 | 1,763 | 2 |
| xɪ Metal industry, ship-building,** etc. | 433·8 | 38 | 11,311 | 9,939 | 21,250 | 28 |
| xɪv Paper industry, etc. | 32·2 | 3 | 1,491 | 655 | 2,146 | 3 |
| xv Textile industry, inc. manufacture of synthetic fibres and yarns | 88·4 | 8 | 2,326 | 2,101 | 4,427 | 6 |
| xvɪɪ Food and tobacco | 160·2 | 14 | 15,633 | 5,234 | 20,867 | 28 |
| Total excl. group xvɪ | 1,091·1 | 96 | 45,912 | 25,930 | 71,842 | 96 |
| xvɪ Public utilities | 42·9 | 4 | 2,944 | — | 2,944 | 4 |
| Total, incl. group xvɪ | 1,134·0 | 100 | 48,856 | 25,930 | 74,786 | 100 |

* Activity units employing at least 10 persons.
† Averages at the end of the 4 quarters.
** Including diamond industry.

*Source:* Netherlands Central Bureau of Statistics.

## 24

Exports by Commodities (in million guilders)

|  | 1950 | 1954 | 1958 | 1965 | 1966 | 1967 | 1968 |
|---|---|---|---|---|---|---|---|
| Food | 1,987 | 2,821 | 3,250 | 5,391 | 5,382 | 5,786 | 6,861 |
| Beverages and tobacco | 64 | 118 | 145 | 283 | 308 | 336 | 388 |
| Raw materials, inedible, except fuel | 393 | 600 | 774 | 1,800 | 2,018 | 2,152 | 2,259 |
| Mineral fuels, lubricants and related materials | 370 | 985 | 1,608 | 2,019 | 1,777 | 2,075 | 2,418 |
| Animal and vegetable oils and fats | 133 | 172 | 161 | 203 | 209 | 223 | 292 |
| Chemicals | 410 | 652 | 1,036 | 2,365 | 2,763 | 3,231 | 4,010 |
| Manufactured goods | 1,052 | 1,936 | 2,556 | 4,555 | 4,851 | 5,071 | 5,682 |
| Machinery and transport equipment | 633 | 1,462 | 2,041 | 4,896 | 5,267 | 5,379 | 6,025 |
| Commodities not mentioned elsewhere | 240 | 426 | 655 | 1,632 | 1,868 | 2,128 | 2,261 |
| Total | 5,282 | 9,172 | 12,226 | 23,144 | 24,443 | 26,381 | 30,197 |

25

Postwar Foreign Investments in the Netherlands; Wholly-owned Establishments and Participations in or Co-operations with Netherlands Industry (December 31, 1968)

*Numbers according to country of origin*

| | Wholly-owned establishments | Participations/ co-operations | Total |
|---|---|---|---|
| United States | 249 | 129 | 378 |
| United Kingdom | 90 | 91 | 181 |
| Belgium | 35 | 29 | 64 |
| West Germany | 62 | 74 | 136 |
| Switzerland | 40 | 49 | 89 |
| Sweden | 38 | 13 | 51 |
| France | 12 | 16 | 28 |
| Other countries | 28 | 33 | 61 |
| Total | 554 | 434 | 988 |

*Distribution according to branches of industry*

| | Wholly-owned establishments | Participations/ co-operations | Total |
|---|---|---|---|
| Metalworking | 222 | 149 | 371 |
| Electrical | 40 | 9 | 49 |
| Chemical | 111 | 85 | 196 |
| Textile | 30 | 45 | 75 |
| Food | 33 | 24 | 57 |
| Rubber | 7 | 11 | 18 |
| Miscellaneous | 111 | 111 | 222 |
| Total | 554 | 434 | 988 |

26

Number of Dwellings Completed after the War

| Year | Private building* | % | Housing Act dwellings† | % | Building by Government | % | Total number of dwellings |
|------|-------------------|-----|------------------------|------|------------------------|------|---------------------------|
| 1945 | 326 | 83·8 | 60 | 15·4 | 3 | 0·8 | 389 |
| 1946 | 992 | 62·3 | 360 | 22·6 | 241 | 15·1 | 1,593 |
| 1947 | 2,865 | 31·0 | 5,600 | 60·6 | 778 | 8·4 | 9,243 |
| 1948 | 7,666 | 21·1 | 27,480 | 75·5 | 1,245 | 3·4 | 36,391 |
| 1949 | 12,582 | 29·4 | 29,000 | 67·8 | 1,209 | 2·8 | 42,791 |
| 1950 | 18,815 | 39·8 | 27,500 | 58·1 | 985 | 2·1 | 47,300 |
| 1955 | 31,607 | 52·0 | 28,643 | 47·1 | 569 | 0·9 | 60,819 |
| 1960 | 44,593 | 53·2 | 38,861 | 46·4 | 361 | 0·4 | 83,815 |
| 1965 | 64,393 | 56·0 | 49,963 | 43·4 | 671 | 0·6 | 115,027 |
| 1966 | 61,258 | 50·3 | 60,034 | 49·3 | 407 | 0·4 | 121,659 |
| 1967 | 57,466 | 45·1 | 69,440 | 54·5 | 527 | 0·4 | 127,433 |
| 1968 | 60,045 | 48·9 | 62,071 | 50·6 | 657 | 0·5 | 122,773 |

* Building under the subsidy scheme for private building and building without government support (including premium building by municipalities and house-building corporations).

† Rented houses and flats built by recognised house-building associations and municipalities.

27

Migrant Workers, 1968

| Nationality | Men | Women |
|-------------|-----|-------|
| Italians | 8,426 | 1,080 |
| Spaniards | 9,607 | 2,533 |
| Turks | 13,243 | 400 |
| Moroccans | 14,072 | 24 |
| Greeks | 1,259 | 357 |
| Portuguese | 1,648 | 628 |
| Yugoslavs | 1,181 | 262 |
| Others (Germans, French, British, Americans, etc.) | 20,760 | 4,860 |
| Total | 70,196 | 10,144 |

*Source:* Ministry of Social Affairs and Public Health.

# Notes and References

## 1. Before the Revolt

1. See P. C. J. A. Boeles, *Friesland tot de elfde eeuw*, The Hague 1951, pp. 69–80.
2. Johan van Veen, *Dredge, Drain, Reclaim, The Art of a Nation*, The Hague 1948, p. 18.
3. Ibid., p. 16.
4. Pliny, *Natural History*, London 1945, Vol. IV, pp. 387–9.
5. Ibid., pp. 389–91.
6. Bernard H. M. Vlekke, 'The Dutch before 1581', Bartholomew Landheer (ed.), *The Netherlands*, Berkeley and Los Angeles 1943, p. 20.
7. Quoted in J. S. Lingsma, *Holland and the Delta Plan*, Rotterdam —The Hague 1963, p. 13.
8. Van Veen, op. cit., pp. 25–6.
9. Lodovico Guicchardini, *The Description of the Low Countreys and of the Provinces thereof*, London 1593, p. 9.

10. Aksel E. Christensen, 'Dutch Trade to the Baltic about 1600', *Studies in the Sound Toll Register and Dutch Shipping Records*, Copenhagen—The Hague 1941, p. 20.
11. Cf. Frank E. Huggett, *Modern Belgium*, London 1969, pp. 2–3.
12. See Gerald L. Burke, *The Making of Dutch Towns, A Study in Urban Development from the Tenth to the Seventeenth Centuries*, London 1956, passim.
13. Nelly Johanna Martina Kerling, *Commercial relations of Holland and Zeeland with England from the late 13th century to the Close of the Middle Ages*, Leiden 1954, pp. 173–5.
14. Ibid., p. 183.
15. Ibid., pp. 194–5.
16. See Richard Vaughan, *Philip the Bold, the Formation of the Burgundian State*, London 1962, part. pp. 81–112.
17. George Edmundson, *History of Holland*, Cambridge 1922, p. 21.
18. Kerling, op. cit., p. 185.
19. G. W. Hoogerwerff, 'Uit de Geschiedenis van het Nederlandsch Nationaal Besef, Tijdschrift voor Geschiedenis', No. 2, 1929, quoted in G. J. Renier, *The Dutch Nation, An Historical Study*, London 1944, p. 15.
20. W. Aglionby, *The Present State of the United Provinces of the Low Countries*, London 1669, Book II, p. 83.
21. See B. M. Vlekke, *Evolution of the Dutch Nation*, New York 1945, pp. 162–6; and for further details of government, Renier, op. cit., pp. 17–21; and Edmundson, op. cit., pp. 3–6.
22. Edmundson, op. cit., p. 33.
23. Aglionby, op. cit., Book I, p. 39.
24. E. Grimeston, *A General Historie of the Netherlands*, London 1608, pp. 383–4.
25. See J. H. Elliott, *Imperial Spain, 1469–1716*, London 1963, pp. 225–6.

## 2. *The Eighty Years' War*

1. G. N. Clark, 'The Birth of the Dutch Republic', *The Raleigh Lecture in History from the Proceedings of the British Academy*, London 1946, pp. 3–4.
2. The standard work in English is Pieter Geyl, *The Revolt of the Netherlands, 1555–1609*, Benn 1962, and *The Netherlands in the Seventeenth Century, 1609–1648*, Benn 1961, and in Dutch, *Algemene Geschiedenis der Nederlanden*, Utrecht 1949–58, 12 vols, Vol. v, *De Tachtigjarige Oorlog*, Utrecht 1952.

3. See K. H. Heeroma, 'The Dutch Language in the World', *Higher Education and Research in the Netherlands*, The Hague, Vol. XI, No. 2, p. 15.
4. Cf., for example, Charles Wilson, *The Dutch Republic and the Civilisation of the Seventeenth Century*, London 1968, pp. 8–15, and Elliott, op. cit., p. 390.
5. Violet Barbour, *Capitalism in Amsterdam in the Seventeenth Century*, Baltimore 1950, p. 13.
6. Clark, op. cit., p. 18.
7. C. V. Wedgwood, *William the Silent*, London 1967, p. 253.
8. See P. A. M. Geurts, *De Nederlandse Opstand in de Pamfletten*, *1566–1584*, Nijmegen-Utrecht 1956, pp. 131–56.
9. Clark, op. cit., p. 8.
10 Wedgwood, op. cit., p. 31.
11. Kervyn de Lettenhove, *Les Huguenots et Les Gueux*, Bruges, Vol. II, 1884, p. 409.
12. Ibid., p. 413.
13. Sir Roger Williams, *The Actions of the Low Countries*, London 1618, p. 62.
14. For a different version, see, for example, Williams, op. cit., pp. 61–2.
15. See Geyl, *The Revolt of the Netherlands*, pp. 122–7.
16. For a thorough account see Douglas Nobbs, *Theocracy and Toleration, A Study of Disputes in Dutch Calvinism from 1600 to 1650*, Cambridge 1938, passim.
17. Ibid., p. x, introduction.
18. See H. A. Enno van Gelder, *The Two Reformations in the Sixteenth Century*, The Hague 1961, part. pp. 309–27.

## 3. The Golden Age

1. Geyl, op. cit., *The Revolt of the Netherlands*, p. 131.
2. Christensen, op. cit., p. 218.
3. Grimeston, op. cit., p. 655.
4. Aglionby, op. cit., Book III, p. 360.
5. Barbour, op. cit., p. 17.
6. Ibid., p. 24.
7. See Christensen, op. cit., pp. 401–4.
8. Ibid., pp. 93–4.
9. For further details, see Boxer, op. cit., passim.
10. F. Gunther Eyck, *The Benelux Countries, An Historical Survey*, D. Van Nostrand Co., Inc. 1959, p. 35.
11. Christensen, op. cit., pp. 112–14 and pp. 190–3.

12. *A Trip to Holland, being a description of the Country, People and Manners: as also some select Observations on Amsterdam*, London 1699, p. 14.
13. *A New Description of Holland and the Rest of the United Provinces in General*, London 1701, p. 62.
14. See Renier, op. cit., p. 99.
15. Aglionby, op. cit., Book III, p. 222.
16. For a recent comprehensive survey in English see Charles Wilson, *The Dutch Republic and the Civilisation of the Seventeenth Century*, London 1968.
17. Van Veen, op. cit., p. 53.
18. See J. A. Leeghwater, *Haarlemmer-Meer-Boeck*, Amsterdam 1710, passim.

## 4. The Collapse of the Dutch Republic

1. Bernard H. Slicher van Bath, 'Historical Demography and the Social and Economic Development of the Netherlands', *Daedalus*, Boston 1968, p. 609.
2. Jill Lisk, *The Struggle for Supremacy in the Baltic, 1600–1725*, London 1967, p. 20.
3. Charles Wilson, *Profit and Power, a Study of England and the Dutch Wars*, London 1957, p. 149.
4. Ibid., p. 155.
5. Maurice Ashley, *England in the Seventeenth Century*, Harmondsworth 1952, p. 127.
6. *The Treaty and Articles of Agreement between the Estates of Holland, the Prince of Orange and the Magistrates of Amsterdam*, London 1650, p. 5.
7. Boxer, op. cit., p. 275; for the reasons for this decline see J. S. Bartstra, *Vlootherstel en Legeraugmentaties, 1770–1780*, Assen 1952, passim.
8. Charles Wilson, *Anglo-Dutch Commerce and Finance in the Eighteenth Century*, Cambridge 1941, p. 23.
9. Aglionby, op. cit., Book III, p. 234.
10. Boxer, op. cit., p. 273.
11. Onslow Burrish, *Batavia Illustrata*, London 1728, Vol. II, p. 252.
12. Wilson, *Anglo-Dutch Commerce*, op. cit., pp. 16–17.
13. R. Fell, *A Tour through the Batavian Republic during the latter part of the year 1800*, London 1801, pp. 359–60.
14. Cornelius Cayley, Junior, *A Tour through Holland, Flanders and part of France*, Leeds 1777, 2nd ed., pp. 7–8.
15. Ibid., p. 13.

16. See K. W. Swart, *Sale of Offices in the Seventeenth Century*, The Hague 1949, p. 68 and p. 77.
17. Van Bath, op. cit., p. 616.
18. See Thomas Bowdler, *Letters written in Holland in the months of September and October, 1787*, London 1788, passim, part. pp. 9, 25, 45 and 155.
19. Fell, op. cit., p. 282.

5. *The Kingdom of the Netherlands*

1. Quoted in Yves Schmitz, *Guillaume Ier. et la Belgique*, Paris 1945.
2. See Huggett, op. cit., pp. 19 23.
3. Edmundson, op. cit., p. 406 and J. C. Boogman, 'The Dutch Crisis in the Eighteen-Forties', J. S. Bromley and E. H. Kossmann, *Britain and the Netherlands*, London 1960, p. 197.
4. See Gerlof D. Homan, 'Catholic Emancipation in the Netherlands', *Catholic Historical Review*, July 1966, Washington D.C., pp. 201–3.
5. Gerlof D. Homan, 'Constitutional Reform in the Netherlands in 1848', *The Historian*, Allentown, Penn., May 1966, p. 421.
6. L. Girard, 'Transport', H. J. Habbakuk and M. Postan (eds), *The Cambridge Economic History of Europe*, Vol. VI, Cambridge 1965, p. 236.
7. Richard M. Westebbe, 'The Iron Age in the Netherlands', *Explorations in Entrepreneurial History*, Vol. IX, No. 3, Cambridge, Mass. 1957, p. 175.
8. See H. Bavinck, *Mental, Religious and Social Forces, A General View of the Netherlands*, No. XVII, The Hague 1915, p. 15.
9. *Digest of the Netherlands, Constitutional Aspects*, The Hague, 4th ed. 1966, p. 58.
10. Johan Goudsblom, *Dutch Society*, New York 1967, p. 84.
11. For details see M. M. Lourens, 'Labour in the Netherlands', Batholomew Landheer (ed.), *The Netherlands*, op. cit., p. 199.
12 Amry Vandenbosch, *Dutch Foreign Policy since 1815, A Study in Small Power Politics*, The Hague 1959, p. 56 and passim for a comprehensive survey of Dutch foreign policy since 1815.
13. Ibid., p. 4.
14. Ibid., p. 57.
15. For the wartime story see Werner Warmbrunn, *The Dutch under German Occupation, 1940–1945*, Stanford and London 1963 and Louis de Jong, *Het Koninkrijk der Nederlanden in de Tweede Wereldoorlog*, The Hague, 3 vols, 1969–70, passim.

## 6. Changes in Society

1. Goudsblom, op. cit., p. 44.
2. Editorial addresses: 71 Fleet Street, London, EC4, and Antwon van Zuilen, United Dutch Publishing Companies Inc., 55, West 42nd Street, New York, NY 10036.
3. *Endeavour*, No. 55, December 1969, p. 5.
4. *The Times*, June 27, 1967.
5. *Assistance given to Unmarried Mothers and their Children in the Netherlands*, Rijswijk, May 1965, p. 2 (typewritten).
6. See *Endeavour*, No. 55, Amsterdam, August 1969, p. 1, and P. E. Treffers, 'Abortion in Amsterdam', *Population Studies, A Journal of Demography*, Part 3, Vol. 20, London 1967, pp. 295–311.
7. See *Endeavour*, Amsterdam, No. 50, May 1968, pp. 1–2, and H Pathius and J. van der Spek, *The Netherlands, Work and Prosperity*, 2nd edn, 1967, pp. 21–2.
8. L. B. van Ommen, *Cultural Aspects of Welfare Policy*, Rijswijk 1969, p. 44.
9. *Endeavour*, Amsterdam, No. 53, February 1969, pp. 1–3.
10. For a survey of smoking and drinking habits, see Ivan Gadourek, 'Drinking and Smoking Habits and Feeling of Well-being', *Sociologia Neerlandica*, Vol. 3, No. 1, 1965–6, Assen, pp. 28–44.
11. Clark, *The Birth of the Dutch Republic*, op. cit., p. 19.
12. J. H. Huizinga, 'Holland Revisited', *Delta*, autumn 1966, p. 84.
13. Ibid., p. 84.
14. Goudsblom, op. cit., p. 29.
15. Duke de Baena, *The Dutch Puzzle*, The Hague 1968, p. 118.
16. E. W. Hofstee, 'Labour at the Cross roads', *Sociologia Neerlandica*, Assen, Vol. 4, No. 2, 1968, p. 114.
17. 'The Faults of the Dutch', a poll, *Delta*, winter 1964–5, p. 17.
18. Otto J. de Jong, 'Dutch Protestantism', *Delta*, Vol. 9, No. 4, winter 1966–7, p. 5.
19. Arend Lijphart, *The Politics of Accommodation, Pluralism and Democracy in the Netherlands*, Berkeley and Los Angeles 1968, p. 19.
20. *Statistisch Zakboek '69*, The Hague 1969, p. 193.
21. For these facts about the formation of the movement, I am indebted to Lucas van der Land, 'Provo is as Provo Does; A General Introduction', in an excellent special issue of *Delta*, autumn 1967, on the Provo movement.
22. *Financial Times*, June 16, 1966.
23. *The Times*, June 17, 1966.
24. Ibid.,

25. See Report of conference on 'Refractory Amsterdam', organised by the Netherlands Sociological Society, *Sociologia Neerlandica*, Assen, Vol. IV, No. 1, 1966–7, pp. 81–4.
26. See Huggett, op. cit., pp. 151–2.
27. *The Times*, April 29, 1967.


7. *The Churches*

1. The most comprehensive account in English is contained in Lijphart, op. cit., passim.
2. William Petersen, 'Fertility Trends and Population Policy', *Sociologia Neerlandica*, Vo. 3, No. 2, Assen, 1966, pp. 8–9.
3. Ibid., p. 11.
4 *New York Times*, January 16, 1967, and *The Times* (London), January 21, 1970.
5. John Horgan, 'The Church in Holland', *The Dublin Review*, London, No. 512, summer 1967, p. 124.
6. M. Kok, *The Old Catholic Church of the Netherlands*, Utrecht 1948, p. 10.
7. Conference by Cardinal Alfrink at the Villa Nova University, June 26, 1969, Utrecht, p. 5 (typewritten).
8. Ibid., p. 5.
9. *New York Times*, August 9, 1967.
10. Conference by Alfrink, op. cit., p. 10.
11. Horgan, op. cit., p. 124.
12. See John T. McNeill, *The History and Character of Calvinism*, New York 1954, pp. 368–9.


8. *Mass Media and Culture*

1. For a full description of the system, see H. Schaafsma, 'Mirror of a Pillarised Society: Broadcasting in the Netherlands', *Delta*, Vol. IV, No. 4, winter 1966–7, passim.
2. Among Common Market countries, the Netherlands ranks second after Germany for the number of television sets in use: 200 per 1,000 of the population in 1967. Comparative figures for Britain were 259 and for the United States 376. Source: *The Common Market and the Common Man*, European Communities, Press and Information Service, Brussels 1969, p. 21.
3. *Daily Telegraph*, March 5, 1965.
4. *Financial Times*, March 4, 1965.
5. *Le Monde*, February 15, 1968.
6. Kenneth E. Olson, *The History Makers, The press of Europe from its Beginnings through 1965*, Baton Rouge 1966, p. 152.

7. See G. W. Marsman, 'De Katholieke Dagbladpers', *Sociologisch Perspectief*, Assen, n.d., pp. 185–97, and p. 223 for details of mergers of Catholic papers.
8. *Guardian*, November 25, 1967.
9. *Neue Zürcher Zeitung*, May 17, 1968.
10. *The Times*, May 8, 1965.
11. See Maarten Rooij, 'The Daily Press in the Netherlands since 1945', *Gazette, International Journal of the Science of the Press*, Leiden, Vol. III, Nos. 1–2, 1957, p. 1.
12. See 'Increased Leisure–What use is made of it', *Benelux Press Tour, May 16–20, 1966*, Rijswijk, n.d., p. 12.
13. John Percival, 'Double Dutch in Dance', *The Times*, April 9, 1969.
14. For an excellent survey of modern trends in Dutch art, see *Delta*, winter 1969–70; and for an equally good number on design, see *Delta*, spring 1969.
15. Heeroma, op. cit., p. 15.
16. Theodoor Weevers, *Poetry of the Netherlands in its European Context, 1170–1930*, London 1960, p. 3.
17. See Gerald K. Schippers, 'Bestsellers and Blasphemy: A Letter from Amsterdam', *Delta*, spring–summer 1967, pp. 55–63.

## 9. The Political Parties

1. *Nieuwe Rotterdamse Courant*, February 16, 1967, and *Statistisch Zakboek, '69*, op. cit., p. 41.
2. Stanley Henig and John Pinder (eds), *European Political Parties*, London 1969, p. 256.
3. *Christian Science Monitor*, April 4, 1970, *The Times*, March 20, 1970, and *Frankfurter Allgemeine Zeitung*, March 20, 1970.
4. *New York Times*, February 15, 1967.
5. There is a summary of the political parties' programmes in *Digest of the Kingdom of the Netherlands, Constitutional Organisation*, The Hague, 4th edn, 1966, pp. 68–76.
6. *The Times*, February 7, 1967.
7. Henig and Pinder, op. cit., pp. 269–70.
8. *Le Monde*, November 15, 1967.
9. *Guardian*, March 10, 1969.
10. See Frits Kool, *Communism in Holland: A Study in Futility*, Problems of Communism, United States Information Agency, Vol. IX, No.5, September–October 1960, p. 18.
11. Radio Free Europe Research, April 13, 1966.
12. Ibid., August 6, 1969.

I

13. *Observer*, Foreign News Service, June 26, 1968.
14. *The Times*, February 17, 1967.


*10. System of Government*

1. For a brief summary of the voting system, see *Digest of the Kingdom of the Netherlands, Constitutional Organisation*, op. cit., pp. 53–5, and for more details E. van Raalte, *The Parliament of the Kingdom of the Netherlands*, London/The Hague 1959.
2. Van Raalte, op. cit., p. 105.
3. Hans Daalder, *Parties and Politics in the Netherlands*, The Hague, n.d., p. 10 (typewritten).
4. Quoted in Daalder, op. cit., p. 10 from C. W. de Vries (ed.), *Bijdrage Tot de Herziening der Grondwet*, 1948, p. 19.
5. See M. Dogan and M. Scheffer-van der Veen, 'Le Personnel Ministériel hollandais, 1848–1958', *L'Année Sociologique*, Paris 1957–8, p. 100.
6. Ibid., pp. 98–9.
7. For the place of women in politics, see J. C. Shokking, *De Vrouw in de Nederlandse Politiek*, Assen, n.d.
8. A. Hoogerwerf, 'Latent Socio-Political Issues in the Netherlands', *Sociologia Neerlandica*, Assen, Vol. II, No. 2, summer 1965, p. 174.
9. *Financial Times*, February 14, 1967.
10. Daalder, op. cit., p. 17.


*11. Crown and Constitution*

1. *The Times*, October 27, 1965.
2. *Endeavour*, Amsterdam, No. 39, 1965, p. 4.
3. *The Times*, March 9, 1966.
4. Quoted in *Le Monde*, September 14, 1969.
5. W. L. Brugsma, 'Party System Crumbling, The Netherlands, A Special Report', *The Times*, December 5, 1968.
6. *Observer*, Foreign News Service, June 20, 1969.
7. The text may be studied in A. J. Peasley, *Constitutions of Nations*, 2nd edn, The Hague 1956, 3 vols. The classic work is P. J. Oud, *Het Constitutionele Recht van het Kroninkrijk der Nederlanden*, Zwolle 1947.
8. See Huggett, op. cit., pp. 113–14.
9. *Digest of the Kingdom of the Netherlands, Constitutional Organisation*, op. cit., p. 80.
10. See Hans Daalder, *The Netherlands: Opposition in a Segmented Society*, Robert A. Dahl (ed.), *Political Oppositions in Western Democracies*, Yale University Press 1966, pp. 195–6.

11. Robert L. Morlan, 'Cabinet Government at the Municipal Level: The Dutch Experience', *Western Political Quarterly*, Salt Lake City, Vol. xvii, No. 2, June 1964, p. 323.
12. Ibid., p. 324.
13. For further details see *Criminal Law and the Treatment of Offenders*, Ministry of Justice, The Hague, n.d. passim (typewritten).

*12. Education*

1. W. Voster, 'The Structure of Education in the Netherlands', *Planning and Development in the Netherlands*, Vol. iii, Nos. 1–2, Assen, p. 2.
2. Goudsblom, op. cit., p. 103.
3. See R. Ruiter, 'Education and Manpower Forecasts', *Planning and Development in the Netherlands*, op. cit., pp. 175–80.
4. Goudsblom, op. cit., p. 97.
5. Ruiter, op. cit., p. 99.
6. F. H. Molyneux and G. Linker, 'Schools in Transition—The Dutch Approach', *Trends in Education*, London, January 1970, p. 49.
7. For further details of technical training, see F. J. W. Farius, *Vocational Training in the Netherlands*, distributed by Ministry of Education and Science, The Hague, n.d., passim.
8. Hofstee, op. cit., p. 108.
9. W. Voster, 'Innovation of Education', *Planning and Development in the Netherlands*, op. cit., p. 18.
10. See Huggett, op. cit., p. 183.
11. *Digest of the Kingdom of the Netherlands, Education, Arts and Sciences*, The Hague, n.d., p. 18.
12. *Summary of the Post-Primary Education Act in the Netherlands*, Ministry of Education and Science, The Hague 1968, p. 10.
13. H. Veldkamp, 'The Planning of Non-University Education', *Planning and Development in the Netherlands*, op. cit., p. 33.
14. See Daniel de Lange, 'Dutch Catholicism', *Delta*, Vol. ix, No. 4, winter 1966–7, p. 26.
15. Ruiter, op. cit., p. 112.
16. F. P. Thomassen, 'University Education in the Netherlands', *Higher Education and Research in the Netherlands*, The Hague, Vol. xiii, No. 2, 1969, to whom I am indebted for many of the facts on university education.
17. *The Times*, June 13, 1969.
18. Thomassen, op. cit., p. 13.
19. For further details see *Summary of the Draft Bill Reform Universities Administration 1970*, The Hague 1969, passim.

*13. Social Welfare*

1. Cayley, op. cit., p. 32.
2. See *The Common Market and the Common Man*, op. cit., p. 28.
3. Ibid., p. 29.
4. Full details may be studied in *Digest of the Kingdom of the Netherlands, Social Aspects*, op. cit., pp. 5–28, and Pathius and van der Spek, op. cit., pp. 44–55.
5. *State Supervision of Public Health in the Netherlands*, The Hague 1969, p. 3.
6. See *Digest of the Kingdom of the Netherlands, Social Aspects*, op. cit., pp. 73–4.
7. A. Querido, *The Development of Socio-Medical Care in the Netherlands*, London 1968, p. 101.
8. *Mental Health in the Netherlands*, The Hague, n.d., p. 34.
9. *Social Employment in the Netherlands*, The Hague, n.d., p. 5.
10. See *Endeavour*, op. cit., No. 51, August 1968, pp. 13–15.
11. Cf. *Overijssel Family Re-adaptation*, Hardenberg 1967, passim (typewritten).
12. H. J. P. F. Goedmakers, 'Care for the Aged in the Netherlands', address given at the opening of Congress on Security for the Aged in Brussels, October 21–3, 1965, Rijswijk, n.d., p. 1.
13. Ibid., p. 5.
14. *Digest of the Kingdom of the Netherlands, Economy*, op. cit., p. 109.
15. See *Repatriation*, Rijswijk 1965, pp. 1–5 (typewritten).
16. Ibid., pp. 6–10.
17. J. M. M. van Amersfoorts, *Surinamese Immigrants in the Netherlands*, The Hague 1969, p. 51.
18. Ibid., p. 48.
19. See 'Adaptation and Integration of the Migrant Worker and his Family', *Synthesis Report prepared for Sixth Conference of ministers responsible for Family Affairs* (Palermo) 1964, Italian Ministry of Labour and Social Security, pp. 19 and 24.
20. B. P. Hofstede, 'Those Who Went and those Who Stayed: Dutch Post-War Overseas Emigration', *Delta*, spring–summer 1967, p. 54.

*14. The Economy*

1. P. S. Gerbrandy, *Indonesia*, London 1950, p. 73.
2. For details see S. I. P. van Campen, *The Quest for Security*, The Hague 1958, Appendix 5, pp. 205–18.
3. See J. Zijlstra, 'Recipe for Growth', *The Times Supplement* on The Netherlands, December 5, 1968, p. III.

4. *Digest, Economy*, p. 16.
5. *European Community*, Brussels, February 1970, pp. 8 and 9.
6. Ibid., p. 8.
7. *The Times*, January 21, 1970—Report of United States Department of Labor, Bureau of Labor Statistics.
8. *Central Economic Plan 1970*, The Hague, n.d., p. 2 (typewritten).
9. *Financial Times Supplement* on the Netherlands, October 27, 1969, p. 11.
10. See Louis Metzemaekers, 'Dominant Giants', *The Times Supplement*, op. cit., p. v.
11. See John L. Enos, 'The Mighty Adversaries', *Entrepreneurial History*, Vol. x, Nos. 3–4, Harvard University 1958, p. 140.
12. Barton William-Powlett, 'The Trans-National Companies, No. 3, Philips', *The Times*, January 7, 1970.
13. J. E. Hartshorn, *Oil Companies and Governments*, London 1967, p. 261.
14. Metzemaekers, *Dominant Giants*, op. cit.
15. *The Times*, April 9, 1970.
16. For a general survey of industry see *Digest, Economy*, op. cit., pp. 29–41.
17. See *Le Monde*, September 11, 1968, and *Digest Economy*, p. 37 for details.
18. *Le Monde*, October 29, 1968.
19. See J. Kymmell, 'Rich in People', *The Times Supplement* on the Netherlands, op. cit., p. 3, and *International Herald Tribune*, December 11, 1969.
20. *Digest, Economy*, op. cit., p. 80. Of the 150 million tons which passed through Dutch ports in 1965, 123 million tons were handled in Rotterdam and over 14 million tons in Amsterdam.
21. Hartshorn, op. cit., p. 92.
22. *Christian Science Monitor*, December 1, 1969.
23. *Digest, Economy*, p. 108.
24. *Common Market and Common Man*, op. cit., p. 21.
25. *Housing in the Netherlands*, The Hague 1966, p. 21.
26. *Pathius and van der Spek*, op. cit., p. 69.
27. *Digest, Economy*, op. cit., p. 109.
28. For a comprehensive survey of modern architecture, see R. Blijstra, *Dutch Architecture after 1900*, Amsterdam 1966, passim.
29. *Some data on house building in the Netherlands*, The Hague 1969, Table F.
30. For the full story, see J. S. Lingsma, *Holland and the Delta Plan*, Rotterdam–The Hague 1963, passim.
31. *The Delta Project*, The Hague, March 1967, p. 7.

32. See John Lambert, 'Holland's Fight to Dam Disaster', *Sunday Times*, May 25, 1969.
33. *The Zuider Zee Works*, The Hague 1967, p. 23.
34. For the present state of Dutch thought in this field, see second Report on *Physical Planning in the Netherlands*, condensed edn, The Hague 1966, 2 vols.
35. See Burke, op. cit., pp. 64–5, and for recent developments, R. Blijstra, *Town Planning in the Netherlands since 1900*, Amsterdam, n.d.
36. Peter Hall, *The World Cities*, London 1966, p. 121.
37. Ibid., p. 121.
38. See second report on *Physical Planning*, op. cit., part 1, p. 44.
39. See Louis Metzemaekers, 'The EEC. Still a Boon to Farmers', *Financial Times Supplement*, op. cit., p. 18.
40. *Digest, Economy*, p. 59.
41. Ibid., pp. 59 and 61.
42. Metzemaekers, 'The EEC. Still a Boon to Farmers', op. cit.
43. *Digest, Economy*, pp. 72–5 for more details.
44. See 'Agricultural Extension in the Netherlands', *Sociologia Neerlandica*, Vol. II, No. 2, summer 1965, passim.
45. For full details see *The Co-operative Movement in the Netherlands*, The Hague 1964.
46. *Common Market and the Common Man*, op. cit., p. 4.
47. *Guardian*, January 22, 1966.
48. C. Westrate, *Economic Policy and Practice: The Netherlands, 1950–1957*, Leiden 1959, p. 179.
49. Ibid., p. 182.
50. Radio Free Europe Research, April 13, 1966.
51. P. S. Pels, 'Organised Industry and Planning in the Netherlands', *International Labour Review*, Geneva, Vol. 94, No. 3, September 1966, p. 279.
52. *Common Market and the Common Man*, p. 22.
53. J. Bosma, 'Youth Makes its Demands', *The Times Supplement* on the Netherlands, op· cit., p. v.
54. *Financial Times*, May 28, 1968.
55. Ibid., September 18, 1968.
56. *Le Monde*, February 26, 1969.
57. *Financial Times*, February 25, 1969.

*15. Foreign Policy and Defence*

1. See van Campen, *The Quest for Security; some Aspects of Netherlands Foreign Policy, 1945–50*, The Hague 1958, pp. 150–1 (footnote).

2. Vandenbosch, op. cit., p. 34.
3. Ibid., pp. 29–30.
4. Ibid., p. 41.
5. Quoted in van Campen, op. cit., p. 150 (footnote).
6. Warmbrunn, op. cit., p. 5.
7. There is still some controversy over whether this was due to faulty German communications or to a deliberate act of terrorism. Cf. ibid., pp. 9–10 (footnote).
8. A graphic account of life in Westerbork by Philip Mechanicus, *Waiting for Death*, London, was published posthumously.
9. See van Campen, op. cit., pp. 57–88.
10. Quoted in van Campen, op. cit., p. 14.
11. Robert W. Russell, 'The Atlantic Alliance in Dutch Foreign Policy', *Internationale Spectator*, The Hague–Brussels, July 1969, p. 1197.
12. J. M. A. H. Luns, Foreword to special issue of *Internationale Spectator*, 'European and Atlantic Co-operation, The Dutch Attitude', op. cit., April 1965, p. 434.
13. J. L. Heldring, *Europe a "Greater Holland"?* in ibid., p. 544.
14. For the development of Benelux, see Huggett, op. cit., pp. 246–252.
15. *Evening Standard*, September 15, 1969.
16. Russell, op. cit., p. 1207.
17. Ibid.
18. *Le Monde*, December 29, 1968.
19. *The Times*, June 16, 1966.
20. *Financial Times*, June 30, 1967.
21. *Wapenbeheersing en wapenbeperking, etc.*, The Hague, n.d., p. 6.
22. Ibid., pp. 8–9.
23. *Europa Year Book*, 1969, Vol. I, London, p. 897.

16. *Loss of an Empire*

1. Leslie H. Palmier, *Indonesia*, London 1965, p. 42.
2. Quoted in K. M. Panikkar, *Asia and Western Dominance*, London 1961, fifth imp., p. 49.
3. Brian Harrison, *South-East Asia, A Short History*, London 1954, p. 113.
4. J. M. van der Kroef, *Indonesia in the Modern World*, Bandung 1954, part I, p. 4.
5. See Huggett, op. cit., pp. 63–5.
6. Palmer, *Indonesia*, op. cit., p. 69.
7. Van der Kroef, op. cit., pp. 6–7.

8. Multatuli, *Max Havelaar* (trans. W. Siebenhaar), New York and London 1927, p. 56.
9. Quoted in Victor Purcell, *The Revolution in South-East Asia*, London 1962, p. 123.
10. See Bruce Grant, *Indonesia*, London and New York 1964, pp. 40–1.
11. See Van der Kroef, op. cit., p. 12; and Palmier, *Indonesia*, op. cit., pp. 96–7.
12. Grant, op. cit., p. 19.
13. Panikkar, op. cit., p. 92.
14. Harrison, op. cit., p. 216.
15. Hugh Tinker, *Ballot Box and Bayonet*, London, New York and Toronto 1964, p. 10.
16. Grant, op. cit., pp. 17–18
17. Ibid., p. 17.
18. Henri Baudet, "The Netherlands after loss of Empire", *Journal of Contemporary History*, London, Vol. IV, No. 1, January 1969, pp. 132–3.
19. P. S. Gerbrandy, *Indonesia*, London 1950, p. 90.
20. Van der Kroef, op. cit., p. 20.
21. Gerbrandy, op. cit., p. 72.
22. Ibid., p. 100.
23. See Leslie H. Palmier, *Indonesia and the Dutch*, London 1962, p. 50.
24. See for example, Friedrich Weinreb, *Collaboratie en Verzet*, Meulenhoff, Amsterdam 1969.
25. Purcell, op. cit., p. 130.
26. Palmier, *Indonesia and the Dutch*, op. cit., p. 108.
27. Hartshorn, op. cit., p. 261.
28. See *Charter for the Kingdom of the Netherlands*, The Hague, n.d., passim and particularly p. 21.

*17. Prospect and Retrospect*

1. *The Times*, May 2, 1970.
2. Ibid., September 16, 1970.

# Bibliography

'Adaptation and Integration of the Migrant Worker and His Family', *Synthesis Report prepared for Sixth Conference of Ministers Responsible for Family Affairs* (Palermo) 1964, Italian Ministry of Labour and Social Security, n.d.

Aglionby, W., *The Present State of the United Provinces of the Low Countries*, London 1669.

'Agricultural Extension in the Netherlands', *Sociologia Neerlandica*, van Gorcum, Assen, Vol. II, No. 2, summer 1965.

Alfrink, Cardinal, *Conference at Villa Nova University, June 26, 1969*, Utrecht, n.d. (typewritten).

*A New Description of Holland and the rest of the United Provinces in General*, Anon., London 1701.

Ashley, Maurice, *England in the Seventeenth Century, 1603-1714, The Pelican History of England*, Vol. 6, Penguin Books, Harmondsworth 1952.

*Assistance given to Unmarried Mothers and their Children in the Netherlands*, Ministry of Cultural Affairs, Recreation and Social Welfare, Rijswijk 1965.

257

*A Trip to Holland, being a Description of the Country, People and Manners: as also some select Observations on Amsterdam,* London 1699.

Barbour, Violet, *Capitalism in Amsterdam in the Seventeenth Century,* Johns Hopkins University Studies in Historical and Political Science, Series LXVII, No. 1, The Johns Hopkins Press, Baltimore 1950.

Bartstra, J. S., *Vlootherstel en Legeraugmentatie, 1770–80,* van Gorcum, Assen 1952.

Baudet, Henri, 'The Netherlands after the Loss of Empire', *Journal of Contemporary History,* January 1969, Vol. 4, No. 1, Weidenfeld and Nicolson, London.

Bavinck, H., *Mental, Religious and Social Forces, A General View of the Netherlands,* No. XVII, The Netherlands Ministry of Agriculture, Industry and Commerce, The Hague 1915.

Blijstra, R., *Dutch Architecture after 1900,* P. N. van Kampen, Amsterdam 1966.

——— *Town-Planning in the Netherlands since 1900,* P. N. van Kampen, Amsterdam, n.d.

Bodenheimer, Susanne J., *Political Union: A Microcosm of European Politics, 1960–1966,* A. W. Sijthott, Leiden; Humanities Press, New York 1967.

Boeles, P. C. J. A., *Friesland tot de elfde eeuw,* Martinus Nijhoff, The Hague 1951.

Boogman, J. C., 'The Dutch Crisis in the Eighteen-Forties', J. S. Bromley and E. H. Kossmann, *Britain and the Netherlands, Papers delivered to the Oxford-Netherlands Historical Conference, 1959,* Chatto & Windus, London 1960.

Bowdler, Thomas, *Letters written in Holland in the Months of September and October, 1787,* London 1788.

Boxer, C. R., *The Dutch Seaborne Empire, 1600–1800,* Hutchinson, London; Knopf, New York 1965.

Bromley, J. S. and Kossmann, E. H., *Britain and the Netherlands in Europe and Asia, Papers delivered to the Oxford-Netherlands Historical Conference. 1959,* Chatto and Windus, London 1960; St. Martin's, New York 1968.

——— *Britain and the Netherlands, Papers delivered to the Anglo-Dutch Historical Conference, 1962,* J. B. Wolters, Groningen 1964.

Burke, Gerald L., *The Making of Dutch Towns, A Study in Urban Development from the Tenth to the Seventeenth Centuries,* Cleaver-Hume Press, London 1956.

Burkett, Jack, *Special Libraries and Documentation Centres in the Netherlands,* Pergamon, Oxford 1969.

Burrish, Onslow, *Batavia Illustrata,* London 1728, 2 vols.

Cayley, Cornelius, *A Tour through Holland, Flanders and Part of France*, Leeds 1777, 2nd edn.

*Central Economic Plan, 1970*, Press Service Department, Ministry of Economic Affairs, The Hague, n.d. (typewritten).

*Charter for the Kingdom of the Netherlands*, Vice-Prime Minister's Cabinet Department, The Hague, n.d.

Christensen, Aksel E., 'Dutch Trade to the Baltic about 1600', *Studies in the Sound Toll Register and Dutch Shipping Records*. Einar Munksgaard, Copenhagen; Martinus Nijhoff, The Hague 1941.

Clark, G. N. 'The Birth of the Dutch Republic', *The Raleigh Lectures on History, from the Proceedings of the British Academy*, Geoffrey Cumberlege, London 1946.

Clark, Sir George, *The Dutch Influence on the English Vocabulary*, Clarendon Press, Oxford 1935.

——— *War and Society in the Seventeenth Century*, University Press, Cambridge 1958.

Cole, W. A. and Deane, Phyllis, 'The Growth of National Income', H. J. Habakkuk and M. Postan (eds), *The Cambridge Economic History of Europe*, Vol. VI, University Press, Cambridge 1965.

*Common Market and the Common Man, The: Social Policy and Working and Living Conditions in the European Community*, European Communities, Press and Information Service, Brussels 1969.

*Community Development for Special Groups: particularly for Foreign Workers*, Ministry of Cultural Affairs, Recreation and Social Welfare, Rijswijk 1968.

*Community Development in the Netherlands*, Nederlands Instituut voor Maatschappelijke Opbouw, The Hague, n.d.

*Co-operative Movement in the Netherlands*, Nationale Coöperatieve Raad, The Hague 1964, 3rd imp.

Cornelisse, Suzanne, *The Dutch Royal Family*, De Bezige Bij, Amsterdam, n.d.

*Criminal Law and the Treatment of Offenders*, Ministry of Justice, The Hague, n.d. (typewritten).

Daalder, Hans, *Parties and Politics in the Netherlands*, Netherlands Universities Foundation for International Co-operation, The Hague, n.d. (typewritten).

——— 'The Netherlands: Opposition in a Segmented Society', Robert A. Dahl (ed), *Political Oppositions in Western Democracies*, Yale University Press 1966.

De Baena, Duke, *The Dutch Puzzle*, L. J. C. Boucher, The Hague 1968, 5th edn.

De Jong, Louis, *Het Koninkrijk der Nederlanden in de Tweede Wereldoorlog*, Martinus Nijhoff, The Hague 1969–70, 3 vols.

De Jong, Otto J. 'Protestantism', *Delta*, Amsterdam 1966–7.

De la Court, Piet, *The True Interest and Political Maxims of the Republick of Holland and West Friesland*, London 1702.

De Lange, Daniel, 'Dutch Catholicism', *Delta*, Amsterdam 1966–7.

De Lettenhove, Baron Kervyn, *Les Huguenots et Les Gueux*, Bruges 1883–5, 6 vols.

*Delta, A Review of Arts, Life and Thought in the Netherlands*, Amsterdam, quarterly.

*Delta Project*, Ministry of Transport, The Hague 1967.

*Digest of the Kingdom of the Netherlands*, Government Printing Office, The Hague, 5 vols.

*Documentation in the Field of Cultural Affairs, Recreation and Social Welfare*, Ministry of Cultural Affairs, Recreation and Social Welfare, Rijswijk 1968, 7th edn.

Dogan, M. and Scheffer-van der Veen, M., 'Le personnel ministériel hollandais, 1848–1958', *L'Année Sociologique*, Paris 1957–8.

East, W. G. and Spate, O. H. K., *The Changing Map of Asia, A Political Geography*, Methuen, London 1960; Barnes and Noble, New York 1970, 5th edn.

Edmundson, George, *History of Holland*, Cambridge University Press, Cambridge 1922.

*Educational Care of the Handicapped Child*, Ministry of Education and Science, The Hague 1969.

Elliott, J. H., *Imperial Spain, 1469–1716*, Edward Arnold, London; St. Martin's, New York 1963.

*Endeavour, Information about Women in the Netherlands*, Amsterdam, monthly.

Enos, John L., 'The Mighty Adversaries: Standard Oil Company (New Jersey) and Royal Dutch-Shell', *Explorations in Entrepreneurial History*, Research Centre in Entrepreneurial History, Harvard University, Mass. 1958.

*Europa Year Book, The*, Europa Publishing Ltd, London 1969.

Eyck, F. Gunther, *The Benelux Countries, An Historical Survey*, An Anvil Original, No. 44, D. van Nostrand Co. Inc., New Jersey 1959.

Fabius, F. J. W., *Vocational Training in the Netherlands*, distributed by the Ministry of Education and Science, The Hague, n.d.

'Faults of the Dutch, The, a Poll', *Delta*, Amsterdam 1964–5.

Fell, R., *A Tour through the Batavia Republic during the latter part of the year 1800*, London 1801.

Gadourek, Ivan, 'Drinking and Smoking Habits and Feeling of Well-Being', *Sociologia Neerlandica*, van Gorcum, Assen, Vol. III, No. 1, 1965–6.

Gastmann, Albert L., *The Politics of Surinam and the Netherlands Antilles*, University of Puerto Rico, Puerto Rico.

Gerbrandy, P. S., *Indonesia*, Hutchinson, London 1950.

Gerretson, F. C., *History of the Royal Dutch*, E. J. Brill, Leiden 1953, 4 vols.

Geurts, P. A. M., *De Nederlandse Opstand in de Pamfletten, 1566–1584*, Dekker and Van de Vegt, Nijmegen-Utrecht 1956.

Geyl, Pieter, *The Netherlands in the Seventeenth Century, 1609–1648*, Benn, London; rev. edn., Barnes and Noble, New York 1961.

—————— *The Revolt of the Netherlands, 1555–1609*, Benn, London; 2nd edn., Barnes and Noble, New York 1958.

Girard, L., 'Transport', H. J. Habbakuk and M. Postan (eds), *The Cambridge Economic History of Europe*, Vol. VI, Cambridge University Press 1965.

Goedmakers, H. J. P. F., 'Care for the Aged in the Netherlands', *Address given to the opening of Congress on Security for the Aged in Brussels, October 21 to 23, 1965*, Ministry of Cultural Affairs, Recreation and Social Welfare, Rijswijk, n.d.

Goudsblom, Johan, *Dutch Society*, Random House, New York 1967.

Grant, Bruce, *Indonesia*, Melbourne University Press, Cambridge University Press, London and New York 1964.

Grimeston, E., *A Generall Historie of the Netherlands continued into this present yeare of Our Lord 1608, out of the best authorities that have written of that subject*, London 1608.

Guicchardini, Lodovico, *The description of the Low Countreys and of the Provinces thereof*, London 1593.

Hall, Peter, *The World Cities*, World University Library, Weidenfeld and Nicolson, London; McGraw Hill, New York 1966.

Harrison, Brian, *South-East Asia, A Short History*, 3rd edn., St. Martin's, New York 1966.

Hartshorn, J. E. *Politics and World Oil Economics*, rev. edn., Praeger, New York 1967.

Heeroma, K. H., 'The Dutch Language in the World', *Higher Education and Research in the Netherlands*, Netherlands Universities Foundation for International Co-operation, The Hague, Vol. XI, No. 2, 1967.

Hendriks, G., *Social Dynamics of the Family in a Changing Society*, Ministry of Cultural Affairs, Recreation and Social Welfare, Rijswijk 1968.

Henig, Stanley and Pinder, John (eds), *European Political Parties*, *Political and Economic Planning*, Allen and Unwin, London; Praeger, New York 1969.

Hofstede, B. P., 'Those who went and those who stayed: Dutch Post-war Overseas Emigration', *Delta*, spring-summer 1967
—— *Thwarted Exodus, Post-War Overseas Migration from the Netherlands*, Martinus Nijhoff, The Hague 1964.

Hofstee, E. W., 'Labour at the Crossroads', *Sociologia Neerlandica*, van Gorcum, Assen, Vol. IV, No. 2, autumn 1968.

Homan, Gerlof D., 'Catholic Emancipation in the Netherlands', *The Catholic Historical Review*, The Catholic University of America, Washington, D.C., Vol. III, No. 2, July 1966.
—— 'Constitutional Reform in the Netherlands in 1848', *The Historian, A Journal of History*, Phi Alpha Theta, Allentown, Penn., Vol. XXVIII, No. 3, May 1966.

Hoogerwerf, A., 'Latent Socio-Political Issues in the Netherlands' *Sociologia Neerlandica*, van Gorcum, Assen, Vol. II, No. 2, summer, 1965.

Horgan, John, 'The Church in Holland', *The Dublin Review*, London, No. 512, summer 1967.

*Housing in the Netherlands*, Ministry of Housing and Physical Planning, The Hague 1966.

Huggett, Frank E., *Modern Belgium*, Pall Mall, London; Praeger, New York 1969.

Huizinga, J. H., 'Holland Revisited', *Delta*, Amsterdam, 1966.

Huxley, Aldous, 'Views of Holland', *Along the Road, Notes and Essays of a Tourist*, Chatto and Windus, London 1925.

'Increased Leisure—What Use is Made of It?', *Benelux Press Tour, May 16–20, 1966*, Ministry of Culture, Recreation and Social Welfare, Rijswijk, n.d.

*International Spectator*, Tijdschrift voor Internationale Politiek, The Hague, Brussels, Special Issue on 'European and Atlantic Co-operation. The Dutch Attitude', April 1965.

Ishwaran, *Family Life in the Netherlans*, van Keulen, The Hague, n.d.

Kerling, Nelly Johanna, *Commercial Relations of Holland and Zeeland with England from the late 13th century to the close of the Middle Ages*, E. J. Brill, Leiden 1954.

Kok, M., *The Old Catholic Church of the Netherlands*, Utrecht 1948.

Kool, Fritz, *Communism in Holland: A Study in Futility. Problems of Communism*, United States Information Agency, Washington, Vol. IX, No. 5, September-October 1960.

Krahn, Cornelius, *Dutch Anabaptism: Origin, Spread, Life and Thought*, Martinus Nijhoff, The Hague.

Krul, W. F. J. M., *Environmental Health in the Netherlands*, Ministry of Social Affairs and Public Health, The Hague 1968.

Landheer, Bartholomew (ed), *The Netherlands*, University of California Press, Berkeley and Los Angeles 1943.

Leeghwater, J. A., *Haarlemmer-Meer-Boeck*, Amsterdam 1710.

Ligtvoet, J. C., 'Education in the Netherlands', *A General View of the Netherlands*, Ministry of Agriculture, Industry and Commerce, The Hague, No. xv, 1915.

Lijphart, Arend, *The Politics of Accommodation, Pluralism and Democracy in the Netherlands*, University of California Press, Berkeley and Los Angeles 1968.

Lingsma, J. S., *Holland and the Delta Plan*, Nijgh and van Ditmar, Rotterdam, The Hague 1963.

Lisk, Jill, *The Struggle for Supremacy in the Baltic, 1600–1725*, University of London Press, London; Funk and Wagnalls, New York 1967.

Marsman, G. W., 'De Katholieke Dagbladpers', *Sociologisch Perspectief*, van Gorcum, Assen, n.d.

McNeill, John, *The History and Character of Calvinism*, Oxford University Press, New York 1954.

Mechanicus, Philip, *Waiting for Death*, Calder and Boyars, London, Hawthorn Books, New York 1968.

*Mental Health in the Netherlands*, Ministry of Social Affairs and Public Health, The Hague, n.d.

Molyneux, F. H. and Linker, G., 'Schools in Transition—the Dutch Approach', *Trends in Education, No. 17*, Department of Education and Science, London, January 1970.

Mooyman, J. A., *The Care of the Homeless in the Netherlands*, Ministry of Cultural Affairs, Recreation and Social Welfare, October 1965 (typewritten).

Morlan, Robert L., 'Cabinet Government at the Municipal Level: The Dutch Experience', *Western Political Quarterly*, University of Utah, Salt Lake City, Vol. xvii, No. 2, June 1964.

Motley, John *The Rise of the Dutch Republic*, George Routledge & Son, London and New York 1882.

Multatuli, *Max Havelaar* (trans. W. Siebenhaar), Alfred A. Knopf, New York and London 1927.

Muntendam, P., *Public Health in the Netherlands*, Ministry of Social Affairs and Public Health, The Hague 1968.

*Nederlandse Hervormde Kerk, The Bible Speaks Again* (trans. A. Mackie), S.C.M. Press, London 1969.

'Netherlands, The', *Financial Times Supplement*, October 27, 1969.

'Netherlands, The, A Special Report', *The Times*, London, December 5, 1968.

Nobbs, Douglas, *Theocracy and Toleration, A Study of Disputes in Dutch Calvinism from 1600 to 1650*, Cambridge University Press 1938.

Nuis, A., 'Amsterdam Provoked', *Delta*, Amsterdam, autumn 1967.

Olson, Kenneth E., *The History Makers, The Press of Europe from its Beginnings through 1965*, Louisiana State University Press, Baton Rouge 1966.

Oud, P. J., *Het Constitutioneel Recht van het Koninkrijk der Nederlanden*, Tjeenk Willink, Zwolle 1947, 2 vols.

*Overijssel Family Re-Adaptation*, Hardenberg 1967 (typewritten).

Palmier, Leslie H., *Indonesia*, Thames and Hudson, London 1965; Walker, New York 1966.

—— *Indonesia and the Dutch*, Institute of Race Relations, Oxford University Press, London 1962.

Panikkar, K. M., *Asia and Western Dominance, A Survey of the Vasco da Gama Epoch of Asian History, 1498–1945*, Allen and Unwin, London; Hillary House, New York, rev. edn., 1959.

Pathius, H. and van der Spek, J., *The Netherlands, Work and Prosperity*, 1967, 2nd edn.

Pels, P. S., 'Organised Industry and Planning in the Netherlands', *International Labour Review*, International Labour Office, Geneva, Vol. 94, No. 3, September 1966.

Petersen, William, 'Fertility Trends and Population Policy: Some Comments on the van Heek-Hofstee Debate', *Sociologia Neerlandica*, van Gorcum, Assen, Vol. III, No. 2, 1966.

Pliny, *Natural History* (trans. H. Rackham), The Loeb Classical Library, Heinemann 1945.

Purcell, Victor, *The Revolution in South East Asia*, Thames and Hudson, London 1962.

Querido, A., *The Development of Socio-Medical Care in the Netherlands*, Routledge and Kegan Paul, London; Humanities Press, New York 1969.

'Refractory Amsterdam', Report of Conference organised by the Netherlands Sociological Society, *Sociologia Neerlandica*, van Gorcum, Assen, Vol. IV, No. 1, 1966–7.

Renier, G. J., *The Dutch Nation, An Historical Study*, Allen and Unwin, London 1944.

*Repatriation*, Ministry of Cultural Affairs, Recreation and Social Welfare, Rijswijk, The Hague 1965 (typewritten).

Rooij, Maarten, 'The Daily Press in the Netherlands since 1945', *Gazette. International Journal of the Science of the Press*, Leiden, Vol. III, Nos. 1–2, 1957.

Roorda, D. J., 'The Ruling Classes in Holland in the Seventeenth Century', Bromley and Kossmann, op. cit., Groningen 1964.

Ruiter, R., 'Education and Manpower Forecasts', *Planning and Development in the Netherlands*, Netherlands Universities Foundation for International Co-operation, van Gorcum, Assen, Vol. III, Nos. 1–2, 1969.

Russell, Robert, 'The Atlantic Alliance in Dutch Foreign Policy', *Internationale Spectator*, Tijdschrift voor Internationale Politiek, The Hague–Brussels, July 1969.

Schaafsma, Hank, 'Mirror of a Pillarised Society: Broadcasting in the Netherlands', *Delta*, Amsterdam, winter 1966–7.

Schaper, B. W., 'Religious Groups and Political Parties in Contemporary Holland', Bromley and Kossmann, op. cit., London, 1960; New York 1968.

Schillebeeckx, E., *The Eucharist* (trans. N. D. Smith), Sheed and Ward, New York 1968.

Schippers, Gerald K., 'Best Sellers and Blasphemy: A Letter from Amsterdam', *Delta*, Amsterdam, summer 1967.

Schmitz, Yves, *Guillaume Ier. et la Belgique*, Paris 1945.

Scott, J. W. Robertson, *War Time and Peace in Holland*, Heinemann 1914.

*Second Report on Physical Planning in the Netherlands*, Government Printing Office, The Hague 1966, 2 vols, condensed edn.

Shokking, J. C., *De Vrouw in de Nederlandse Politiek*, van Gorcum, Assen, n.d.

Smith, J. M., 'The Present Position of Studies regarding the Revolt of the Netherlands', Bromley and Kossmann, op. cit., 1968.

*Social Employment in the Netherlands, A Brief Survey of the Social Employment Act*, Ministry of Social Affairs and Public Health, The Hague, n.d.

*Some Data on House-Building in the Netherlands*, Ministry of Housing and Physical Planning, The Hague 1969.

Stapel, F. W., *Geschiedenis van Nederlansch Indie*, Amsterdam 1943, 2nd edn.

*State Supervision of Public Health in the Netherlands*, Ministry of Social Affairs and Public Health, The Hague 1969.

*Statistisch Zakboek*, '69, Centraal Bureau voor de Statistiek, The Hague 1969.

*Summary of the Draft Bill Reform Universities Administration*, Ministry of Education and Science, The Hague 1969.

*Summary of the Post-Primary Education Act in the Netherlands*, Ministry of Education and Science, The Hague 1968.

Swart, K. W., *Sale of Offices in the Seventeenth Century*, Martinus Nijhoff, The Hague 1949.

Thoenes, D., *De Elite in de Verzorgings Staat*, Leiden 1962.

Thomassen, 'University Education in the Netherlands', *Higher Education and Research in the Netherlands*, the Netherlands Universities Foundation for International Co-operation, The Hague, Vol. XIII, No. 2, 1969.

Tinker, Hugh, *Ballot Box and Bayonet, People and Government in Emergent Asian Countries*, Royal Institute of International Affairs, Oxford University Press, London, New York and Toronto 1964.

*Treaty and Articles of the Agreement between the Estates of Holland, the Prince of Orange and the Magistrates of Amsterdam*, London 1650.

Treffers, P. E., 'Abortion in Amsterdam', *Population Studies, A Journal of Demography*, London, Vol. XX, Part 3, 1967.

Van Amserfoort, J. M. M., *Surinamese Immigrants in the Netherlands*, Ministry of Cultural Affairs, Recreation and Social Welfare, Government Printing and Publishing Office, The Hague 1969.

Van Bath, Bernard H. Slicher, 'Historical Demography and the Social and Economic Development of the Netherlands', *Daedalus, Journal of the American Academy of Arts and Sciences*, Boston, spring 1968.

Van Campen, S. I. P., *The Quest for Security, Some Aspects of Netherlands Foreign Policy, 1945–50*, Martinus Nijhoff, The Hague 1958.

Vandenbosch, *Dutch Foreign Policy since 1815, A Study in Small Power Politics*, Martinus Nijhoff, The Hague 1959.

Van der Kroef, *Indonesia in the Modern World*, Mara Basu, Bandung 1954.

Van der Land, Lucas, 'Provo is as Provo does: A General Introduction', *Delta*, autumn 1967.

Van der Schaff, Sjoerd, 'The Frisian Movement', *Delta*, Amsterdam, winter 1965–6.

Van der Veen, Adriaan, 'Literature of the Lowlands through Californian Eyes', *Delta*, Amsterdam, autumn 1966.

Van Dillen, J. G., 'Amsterdam's Role in Seventeenth Century Dutch Politics and its Economic Background', Bromley and Kossmann, op. cit., 1968.

Van Gelder, H. A. Enno, *The Two Reformations in the Sixteenth Century, A Study of the Religious Aspects and Consequences of Renaissance and Humanism*, Martinus Nijhoff, The Hague 1961.

Van Ommen, L. B., *Cultural Aspects of Welfare Policy*, Ministry of Cultural Affairs, Recreation and Social Welfare, Rijswijk 1969.

Van Raalte, E., *The Parliament of the Kingdom of the Netherlands*, The Hansard Society for Parliamentary Government, London–The Hague 1959.

Van Veen, J., *Dredge, Drain, Reclaim, The Art of a Nation*, Martinus Nijhoff, The Hague 1948.

——— *Land below Sea-Level, Holland in its age-long Fight against the Waters*, L. J. C. Boucher, The Hague 1953.

Vaughan, Richard, *Philip the Bold, The Formation of the Burgundian State*, Longmans, London; Harvard University Press 1962.

Veldkamp, H., 'The Planning of Non-University Education', *Planning and Development in the Netherlands*, Netherlands Universities Foundation for International Co-operation, van Gorcum, Assen, Vol. III, Nos. 1–2, 1969.

Vlekke, B. M., *Evolution of the Dutch Nation*, New York 1945.

Vlekke, Bernard H. M., 'The Dutch before 1581', *The Netherlands*, Bartholomew Landheer (ed.), op. cit.

Voster, W., 'The Structure of Education in the Netherlands and the Innovation of Education', *Planning and Development in the Netherlands*, Netherlands Universities Foundation for International Co-operation, van Gorcum, Assen, Vol. III, Nos. 1–2, 1969.

Warmbrunn, Werner, *The Dutch under German Occupation, 1940–1945*, Stanford University Press, Oxford University Press, London 1963.

Wedgwood, C. V., *William the Silent*, Cape, Fernhill, New York 1960.

Weevers, Theodoor, *Poetry of the Netherlands in its European Context, 1170–1930*, Athlone Press, London 1960.

Westrate, C., *Economic Policy in Practice: The Netherlands 1950–1957*, H. E. Stenfert Kroese, Leiden 1959.

Wieringa, W. J., 'Social Circumstances and Development of the Dutch Economy in the Nineteenth Century', Bromley and Kossmann, op. cit., 1968.

Williams, Sir Roger, *The Actions of the Lowe Countries*, London 1618.

Wilson, Charles, *Anglo-Dutch Commerce and Finance in the Eighteenth Century*, Cambridge University Press, Cambridge 1941.

—— *Profit and Power, A Study of England and the Dutch Wars*, Longmans, London 1957.

—— *The Dutch Republic and the Civilisation of the Seventeenth Century*, World University Library, Weidenfeld and Nicolson, London; McGraw Hill, New York 1968.

—— *The History of Unilever. A Study in Economic Growth and Social Change*, Cassells, London; Praeger, New York 1968, 3 vols.

Windmuller, John P., *Labor Relations in the Netherlands*, Cornell University Press, New York 1969.

Zijderveld, Anton C., 'History and Recent Development of Dutch Sociological Thought', *Social Research, An International Quarterly of Political and Social Science*, New York, Vol. 33, 1966.

*Zuider Zee Works, The*, Ministry of Transport, The Hague 1967, 8th edn.

Zumthor, Paul, *Daily Life in Rembrandt's Holland*, Weidenfeld and Nicolson, London; Macmillan, New York 1959.

# Index

# Index

# Index

Ships, Shipbuilding: in 15th C., 7–8; in 17th C., 32–3, 41; decline in 18th C., 46; improvement in 19th C., 59; now, 166, 173
Sjahrir, Sutan, 207
Social Democratic Labour Party (SDAP), 61, 63, 114
Social Democratic Union, 63
Social-Economic Council, 130, 184, 187, 189, 220
Social Security, 129, 155–60
Socialism, growth of, 61, 63–4
Socialist broadcasting organisation, 96
Socialist party, 84, 113, 128, 129, 131, 198
Societé Générale des Pays-Bas. . . ., 54
Soviet Union, 115, 116, 192, 198
Spanish rule, 12–29, 30
Spice trade, 32, 33, 200, 202
Staatsmijnen/DSM, 170
Stadtholders, 11, 17, 26, 43, 44, 45
Staphorst, 93–4
States-General, 11, 12, 18, 19, 20, 21, 26, 27, 28, 29
Steen, Jan, 36
Stikker, Dirk, 192
Strikes, 63, 187–9, 190
Student demonstrations, 80, 138, 153–4, 221
Student population and problems, 151
STUW movement, 210, 214
Suffrage, 64
Suharto, President, 215
Sukarno, Achmed, 206, 207, 210, 211, 215
Surinam, 41, 163, 216

Taxation, 47, 55, 129, 190
Television, 96–100
'Tenth Penny' tax, 25
Textile industry, 50, 59, 173, 176
Theatre, 105
Thorbecke, Jan Rudolf, 57, 58, 100, 127
Trade, see Industry and trade
Trade Unions, 63, 186–7, 189; Catholic, 186, 189; Communist, 186; Liberal, 186; Protestant, 186; Socialist, 186, 189
Treaty of Twenty-four Articles, 56
Tromp, Martin, 41, 44

Unilever, 60, 165, 170, 171
Unitarists, 52
United East India Company, 34, 201, 208

United Nations, 194, 215
United Provinces, 19
United States: direct investment in Netherlands, 173; press for sanctions against Dutch over Indonesia, 213, 214; relations with Netherlands, 192
Utrecht 5, 6, 9, 11, 13, 19, 26, 50, 63, 93, 163, 177; Treaty of (1713), 43, 65; Union of (1579), 19; University, 79, 151

Valois dynasty, 15
Van Adrichem, Claes Adriansz, 34–5
Van Gogh, Vincent, 59n., 105
Van Kleffens, E. N., 195
Van Mierlo, Hans, 118–19
Van Mook, R. J., 213–14
Van Oldenbarnevelt, Johan, 26, 27, 28
Verdun, Treaty of (843), 5
Vermeer, Jan, 36
Verolme, Cornelis, 97
Verzuiling, 62, 64, 68, 83, 110, 114, 132; in cultural life, 103; in education, 145, 150; in press, 100; in television, 98, 99; in trade unions, 186

Wages, 78, 167, 185, 189, 219
Walloon provinces, 12, 14
War of the Austrian Succession, 45
War of the League of Augsburg, 42
War of the Spanish Succession, 42, 44
Welfare state, 116, 129
West India Company, Dutch, 27, 31, 34
Wilhelmina, Queen, 133–4, 139, 210
Wilhelmina, wife of William V of Orange, 50, 51
William I, 52, 53–5, 56, 57, 126, 203
William II, 56, 57
William III, 65, 133
William II (the Silent) of Orange, 13, 14, 18–24, 30, 43, 44, 193
William III of Orange, 42, 44
William IV of Orange, 44, 45
William V of Orange, 44, 50, 51
William II, Count of Holland, 5
William Louis, stadholder, 26
Women, status of, 69–70; in politics, 128; and work, 71, 184
Working Incapacity Act (1967), 157

Zeeland, 6, 9, 10, 11, 12, 18, 19, 23, 24, 26, 27, 31, 94, 118; 1953 floods, 91, 179; shipbuilding, 7–8
Zuider Zee, 6, 7, 46, 59, 67, 180, 181, 182